Thomas Knieps-I
Aldegonde Brenninkmeij

Authentic Voices, Discerning Hearts

INTAMS Studies on Marriage and Family / INTAMS-Studien zu Ehe und Familie

edited by / herausgegeben von

Thomas Knieps-Port le Roi
(KU Leuven)

Philippe Bordeyne
(Institut Catholique de Paris)

Jochen Sautermeister
(Universität Bonn)

Claire Watkins
(University of Roehampton)

Volume / Band 1

LIT

Authentic Voices, Discerning Hearts

New Resources for the Church on Marriage and Family

edited by

Thomas Knieps-Port le Roi
and
Aldegonde Brenninkmeijer-Werhahn

LIT

Cover illustration: Nancy Standlee, *Family Abstract* (2014)

Bibliographic information published by the Deutsche Nationalbibliothek
The Deutsche Nationalbibliothek lists this publication in the Deutsche Nationalbibliografie; detailed bibliographic data are available on the Internet at http://dnb.d-nb.de.

ISBN 978-3-643-90760-8

A catalogue record for this book is available from the British Library

Klosbachstr. 107
CH-8032 Zürich
Tel. +41 (0) 44-251 75 05 Fax +41 (0) 44-251 75 06
E-Mail: zuerich@lit-verlag.ch http://www.lit-verlag.ch
Distribution:
In the UK: Global Book Marketing, e-mail: mo@centralbooks.com
In North America: International Specialized Book Services, e-mail: orders@isbs.com
In Germany: LIT Verlag Fresnostr. 2, D-48159 Münster
Tel. +49 (0) 2 51-620 32 22, Fax +49 (0) 2 51-922 60 99, e-mail: vertrieb@lit-verlag.de
In Austria: Medienlogistik Pichler-ÖBZ, e-mail: mlo@medien-logistik.at
e-books are available at www.litwebshop.de

Table of Contents

Part IV. THE SENSE OF THE FAITHFUL

Preface to the Series

INTAMS (the *International Academy for Marital Spirituality*) has published the international theological periodical *INTAMS Review: Journal for the Study of Marriage and Spirituality,* with contributions in English, German, French, and Italian, since 1995. We have had the wish for some time now to launch additionally a series of books on topics specific to marriage and the family. When we now implement our project, this is indirectly thanks to Pope Francis and to his initiative of convoking two successive Synods of Bishops on the theme of marriage and the family: the Extraordinary General Assembly on the theme of "Pastoral Challenges to the Family in the Context of Evangelization" in 2014, and the Ordinary General Assembly on the theme of "The Vocation and Mission of the Family in the Church and in the Contemporary World" in 2015.

No other Synod has ever attracted so much attention worldwide as these two Assemblies on marriage and the family. This was one of the most explosive Synods in recent church history. Its importance is not to be measured on its outcome alone, but on the synodal process and on the dynamic that this has developed throughout the world, as well as on the insight that marriage is understood and lived differently in the various continents and countries.

Through the huge publicity that the Synod received, the last two years have seen a strengthening of the insight that marriage is intimately linked to the core of society and of the church. A rigid enforcement of ecclesiastical ideas about norms in the last three decades meant that this insight was starved of oxygen. This caused a great deal of suffering.

If we are to understand the meaning of the marital covenant, we should not forget the following points.

Every human being is sometimes, and perhaps even for most of the time, alone with his or her own inner thoughts. This also applies to the married woman and to the married man. The success or failure of their shared path of development depends decisively on how the individual partner deals in their togetherness with his or her own world of ideas. The aphorism: *as one thinks, so one lives*, proves true for married people above all in the history of their married life.

Young people who want to get married are often alone with the inner world of their ideas. It is very difficult for them to decide to commit themselves. This is often because they can scarcely find anyone to accompany them, anyone with whom they can have an intimate dialogue.

But young married people too are often insufficiently prepared to give their partner admittance at the right time to their own world of ideas. Many things are suddenly on the line: the new responsibility as parents; the pressure to prove themselves in their professional work; the daily organization of the household; cultivating relationships with their family and friends. But their most intimate concern is the success of their marriage.

In our fast-moving society, married couples who are growing older are often left alone with their thoughts, if they have not learned to communicate their deepest thoughts to each other in the course of their years as a couple. They too are exposed to all kinds of tests as they get older: children who now begin to lead their own life outside the parental home; the forced or natural departure from the world of work; the biological and physical changes that force themselves upon one, and that sometimes can pose a risk to the marital relationship. Besides this, they can be confronted with illnesses that bring a fundamental change to their relationship as partners. Nor should we forget the state of being widowed, which poses its own challenge of being alone. It is hard to feel that one has been left alone. But it is precisely the ability to open oneself to others that remains an important task for widowers and widows. It is all too easy for them, in spite of their rich experiences, to be forgotten by society.

A spirituality of marriage includes the insight that from the day of the marriage vows onwards until the time in which the arch of a life in common sinks down towards its close, the marital relationship encompasses phases of life that affect one profoundly and that one does not simply leave behind. Rather, these phases are like a treasure that accompanies one through life. The beginning and the end of a married life are often beset with a mystery that must be shared in words, even if these words are fragile. It needs to be shared, because the mysterious fire of a sacred love burns within it. Both partners want to see and experience this reciprocal, blessed love. Both want to know that they are joined together and loved by God in their human marital life, even if faith is present only as a very tender shoot; it is a question of God and of being the child of God. In every human being, there lives the hope of experiencing eternally the mysterious blazing fire in a new heaven and a new earth. But the hope that one will be able to live in holy harmony is fulfilled only if one keeps the warm fervor burning continuously along one's path through life. The mysterious love between two persons is not realized all at once; it is achieved only in the course of the years of the marriage, step by step, gradually (if at all). This is because we are, after all, human beings who live in their own time and who are en route, in order to move others on their path in their own time. This holy dynamic means a growth in one's own self, with and through the other person. And this creates the possibility of building up a reciprocal and intimate culture of dialogue.

Many marriages are put to the test early on. This is now the time – if the couple has not yet done so – to put into words, with each other and for each other, essential aspects of the mysterious fire of a sacred love. They should not keep this to themselves, but should practice dialogue, in order thus to build up their own "domestic rite of marriage". This is an essential building brick for the covenant of their life, and helps them to "grow into" their relationship as partners. If they dialogue with each other regularly, at a time they agree upon, they each learn how to communicate to the other their own spiritual goods in a calm conversation. Every marital relationship that takes itself seriously demands this rhythm, in order thus to construct an intimate shared marriage path through life. This practice has proved its worth. It can inspire the partners to respect each other's spiritual goods and to disclose them with respect and high appreciation. This is where a marriage develops its own very specific and particular marital culture.

This praxis has an incontrovertible validity for the marriage path. A basis of reciprocal trust and reliability can be built up here. This is also the place where one can express one's joys and one's troubles, and practice the virtue of mutual acceptance. On yet another level, the challenges are brought into unity in a marriage by trust in God and faith in the Gospel and in Jesus Christ, whose life shows us the path that we must take. This is the starting point of the church in the household.

This brings me to the present book, the first volume in the series *INTAMS Studies on Marriage and the Family.* This series seeks to bring together contemporary and fresh works of scholarship and reflections on central themes that are specific to marriage.

The first volume contains contributions to two academic symposia that INTAMS organized in connection with the Synods of Bishops. In the spring of 2015, INTAMS convoked a group of thirty-three experts in Rome for conversations in the period before the Ordinary General Assembly. These conversations were intensive and had a high academic standard; at the same time, they were held in an open and intimate atmosphere. The principal motivation was to provide thematic help to the European church and its members at the Synod.

The insights that were gained there flowed into the two-days INTAMS symposium in September 2015, likewise in Rome, on the theme: "Authentic Voices, Discerning Hearts: Marriage and Family in Church and Society". This generated a deeper discussion by theologians and scholars from other disciplines, experts and laypersons in the field of marriage and family, married persons and celibates, women and men from Northern, Southern, Western, and Eastern Europe.

The way in which people think about the family today, the way in which it is lived and understood, has changed the understanding of marriage. But marriage and the family have not lost their importance even today, in the twenty-first century. On the contrary, men and women who grow into adulthood with the desire to live in a convincing ethical marriage bond continue to form the majority, as the European Values Studies show us in their Human Values Scale. The official documents of the church have so often expressed a catalogue of challenges to marriage, all of which are described in negative terms (see *Evangelii gaudium*, 83). Precisely because the married state continues to enjoy such high esteem in the public sphere, this series of *INTAMS Studies on Marriage and the Family* endeavors to understand marriage in a realistic way, in order to affirm it in its deep core. This is what Jesus teaches us in Matthew 19,3–12: we must give a meaning to the life that a couple shares; we must live responsible parenthood in the image of God (Genesis 1,27); we ought to understand marriage in its entirety as a pilgrimage path, and to perceive it as the shared adventure of a path through life with its various segments and stages.

This series of books on marriage and the family gives us the opportunity to express our joy at having been permitted to work on this topic for almost thirty years. For my part, this is accompanied by the joy at fifty successful years of marriage with my husband Hubert. The paths we took were sometimes bumpy, but they have helped us to grow together. Last but not least, they have inspired the work of INTAMS in a good and natural way.

A special word of thanks is owed here to our deceased friend Klaus Demmer, who helped to give INTAMS its shape. He encouraged us to let INTAMS see the light of day, strengthening our resolve and supporting us.

We are very grateful, and our hope is that this series can offer much information and deeper insights into marriage and the family in the present century.

I address you in complete human confidence, unknown reader, and I hope that you will find pleasure in this series of books. I wish you good and informative hours of reading and enriching conversations with your colleagues, students, and partners.

Aldegonde Brenninkmeijer-Werhahn
Sint-Genesius-Rode (Brussels)
Pentecost 2016: The Sending-out of all the Baptized

Introduction

It seems that marriage and family life have currently become the domains par excellence in which the Christian communities have to reconsider and redefine their position towards and in the late-modern world. The Roman Catholic Church had made a major attempt to reconcile with modernity in the early 1960s at the Second Vatican Council. In one sense, however, the council's clearest and most successful achievements were related to debates dating from the nineteenth and early twentieth centuries, such as the church's relationship to democracy, religious liberty and the understanding of Holy Scripture. In many of the other, theologically more sensitive, domains its outcome was much less conclusive, bearing the marks of fierce internal controversies which in many cases could be overcome only with the help of compromise formulations. This is also true of the issue of marriage and family, to which the Pastoral Constitution on the Church in the Modern World, *Gaudium et spes,* dedicated its chapters 47–52, in which the Catholic Church finally came to terms with the perception of twentieth-century Christian couples who, along with their secular contemporaries, had come to regard marriage as the loving commitment of two partners who freely consent to share their lives together. But alongside the passages in which this personalist vision was spelled out for the first time in a document of the magisterium, the conciliar text still maintained the traditional natural-law approach with its primarily institutional logic, according to which the spouses give themselves over to a marital state that was instituted by God and ordered by divine and natural laws. In some areas, therefore, the council thus left unfinished the task on which it had so impressively embarked in others.

It is possible that the council simply came too early to address the questions that swept over Christianity and Catholicism in the wake of the sexual revolution.[1] There is little doubt, however, that although the popes in the post-conciliar era made marriage and family issues a matter of decision at the highest level, they did not succeed in reconciling the tensions that are laid bare in the council document. This was obvious in the way in which Pope Paul VI dealt with the question of birth control in *Humanae vitae*. But it finally turned out that also John Paul II's reading of *Gaudium et spes* was not able to avert the growing discrepancy between the church's moral teaching in these matters and the moral insights of a large

---

1 See R. Douthat: "A Crisis of Conservative Catholicism", 2016, http://www.firstthings.com/article/2016/01/a-crisis-of-conservative-catholicism; retrieved 30.03.2016.

portion of the Catholic faithful. The Synod of Bishops which Pope Francis called in 2014 and 2015 and his Postsynodal Apostolic Exhortation *Amoris laetitia* can be regarded as a new attempt by the teaching authority to come to terms with the questions that emerged on the horizon already in the 1960s.

While the media attention covering the two synods focused almost exclusively on what the late-modern zeitgeist had long before perceived as "hot topics" (the Catholic Church's way of dealing with unmarried cohabitation, divorce and remarriage, and same-sex relationships), a number of scholarly publications of high quality had undertaken to point to a number of substantial theological questions that had been lingering in the background since the times of the council.[2] Peter Hünermann, for instance, has identified three major theological misunderstandings which the magisterium ought to urgently correct: a distorted conception of "natural law" which has led some to overlook the fact that marriage is the result of historical and cultural developments that are also shaped by human freedom; a fundamentalist reading of biblical passages, which have sometimes been directly translated into ecclesiastical regulations about marriage; and finally, a misunderstanding of what constitutes the sacramental sign in Christian marriage, which is, in fact, the personal, lifelong commitment of the spouses rather than an instantaneous contractual agreement between them.[3] In a similar vein, during a study day organized jointly by the German, French and Swiss Bishops' Conferences in May 2015, several theological desiderata were formulated with regard to church teaching. The various contributors asked for a hermeneutics that, based on Jesus' teaching about God's Kingdom, reads biblical passages within their literal and historical context; for a stronger validation in ethical-theological discourse of people's personal biographies and experiences as well as of new insights from the

---

2 I refer here, among others, to the following publications: K. HILPERT/B. LAUX (eds.): *Leitbild am Ende? Der Streit um Ehe und Familie*, Freiburg-Basel-Wien: Herder, 2014; G. AUGUSTIN/I. PROFT (eds.): *Ehe und Familie. Wege zum Gelingen aus katholischer Perspektive*, Freiburg-Basel-Wien: Herder, 2014; U. RUH/M. WIJLENS (eds.): *Zerreißprobe Ehe: Das Ringen der katholischen Kirche um die Familie*, Freiburg-Basel-Wien: Herder, 2015; F.X. BISCHOF/C. LEVIN (eds.): *Ehe – Familie – Kirche. Biblische Überlieferung, Historische Weiterentwicklung, Aktuelle Perspektiven*, Wiesbaden: Berlin University Press, 2015; H. LANGENDÖRFER/O. RIBADEAU DUMAS/E. TANNER (eds.): *Theologie der Liebe. Zur aktuellen Debatte um Ehe und Familie*, Freiburg-Basel-Wien: Herder, 2015; "'Between Two Synods: Journeying Together': Proceedings of the European Conference on the Family, Malta, 20 February 2015", in: *Melita theologica* 65/1 (2015); "*La vocation et la mission de la famille dans l'Eglise et dans le monde contemporain": Vingt-six théologiens répondent*, Paris: Bayard, 2015; A. SPADARO (ed.): *La famiglia, ospedale da campo: Dibattito biblico, teologico e pastorale sul matrimonio nei contributi degli scrittori de La Civiltà Cattolica*, Queriniana: Brescia, 2015.

3 See P. HÜNERMANN: "'Revolutionierung der Ehe': Theologiegeschichtlich-systematische Reflexionen und Konsequenzen für das kirchliche Lehramt", in: U. RUH/M. WIJLENS (eds.): *Zerreißprobe Ehe*, 45–78.

human sciences; for a deeper understanding of the gradualness of moral life on its way to perfection and an acknowledgment of the positive and constructive elements in those forms of living together which do not correspond to the church's ideal; and for a revision of central theological concepts such as sacramental marriage and consummation.[4]

In his Postsynodal Apostolic Exhortation *Amoris laetitia,* Pope Francis has himself pointed to some of these underlying theological issues and pleaded for a revisiting of positions previously held by the church's teaching authority. This is, for example, the case when he admonishes that natural law is not to be understood "as an already established set of rules that impose themselves a priori on the moral subject" but rather as "a source of objective inspiration for the deeply personal process of making decisions". He invites to a similar theological reconsideration with regard to the role of conscience in moral decision making, the concept of gradualness in the moral life, the relevance of *epikeia* in the application of general norms to concrete situations, and the scope of the magisterium's language about "objectively disordered" situation or actions. Although Francis does not further elaborate on these issues, he clearly recognizes their complexity and therefore encourages "continued open discussion of a number of doctrinal, moral, spiritual, and pastoral questions".

This is what the present publication undertakes to do, thus joining the various scholarly initiatives that have provided both a profound and critical analysis of the status quo of and new and constructive perspectives for the church's teaching on marriage and family. From 18–19 May 2015 INTAMS had invited an international group of experts to reflect on the theological agenda in view of the 2015 Ordinary Assembly of the Synod of Bishops. These reflections fed into the international symposium that was held from 10–12 September 2015 in Rome, two weeks before the bishops gathered. The key note papers presented at this conference are collected in this volume.

Four central issues structured the reflections at the expert seminar in May as well as the inputs at the international symposium in September 2015. They also provide the general structure for this volume. The first addresses a real theological concern that many observers shared during the entire synodal process. It had to do with the more or less tacit agreement among the synod fathers that their deliberations should be about the applicability but not the contents of the Church teaching, about pastoral care but not about moral doctrine as such.[5] That such a

4 See H. LANGENDÖRFER ET AL. (eds.): *Theologie der Liebe*, 85–92.

5 Only few bishops seemed to be willing to question this agreement, such as the Bishop of Antwerp, Johan Bonny: "In these last months of preparation for the Synod, I have heard or read the following on numerous occasions: 'Agreed that the Synod should support greater pastoral flexibility, but it will not be able to touch Church doctrine'. Some create the impression

divide between doctrine and practice, between teaching and ministry cannot be justified, either on theological or on pastoral grounds, is the conviction of both the authors in this first section of the book. *Clare Watkins* blurs the boundaries between a neat, rationally worked-through doctrinal account and the sometimes messy reality of Christian practice by referring to the theology of Revelation set out in Vatican II's constitution *Dei verbum*. She presents the Christian household – which the more recent tradition calls a "domestic church" – as both a practical and doctrinal ecclesial locus where, in a conversational method of discernment, truth is discerned, the reception of revelation is realized, and evangelization is carried out. *Emmanuel Agius* agrees that the distinctive feature of teaching is not imparting knowledge, but educating one's heart and promoting one's internal growth and health – which is exactly the task of pastoral ministry as well. With his empirical-critical-theological approach, he suggests a concrete hermeneutical method by which doctrine and pastoral practice can be harmonized.

In the second part, a central ethical and theological question is raised, which summarizes in a nutshell what Pope Francis had asked the bishops' synods beforehand to reflect upon. How can the church, its pastors and all faithful remain close to and accompany "with mercy and patience" (*Evangelii gaudium,* 44) individuals, partners, spouses and families who live their relationships in sometimes difficult and painful situations, also (and particularly) those who do not comply with the Church's moral standards? *Roger Burggraeve*'s answer is straightforward: if only we understand the human person and her moral life as "on the way", we can develop an ethics of gradualness and growth that values what is morally attainable and at the same time calls forward toward greater perfection. Only then can one avoid the assertion that mercy comes "after ethics". Only such an "ethics of mercy" provides an ethics that is pastoral in itself. While Burggraeve's approach lends itself to come to terms with the social reality of premarital cohabitation, *Jochen Sautermeister* enlarges the perspective and includes, next to growth, failure as a category of human biographies. Whether related to contingency or guilt, human failure urges theological and ethical reflection to focus not primarily on moral ideals, but on individual biographies and on personal conscience. A Christian ethics of gradualness is at its best only when it also recognizes the struggle

---

that the Synod will only be free to speak about the applicability of the Church's teaching and not about its content. In my opinion, however, such an antithesis between 'pastoral care' and 'doctrine' is inappropriate in both theological and pastoral terms and it has no foundation in the tradition of the Church. Pastoral care has everything to do with doctrine and doctrine everything to do with pastoral care. Both will have to be dealt with during the Synod if the Church wants to open new avenues towards the evangelization of marriage and family life in today's society." J. BONNY: *Synod on the Family. Expectations of a Diocesan Bishop*, 2015, 6f., http://archief.kerknet.be/admin/files/assets/subsites/4/documenten/SYNOD_ON_FAMILY_ENG.pdf; retrieved 30.03.2016.

for a realization of moral values in the lives of those for whom it is impossible to live the religious and moral ideal of marital love.

The third part focuses on the theology of marriage and on the teaching about indissolubility. The synodal discussions were largely dominated by a controversy between those who endorsed Cardinal Walter Kasper's proposal to admit, in individual cases and after a proper process of discernment in the internal forum, divorced and remarried persons to the eucharist (on the one hand) and those who firmly refused such a pastoral solution (on the other).[6] Underneath this disciplinary move there lies, however, a profound theological question which touches upon the understanding of sacramental marriage. *Andrea Grillo* analyses the fundamental shift in cultural experience which distinguishes a premodern from a late-modern understanding of what safeguards the conjugal relationship. As the indivisibility of the matrimonial union has been replaced by the inviolability of individual freedom, a slow work of giving marriage a new theological meaning has to be undertaken in order to liberate it from its former procrustean bed. Mediating between the premodern "objectivity of the bond" and the modern "subjectivity without bonds", Grillo proposes an "intersubjective theory of the freedom of conscience and of the history of the bond" which would allow the theological axiom of the indissolubility of marriage to be translated into the intersubjective non-availability of the conjugal relationship. *Eberhard Schockenhoff* and *Peter Hünermann* second this analysis and comb through the theological tradition with regard to what makes marriage "indissoluble". As Schockenhoff shows, indissolubility is not a normative expectation that is imposed upon marriage from the outside by means of a law or a sacramental symbolism, but rather an inherent requirement of every genuine and authentic loving relationship. This leads him to conclude that a second marriage too, after the failure of the first one, can be thought of theologically as an indissoluble union, and secondly that a first marriage that has broken down in its human reality forfeits its potential to become, in a sacramental reading, a sign and image of God's fidelity to the human person and of Christ's love for his Church. Hünermann appeals to a solid theological tradition ranging from Thomas Aquinas via Roman Neo-scholasticism up to the more recent theological approaches, to argue that the marital sacrament ought no longer to be thought of in static-ontological, but in historical-processual terms. A central argument here is that an erroneous magisterial interpretation has located the in-

---

6 See W. KASPER: *The Gospel of the Family:* New York: Paulist Press, 2014; the opponents of Kasper's proposal presented their arguments, among others, in R. DODARO (ed.): *Remaining in the Truth of Christ: Marriage and Communion in the Catholic Church*, San Francisco: Ignatius Press, 2014, and J.J. PÉREZ-SOBA/S. KAMPOWSKI: *The Gospel of the Family: Going Beyond Cardinal Kasper's Proposal in the Debate on Marriage, Civil Re-Marriage and Communion in the Church*, San Franciso: Ignatius Press, 2014.

dissolubility of marriage in its imaging of Christ's relationship with the Church, whereas this sacramental symbolism is not inherent in marriage itself but is only added to it from a faith perspective. Christian marriage thus does not receive its solidity at the moment when it is entered into, but only in a lifelong process in the course of which the spouses are supported by God's grace which is given to them with the sacrament.

The fourth and last section deals with the "sense of the faithful". One of the main reasons for calling the synods of bishops on the family has been the manifest discrepancy between the moral teaching of the Church on the one side and the moral insights and practices of the faithful on the other. The problem seems to have a quality that cannot simply be referred to in terms of "deviation" from an otherwise widely accepted moral norm. The responses to the Vatican questionnaire in the lead-up to the Extraordinary Synod have unmistakably confirmed that committed Catholics too not only factually depart from church teaching, but also invoke their moral sense and conscience to do so.[7] However one is finally to assess this conceptual and practical dissent, it raises questions with regard to ecclesiology and the process and methods whereby the people of God ascertain the truth of the faith. *Thomas Knieps-Port le Roi* explores the extent to which the Church's infallible "sense of the faith" can also be ascertained with regard to "matters of morals". He argues that in the present context, the question is not so much how the Church contributes to the formation of the believers' moral discernment, but also vice-versa, how the moral sense of the faithful in their daily decision-making and practice can feed into the moral insight of the Church. *Serena Noceti* further develops the idea of the *sensus fidelium* from an ecclesiological point of view, by focusing on the communicative and participatory dynamics that it implies. Recalling the lofty ecclesiological ideas of Vatican II, she pleads for a model of communication which lives from multidirectional networks where each

---

[7] See the extensive summaries of the responses to the Vatican questionnaire published by the German and Swiss Bishops' Conferences: DEUTSCHE BISCHOFSKONFERENZ: *Pastoral Challenges to the Family in the Context of Evangelisation: Summary of the Responses from the German Dioceses and Archdioceses to the Questions Contained in the Preparatory Document for the III Extraordinary General Assembly of the Synod of Bishops 2014*, 2014, http://www.dbk.de/fileadmin/redaktion/diverse_downloads/presse_2014/2014-012b-ENG-Fragebogen-Die-patoralen-Herausforderungen-der-Familie.pdf; retrieved 30.03.2016. SCHWEIZER BISCHOFSKONFERENZ: *"Die Pastorale Herausforderung der Familie im Kontext der Evangelisierung": Synthesebericht der Schweizer Bischofskonferenz über die Umfrage der Diözesen unter Seelsorgenden und Experten in der Schweiz*, http://www.kath.ch/skz/upload/20140211135608.pdf; retrieved 30.03.2016. See also A. DILLEN/T. KNIEPS-PORT LE ROI/K. KRYSINSKA: "A Growing Gap? Catholic Pastoral Workers and Volunteers' Perceptions of Family Life and Church Teaching in Flanders", in: E. OSEWSKA/J. STALA (eds.): *Modern Family: Local and European Perspectives*, Krakow: The Pontifical University of John Paul II in Krakow Press, 2015, 159–177.

point in the network is both a receiver and a transmitter. In such a hermeneutical and synodal community, the word of women, of married couples and of the local church should finally be heard, much more so than has been the case at the recent two synods.

I would like to thank all those who have contributed to make this publication possible: all authors who have provided papers of excellent quality; Dr. Brian McNeil, who has taken on the task of translating the papers that were not originally written in English and of revising those written by non-native speakers; Dr. Hans Storme, who has edited the contributions in his usual conscientious way; Dominique van Haelst who has coordinated the contact with the authors; and last but not least, Dr. Michael J. Rainer from the LIT Verlag, for his willingness to publish this volume and for his constant support along the path toward its publication.

It is to be hoped that the reflections offered in this volume and in many others like them will provide the Church with new resources in order to provide orientation and inspiration for all who consistently live their partnerships, marriages and family lives with dedication and loving commitment.

Thomas Knieps-Port le Roi

Part I

CHURCH DOCTRINE AND PASTORAL CARE

Conversational Methods of Discernment: Learning for Mission from the Domestic Church

Clare Watkins

When I first delivered this paper at the INTAMS Symposium in Rome, in September 2015, I was very conscious of not having been able to deliver the piece for translation ahead of the conference as I had been asked. I felt I had to begin with an apology! I was sorry, of course; but I also reasoned thus: This is what happens when you invite as conference speakers middle aged women, who are mothers of a good number of children at different stages, with elderly and infirm parents to look after, and (demanding in its own way!) a husband to love. Such people – people like me – are just too unreliable to be allowed to do serious theology! Ultimately this seemed to me an important way of introducing the paper, for it is precisely out of these human domestic realities the thoughts and methodology outlined in this paper spring. The ordinary living of family households, in all their messiness, is littered with less-than-finished and perfected projects, conversations and plans, which are fractured by unforeseen events, illnesses, emotional and physical demands. The voices – and theologies – that speak from these places are seldom neatly packaged (or on time!), understandably and by their nature. Yet these are the very voices, I will argue, that are essential, not only in the discernments of the church's approach to marriage, relationship and family at this time, but, more profoundly, to the whole ecclesial vocation and mission. If we take this seriously our ways of working theologically and ecclesially will need to be changed radically.

What follows is, then, both in form and content, an argument for the centrality of the theological and spiritual insights that are gained by the living of Christian households – "domestic churches". My argument is that there must be some constant and ongoing way of enabling these voices and experiences to be an essential part of the dynamic processes of a teaching-and-learning church, if the church is properly to deepen its practical wisdom about its mission in today's world. The embodied theological wisdom of our domestic churches, even the most messy of them, does not just teach us about marriage and family life; it is a wisdom from which the church as a whole must learn at every point, if it is to re-centre itself in those places of the edges – the periphery – where its true mission takes place.

These insights from household living are rarely articulated, and their interrupted nature often makes it hard for them to find a verbal form, even for those who live by them. For this reason, at the heart of my argument, is the developed methodology of a practical theological approach to such theologies in ordinary – theological action research – which involves processes of action research methods and empirical data gathering, followed by conversational practice and discernment. These methods enable the theological wisdom of such hidden, busy and messy corners of our church to gain their own voice. The scope of this paper, however, is such that only a small glimpse of this methodology and its fruits over the last decade can be explored. What I will be concerned with here, is the fundamental theological basis for such practical theological inclusion of voices from practice. I will demonstrate from the Catholic tradition a fundamental theology which not only *supports* these voices being heard by the magisterium of our ecclesial hierarchy (through occasional consultations and the like), but *demands* that they should be made our proper starting place and place of return in all of our theological discernment and mission as church. The domestic church is not simply one area into which the church magisterium is called to teach; it is, itself, an essential place from which to learn.

These theological convictions determine the shape of my argument. I want first to say a little about my experience and approach in working theologically with voices from practice – including family practice. This very brief introduction to the methodology of theological action research will be followed by a dual theological account of the fundamentals that both underpin and make essential something like the practical theological approach described. The first of these accounts draws on the Catholic tradition of *pedagogy*, informed by a doctrine of the person and an epistemology that makes certain and clear demands on teaching-and-learning – and so *doctrinal* – practices for the Christian community. The second account draws heavily from the fundamental theology of revelation set out by the second Vatican Council, and demonstrates, from another perspective, the essential place that the voices of the ordinary Christian household must have in the dynamics of discerning truth and the development of revelation's expression in our world today. Questions will remain as to how such a theology of the household as an essential place of ecclesial learning can be made a constant practice of our communities; but research already undertaken suggests that there is a rich wisdom of practical loving and mission in our families upon which the church as a whole needs to draw. Through these basic ingredients I hope to open up a fresh discussion about marriage and family today, in ways which shape a *whole-theology* (doctrinal-and-pastoral), which not only contributes to a constructive theology of marriage for our time, but also leads to ways which better enable the effective living of marriage and family as Christian witness to, and evangelisation of, the world.

1 "Realities Are More Important Than Ideas": The Theological Reading of Practice

What might be seen as a certain "Franciscan" renewal taking place in the church at the moment is characterized by the Pope's consistent call to contemplate "the real", the fleshly[1] and the practically lived as a locus for theology. In keeping with his Argentinian liberation theology background, and his Ignatian formation in discernment, Pope Francis repeatedly puts before us this challenge to do theology "incarnationally". In a recent address to the International Theological Congress he puts it this way:

> The questions our people pose, their anguish, their quarrels, their struggles, and their concerns all have hermeneutical value we cannot ignore if we are to take seriously the principle of the incarnation ... Our formulations of faith were born of dialogue, encounter, comparison and contact with different cultures, communities and nations in situations calling for greater reflection on matters not previously clarified. For Christians something becomes suspicious when we no longer admit the need for it to be criticised by others. People and the specific conflicts, their peripheries, are not optional but rather necessary for a better understanding of faith. Therefore it is important to ask whom we are thinking of when we engage in theology. Let us not forget that the Holy Spirit in a praying people is the subject of theology. A theology that is not born of this would offer something beautiful but not real.[2]

Whilst recognizing a certain complexity around this apparently naïve use of the language of "the real" (ideas are, in their own, way "real", and there are of course, ontological realities which are not always knowable existentially), what we have

---

1 This is vividly expressed in the Apostolic Exhortation *Evangelii gaudium*, 2013 (http: // w2.vatican.va/content/francesco/en/apost_exhortations/documents/papa-francesco_esortazione-ap_20131124_evangelii-gaudium.html; retrieved 16.11.2015), both in Pope Francis's advice to preachers to contemplate the lives of those they preach to as well as the scriptures (154), but also in his account of the importance of popular devotional practices: "Genuine forms of popular religiosity are incarnate, since they are born of the incarnation of Christian faith in popular culture. For this reason they entail a personal relationship, not with vague spiritual energies or powers, but with God, with Christ, with Mary, with the saints. These devotions are fleshy, they have a face. They are capable of fostering relationships and not just enabling escapism." (90)

2 FRANCIS: "Video Message ... to Participants in an International Theological Congress, held at The Pontifical Catholic University of Argentina, Buenos Aires, 1–3 September 2015", https://w2.vatican.va/content/francesco/en/messages/pont-messages/2015/documents/papa-francesco_20150903_videomessaggio-teologia-buenos-aires.html; retrieved 16.11.2015.

here is a clear sense that the embodied faith lived in ordinary by Christians in their particular, limited contexts has significant and essential theological authority. Such a vision for a renewal of theology and church teaching-and-learning is very welcome to those who, like me, have been working theologically in ways that seek to take practice and lived faith as an important, authoritative source.

For myself this work has taken a particular form through the development of *theological action research*, as a practical process and methodology.[3] This way of thinking theologically uses qualitative research methods and action research as a way of giving a voice to the experiences, insights and wisdom of those who practice faith "in the world". In *Dei verbum*'s language, these data gathering and reflection methods enable the articulation of the voices of faith practice, and the wisdom learnt "through the contemplation and study made by believers, who treasure these things in their hearts (see Luke, 2:19, 51) through a penetrating understanding of the spiritual realities which they experience".[4] At the same time, theological action research seeks to bring this practical wisdom into dynamic and discursive relationship with church teaching, doctrine, the longer tradition, as well as with the insights of the academy. This is not conceptual discursive activity; in keeping with participative action research, it involves real conversations between academics, practitioners and others so as to broaden the hermeneutical activity beyond the lone researcher, or the academic or clerical "experts". The interpretation of practice belongs, above all, to those who live the practices. All this results in a profoundly *conversational method of discernment*, in which the variety of ecclesial and theological voices are heard and responded to, through different places and persons of wisdom and expertise, each with their own particular (if asymmetric) kind of authority. The conversations are, themselves, recorded and reflected

3 The basic textbook setting out these methods is H. CAMERON ET AL.: *Talking about God in Practice: Theological Action Research and Practical Theology*, London: SCM, 2012. The further development of this methodology can be seen in the following publications, among others J. SWEENEY: "Practical Theological Research: A Case Study", in: J. SWEENEY ET AL. (eds.): *Keeping Faith in Practice*, London: SCM, 2010; C. WATKINS: "Practical Ecclesiology: What Counts as Theology in Studying the Church?", in: P. WARD (ed.): *Perspectives on Ecclesiology and Ethnography*, Grand Rapids, MI: Eerdmans, 2012; C. WATKINS/H. CAMERON: "Epiphanic Sacramentality: An Example of Practical Ecclesiology Revisioning Theological Understanding", in: C.B. SCHAREN (ed.): *Explorations in Ecclesiology and Ethnography*, Grand Rapids, MI: Eerdmans, 2012; C. WATKINS/B. SHEPHERD: "The Challenge of 'Fresh Expression' to Ecclesiology: Reflections from the Practice of Messy Church", in: *Ecclesial Practices* 1/1 (2014), 92–110; C. WATKINS: "Practising Ecclesiology: From Product to Process: Developing Ecclesiology as a Non-Correlative Process and Practice through the Theological Action Research Framework of Theology in Four Voices", in: *Ecclesial Practices* 2 (2015), 23–39; C. WATKINS: "Living Marriage, Learning Discipleship, Teaching Church: The Practices of Married Life as Embodied Theology for today's Mission", in: *INTAMS Review* 20/2 (2014), 236–248.

4 *Dei verbum*, 8.

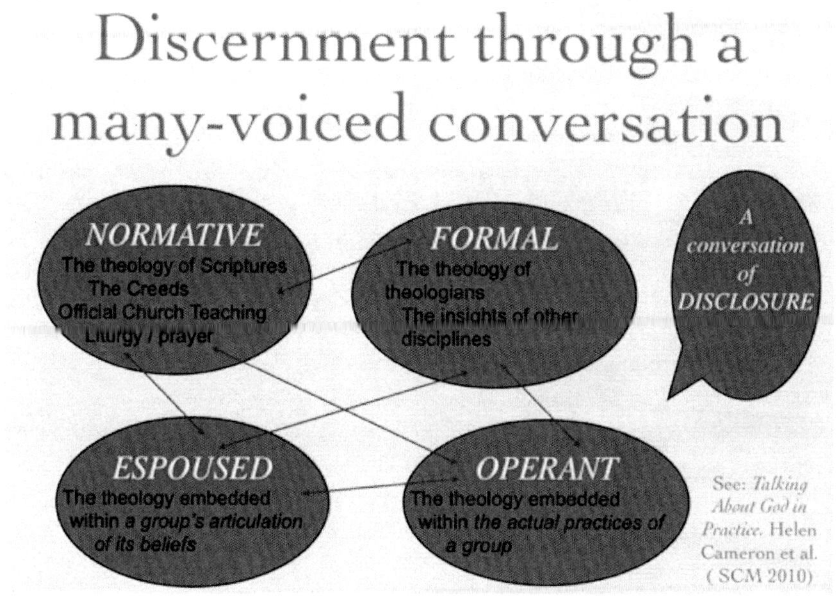

Fig. 1

on as accounts of a "living text", and not so much "analysed", as "theologically discerned". To enable such discernment we have developed a framework for reflection described in terms of "a theology in four voices". This can be diagrammatically presented as in Fig. 1.

What this represents are not four discrete and separate opinions or points of view; for each "voice" is, itself, clearly and complexly dependent on and interpenetrating with the other three. Rather, what the whole depicts is a single conversation between different points of emphasis and expertise, united in the purpose of discerning the way forward in faithfulness and practical wisdom. It is an ecclesial expression of "faith seeking understanding". What is important is not so much any one of these "voices" alone, but rather the insights, or "disclosures", that occur through their mutual – even critical – engagements one with another. Fundamentally there is a certain "apophaticism" involved in using this method, which works on the basis that there is something as yet unarticulated which is to be apparent in the conversational practice. This is not about knowing for sure what any desired outcome is (except in the most general or rather, fundamental, terms – God's mission of love and mercy). It is, rather, about openness to possibilities as yet unforeseen, openness to the Holy Spirit who "blows where he will" (see Jn 3,8).

This is, I suggest, the kind of fundamental practical theology we need in order to speak effectively and authentically about marriage and family today. This is especially so when we remember the curiously distinctive place of the marriage household as the "domestic church", a particular expression of the ecclesial[5] based on the "ecclesial office" of marriage[6], which is, none the less, properly societal, worldly, and, in some important ways, on the edges of the church organisation, whilst continuing to be its beating heart, and one of its central expressions. It is, in Pope Francis's language, that essential periphery of church, which means that, when we seek to discern the theology embodied in marriage and family life, we are also discovering realities and theological wisdom central to the church itself. Marriage and family life, even lived in the brokenness of our fallen-and-redeemed humanity, can here be recognised as an extraordinarily privileged locus for the urgent conversation and pedagogy to which both true doctrine and loving ministry impels us today. The Synodal processes of the last two years cannot *just* be about "marriage and family" as an "issue"; for when we touch this place we open up a powerful energy for the renewal of the whole church and its mission in and for the world.

2 Doctrine and Ministry in a Pedagogical Account of Church as Missionary

I now want to move to the first demonstration of the fundamental theological underpinnings of this kind of approach to the Christian household as a place from which the whole-church must learn. I first will reflect a little on what we mean by "doctrine", before turning to a relocation of this language in the longer pedagogical tradition of our faith.

Arguably one of the greatest difficulties facing contemporary Christian theologies of marriage today is the experience of a certain distance between – even detachment of – the doctrinal vision of marriage and its lived reality. As Catholics we inherit a tradition which is rich in its doctrinal account of even the most immediate and practical aspects of faith-full living, a tradition which has sought to speak of fundamental realities in *ontological* terms – prayer, sacraments, the human person, the church. We have, in modern times, a certain preference for naming "realities" in terms of "pure ontology", rather than in the ways that seem to be suggested by Pope Francis's present use of the term. As a sacrament of the church

[5] As, for example, described by JOHN PAUL II: " ... in its own way the family is a living image and historical representation of the mystery of the Church" (*Familiaris consortio*, 49).

[6] *Catechism of the Catholic Church*, 1631.

such a doctrinal approach is fitting to marriage; but it surely cannot be sufficient. In fact, ours is also a tradition wise in *phronesis* – practical wisdom – which speaks of the existential realities through which the ontological is inevitably experienced, lived, and encountered – all be it in fractured ways. The pastoral theological genius of Pope St. Gregory, the moral theological sensitivity of St. Alphonsus, and the persistent, often unarticulated witness of many pastors through the ages, all reflect the gifts required for pastoral wisdom in complex, and broken human lives. At their heart they are moved by the same Spirit present in Jesus' quietly powerful wisdom before the adulterous woman waiting to be stoned, as she should have been according simply to the law.

What this tradition of *phronesis* recognises is the essential integration of "doctrine" with pastoral care, within a church community characterized by teaching-and-learning. There can be no opposition of the "doctrinal" and "pastoral" – a tendency which has tragically been all too evident in many of the debates around the Synods of 2014 and 2015. The inauthenticity of such opposition becomes clear when we are reminded of the primary nature of doctrine as *teaching*, and the foundational understanding of pastoring as *husbandry*, or farming. In both cases the concern is for health and growth, the bearing of fruit for the nourishment of the common good. Such a resonance of themes draws attention to the significance of the contexts of our discussions of marriage here as properly *pedagogical and missiological.*

Such understanding is a clear part of our longer tradition. The idea of doctrine as pedagogical is clearly attested by that tradition: we need only think of Augustine's classic text *On Christian Teaching*, and his *Enchiridion: on Faith, Hope and Charity.* In both cases the texts set out to speak of catechesis, and doctrine; yet their content is majorly concerned with *how people learn* Christian wisdom and virtue, rather than simply information about the faith that they should know. The concern is with Christian lives bearing fruit, and the blessing of the human processes of teaching and learning rather than, in the first place, correct detailed content, to be remembered, assented to and reproduced unquestioningly.

This pedagogical, personally formative perspective on the place and function of doctrine is underlined by the account Thomas Aquinas gives of how people come to true knowledge. In particular, in question 11 of his *De veritate*, Aquinas tackles the difficult (for him – but interestingly rarely for modern people?) passage of Mt 23,8–10, which calls on Jesus' followers to call no one teacher or instructor, for there is only one Teacher, who is God. For Aquinas the identification of God as the sole true teacher is non-negotiable; it is *only* through the interior activity of the Holy Spirit that the human mind is opened to see and learn what is true. The role of the so-called teacher is simply to facilitate this divine-human tutoring by enabling the learner to hear and understand what the teaching Spirit is leading him or her to. If we are teachers as human beings, it is only by way of analogy, and only in so far as we enable God's own teaching of the person before us.[7]

It is in continuity with this tradition that my own ecclesiological preference has become to refer to our church not simply as a "teaching church", but as a "teaching-and-learning church". Such language draws attention to a particular pedagogy of "deep learning" – women and men conversing and thinking together so as to discern truth, and be shaped towards it in its discernment. This is a way of personal formation which is profoundly transformative. What has here been described concerning doctrine and teaching in our tradition suggests that our commitment to the church as a *teaching* church, and to the body of doctrine as enabling the "deep learning"[8] envisaged in the tradition, must carry with it an appropriate sense of pedagogy. In particular, the pedagogical wisdom of the church concerning the importance of narration and discourse[9], the holistic nature of learning[10], and the necessary freedom of the conscience and the seeking mind in the coming to knowledge of the truth[11], has a bearing on how doctrine is communicated,

7 THOMAS AQUINAS: *De veritate,* Question XI, Article 1 (as found in ID.: *Truth,* trans. J.V. McGlynn, vol. 2, Indianapolis, IN: Hackett Publishing, 1994, 77–87).

8 A term borrowed from contemporary pedagogical theory, which is becoming highly influential across disciplines for an increased awareness of the whole-person significance of learning and teaching. See, for example, http://exchange.ac.uk/learning-and-teaching-theory-guide/deep-and-surface-approaches-learning.html; retrieved 16.11.2015. The traditions of Catholic theologies of learning would find much in common with this approach.

9 Such was the insight of the significant catechist of the 18th century, Claude Fleury, building on the scriptural methods of teaching through narrating God's acts in history. Much of this insight seems to be reflected in the current *Catechism of the Catholic Church* with its proclamative and discursive approach and strong biblical and patristic sourcing. This is in keeping with the aims described by John Paul II: "The presentation of doctrine must be biblical and liturgical. It must be sound doctrine suited to the present life of Christians" (JOHN PAUL II: Apostolic Constitution *Fidei depositum*, 1992, http://www.vatican.va/archive/ccc_css/archive/catechism/aposcons.htm; retrieved 16.11.2015).

10 "For a true education aims at the formation of the human person in the pursuit of his ultimate end" (PAUL VI: *Gravissimum educationis*, 1965, 1, http://www.vatican.va/archive/hist_councils/ii_vatican_council/documents/vat-ii_decl_19651028_gravissimum-educationis_en.html; retrieved 16.11.2015).

11 "It is through his conscience that man sees and recognises the demands of the divine law. He is bound to follow his conscience faithfully in all his activity so that he may come to God, who is his last end. Therefore he must not be forced to act contrary to his conscience. Nor must he be prevented from acting according to his conscience, especially in religious matters" (PAUL VI: Declaration on Religious Freedom *Dignitatis humanae*, 1965, 3, http://www.vatican.va/archive/hist_councils/ii_vatican_council/documents/vat-ii_decl_19651207_dignitatis-humanae_en.html; retrieved 15.11.2015). See also: "The search for truth, however, must be carried out in a manner that is appropriate to the dignity of the human person and his social nature, namely, by free enquiry with the help of teaching or instruction, communication and dialogue. It is by these means that men share with each other the truth they have discovered, or think they have discovered, in such a way that they can help one another

heard, and responded to. This sets up a certain dynamic, of which doctrine is a *part*, whose fundamental theological nature will become clearer in the next section.

The deep learning, participative pedagogy I am suggesting here has far reaching implications for the ways in which a teaching-and-learning church shaped by such an approach understands and practices its mission. In particular, for our purposes, it emphasises the ways in which the communal discernment of God's Word in the church requires not so much a group of expert teachers with a suitably well-behaved cohort of learners; but rather, a pedagogical community, in which, fundamentally *all* are *disciples* – that is, pupils.

Such an understanding of church requires a reshaping of our understanding and practice of pastoral ministry, which refuses simply to see one class of people as those who minister, over against those ministered to (or at!). Whilst exercised in different ways, both the ordained and the married live vocations of *ministerium* in so far as they are living characteristically sacraments "at the service of communion". As the *Catechism of the Catholic Church* makes clear the ministerial nature of both orders and marriage as the "sacraments at the service of communion", orientates the living of these sacraments towards the good of the other:

> Two other sacraments, Holy Orders and Matrimony, are directed towards the salvation of others; if they contribute as well to personal salvation, it is through service to others that they do so. They confer a particular mission in the Church and serve to build up the People of God.[12]

To minister is always to serve the salvation of others: it is always missionary. It is for this reason that the sacrament of orders is characterised as "at the service of the common priesthood. It is directed at the unfolding of the baptismal grace of all Christians".[13]

What this all means, I suggest, is that when we speak of doctrine and pastoral ministry we are speaking always about the one pedagogical dynamic of the Christian life, in which Christian households are intrinsically involved, not just as learners simply, but as part of a deep personal learning dynamic which shapes the whole church in its missionary vocation. This is the life of discipleship, or tutelage, for mission in the world. In this dynamic there is a fundamental sense that all in the church are learning together, all be it that there are different places held by different people and offices within that dynamic. All are disciples or learners; and in some sense (if we follow Aquinas' reading of Mt 23,8–10) all are "teachers",

---

in the search for truth. Moreover, it is by personal assent that men must adhere to the truth that they have discovered." (Ibid.)

12 *Catechism of the Catholic* Church, 1534.

13 Ibid. 1547

as we mutually help one another discern the voice of the Spirit speaking in the hearts of believers, in the traditions of the Christian faith, and in the signs of the times.

3 Fundamental Bases for this "Conversational" Approach to Seeking Truth and Wisdom, and its Implications for Theological Enquiry

Such a pedagogical dynamic as a basis for understanding the relation of pastoral realities and doctrinal realities should really come as no great surprise; the fundamental theology of our Catholic tradition actually demands such an account of faith teaching and practice. It is to something of this fundamental theological tradition that I will now turn, through a reflection on some familiar texts from the Second Vatican Council.

I begin with that remarkable Dogmatic Constitution of the Council *Dei verbum,* On Divine Revelation. In this text it is clear that the contemporary "Franciscan renewal" towards a more "incarnational" theological approach is indeed demanded by the nature of Revelation itself. God speaks to us not only in words, but "deeds and words", these having an "inner unity".[14] Ultimately this historical integrative communication of the divine finds its perfect expression *not* in words, nor simply in "deeds and words", but in a Person, a lived life: "the deepest truth about God and the salvation of man shines out for our sake in Christ, who is both the mediator and the fullness of all revelation".

> This plan of revelation is realised by deeds and words having an inner unity: the deeds wrought by God in the history of salvation manifest and confirm the teaching and realities signified by the words, while the words proclaim the deeds and clarify the mystery contained in them. By this revelation then, the deepest truth about God and the salvation of man shines out for our sake in Christ, who is both the mediator and the fullness of all revelation.[15]

In describing divine revelation in this way, *Dei verbum* makes clear that God's communication with men and women is necessarily contextual; it is always historically and humanly mediated. This divine-human dynamic at the heart of revelation is made especially clear when teaching out what "authorship" might mean for the scriptural texts. Fundamentally God is the true author, as the texts are inspired by the Holy Spirit; this is what gives them their sacred and canonical nature.[16] However, to stop here would not sufficiently attest to the mysterious reality

---

14 *Dei verbum*, 2.
15 Ibid.
16 Ibid. 11.

of the authorship as mediated by the "true authorship" of those men in historical contexts who wrote the texts:

> In composing the sacred books, God chose men and while employed by Him they made use of their powers and abilities, so that with Him acting in them and through them, they, as true authors, consigned to writing everything and only those things which He wanted. Therefore, since everything asserted by the inspired authors or sacred writers must be held to be asserted by the Holy Spirit, it follows that the books of Scripture must be acknowledged as teaching solidly, faithfully and without error *that truth which God wanted put into sacred writings for the sake of salvation.*[17]

The mysterious fact that fallen, contextually and historically particular human beings participate thoroughly in God's self-revealing to the world immediately alerts us to the nature of the scriptural texts as accounts to be *discerned*. So, "since God speaks in Sacred Scripture through men in human fashion, the interpreter of Sacred Scripture, in order to see clearly what God wanted to communicate to us, should carefully investigate what meaning the sacred writers really intended, and what God wanted to manifest by means of their words".[18]

The previous section demonstrated how all talk of doctrine and pastoral care in the church must necessarily be read in a context of a deep learning, participative pedagogy, in which all are (in varying ways) teachers *and* learners. Something of this same dynamic can now be recognised as we move to *Dei verbum*'s account of how the nature of divine revelation makes a holistic demand on the church as the privileged hermeneutical community for the discernment of God's Word. For here, too, this interpretative, missionary task involves a dynamic – even a conversational dynamic – for all "in" the church:

> And so the apostolic preaching, which is expressed in a special way in the inspired books, was to be preserved by an unending succession of preachers until the end of time.
> This tradition which comes from the Apostles develops (*proficit* – proceeds? progresses?) in the Church with the help of the Holy Spirit. For there is a growth in the understanding of the realities and the words which have been handed down. This happens through the contemplation and study made by believers, who treasure these things in their hearts (see Luke, 2:19, 51) through a penetrating understanding of the spiritual realities which they experience, and through the preaching of those who have received through Episcopal succession the sure gift of truth. For as the centuries succeed one another, the Church constantly moves forward toward (*tendit*) the fullness of divine truth until the words of God reach their complete fulfilment in her.[19]

It is important to spell out something of the theological and ecclesiological im-

[17] Ibid. My emphases.
[18] Ibid. 12.
[19] Ibid. 8.

plications of this fundamental theology of revelation. In particular, it seems to require a whole-church commitment to the "development" ("progress"?, "using"? – *proficio*) of the apostolic tradition, as described in *Dei verbum* 8. There is here described a complexity of growth points for the "development" of the tradition, including the hearts and experiences of the faithful, together with magisterial teaching. This is a "living tradition ... poured into the practice and life of the believing and praying church".[20] Here is a fundamental theology of process just as much as of content, and offers a thoroughly discursive vision of the ecclesial discernment of doctrinal realities and the practical wisdom needed for their effective and contextual embodiment in the world.

It is this church teaching on how God "uninterruptedly converses with the bride of His beloved Son" that underpins the approach to "practical theology" which I outlined at the start of this paper. It is a magisterial, authoritative teaching which radically holds itself to account, in locating its heart in the complexities of diverse living and faith-full practice among Christians in their different contexts.

4 Conclusion: In the End, it's All about God's Mission – of Love and Mercy

In October 2015 the Synod Fathers gathered in Rome from all over the world, from very different contexts and cultures, to reflect on marriage and family life. My own position, from the start of this paper, is that this cannot be seen as an event simply dealing with a discrete "topic" or set of difficult "issues" in the church's life. The Synod cannot be an exercise of clerical problem solving on behalf of a laity who've messed things up in their living of the Gospel! Rather, the subject and processes of the two Synods of 2014 and 2015 draw us into much more fundamental ecclesiological questions – a number of which have been set out in this paper. I want to end with a plea that we turn our gaze *outward* in discussing these matters – outward not to households (who in many ways are thorough central, whilst "peripheral", to the church), but to the greater world with which Christian households live in solidarity.

The urgency of the Synod conversation is, I want to suggest, most properly to be understood not as one, first of all, of "moral crisis" or cultural threat, but rather of a missiological type. In slightly different ways both the Extraordinary Synod of 2014 and the General Synod of 2015 seek to locate reflection on marriage and family within "the context of Evangelisation", with the gathering of 2015 clearly setting out that the concern as for "the vocation and mission of the family in the church and in the contemporary world". This is important. It can

20 Ibid.

remind us that, as Pope St. John Paul put it: "The family is not simply the object of the Church's pastoral care; it is also one of the Church's most effective agents of evangelisation."[21] A constructive theology for marriage and family, building on the fundamental theological and ecclesiological teachings of the second Vatican Council already outlined, must find a central place for the ordinary living of this evangelising mystery of the church-in-the-world, without simply jumping to examine its weaknesses and name its "pastoral problems".

In fact, from its earliest modern use in the essentially evangelisation-motivated Council of Vatican II, the "domestic church" has been recognised as an agent of mission in a peculiarly powerful way. First as a "domestic sanctuary of the church"[22], and later as "a place where the Gospel is transmitted and from which the Gospel radiates"[23], the Christian household based in marriage is increasingly developed in magisterial and papal teaching as a crucial element in the renewed work of evangelisation in the late modern world. Not least among the reasons for this, is the recognition of the powerful place the family unit – "the first and vital cell of society"[24] – has as, on the one hand, an embodiment of an ecclesial office of service for the salvation of others (as described above), and, on the other, a human, societal reality, grounded in the very hearts of men and women as they are created by God.[25] In marriage we see a sacramentally graced embodiment of the ecclesial life of faith, deeply embedded in the world. From this the Christian household can be recognised as a place where faithful Christians live in effective solidarity with all those very many people who struggle to live lives of love, faithful relationship and family in the fraught situations of our cultures.

It is this graced solidarity with the women and men of our own context that marks Christian marriage and family out as a powerful place of evangelisation, both of culture and of persons. To make this our primary focus for reflection on marriage is to commit ourselves to a constructive theology of married and family life which begins with the central questions of evangelisation: the relation of the ecclesial to prevailing culture; questions of enculturation and Gospel fidelity; the need for solidarity for missionary effectiveness; and the compassionate reading of the realities of the "mission field".[26] In all this, the ones who evangelise, by virtue

---

21 JOHN PAUL II: *Ecclesia in Asia*, 1999, 46, http://w2.vatican.va/content/john-paul-ii/en/apost_exhortations/documents/hf_jp-ii_exh_06111999_ecclesia-in-asia.html; retrieved 16.11.2015.

22 *Apostolicam actuositatem,* 11.

23 PAUL VI: *Evangelii nuntiandi*, 1975, 71, http://w2.vatican.va/content/paul-vi/en/apost_exhortations/documents/hf_p-vi_exh_19751208_evangelii-nuntiandi.html; retrieved 16.11.2015.

24 *Apostolicam actuositatem,* 11.

25 Ibid.

26 John Paul II's Encyclical *Redemptoris missio* (1990) is an invaluable source here (http://w2.vatican.va/content/john-paul-ii/en/encyclicals/documents/hf_jp-ii_enc_07121990_redemptoris-missio.html; retrieved 16.11.2015).

of their graced solidarity with the world in which they mission, learn a practical wisdom with regard to that world and its ways. This is a wisdom informed by love for, and lived understanding of, that world, as well as by the traditions of Christianity which they seek to share in it.

These brief missiological reflections on marriage and family as a graced and privileged place of evangelisation lead me to make some observations on the consequences of this for contemporary thinking on Christian married living.

A first observation concerns how we can establish, as an essential and permanent dynamic of our living tradition, ways of properly attending to the practice of Christian households, as a necessary part of the church's discerning conversations. If marriage and family life is a privileged locus of ecclesial mission practice, then the "missionaries" – the practitioners of this mission – clearly have a key role in the whole-church pedagogical discernment of practical wisdom for contemporary evangelisation. Appropriate methods, like those I have tried to develop in theological action research, are needed in order to articulate and engage with these "operant voices". This is essential if our practice doctrine and pastoral care are to be authentically integrated in the pedagogical dynamic to which they are, together, called. If the theological understanding outlined in this paper is even a bit true, then it is hard to see how the church can move forward joyfully and confidently without finding ways of establishing the processes, structures and skills needed for such organisational attentiveness to the voices of ordinary living.

Secondly, if the lives and faith of married people, even in their ordinary human brokenness, are such privileged practitioners of mission in and for the world, then – as for all missionaries – there needs to be an appropriate spirituality, developed through their experiences and in critical continuity with other spiritualties of the tradition.[27] Again, this requires the hearing of the ordinary voices of this practical way of holiness; for a spirituality of family-based mission is surely already being lived out, all be it in rather unarticulated ways. The articulation of this way of holiness, based on an inductive reading of it from its heart of day to day living, is potentially a huge and renewing gift for the life of the whole church. We need to ask ourselves with a new urgency, as theologians, pastors, church leaders, and family members, how such a domestic missionary spirituality can be understood and nurtured among ordinary people.

In all this, as a third point, particular attention needs to be paid as to how faithful Christians living marriage and family life understand the cultural contexts in which they find themselves, and how they discern appropriate responses to the Christian living of that culture. A central question here would be: Is the mission of

---

27 Reflection on "missionary spirituality" set out in *Redemptoris missio*, 87–91, as a stimulus for the articulation of the spirituality of the domestic church might prove fruitful here.

the family characterised by a more, or less, counter cultural stance, or a more, or less, enculturating attitude? As families negotiate the complexities of late modern and globalised cultures, they will have learnings to share, and insights particular to their situations which are essential to the effectiveness of our whole-church vocation to evangelise.

As a final observation I return to the journalistic accounts that have accompanied the Synod, and the ways in which they have been in danger of reducing what is happening here to a quasi-political procedure focusing on a few difficult issues – an act of clerical problem solving on behalf of a benighted laity. The more fundamental and ecclesiologically far reaching account I have given here suggests that the genius of this synodal process has been *not* in such sorting out of issues, but rather in the re-orientating of the church in such a way that it might be better equipped to deal with these, and much more fundamental questions of mission and vocation. For it is through the Christian household's understanding of the practices of Christian wisdom in the heart of the world, that many of the "difficult questions" concerning marriage and family can be re-encountered. In the domestic church these "problems" – whilst often still problematic – are experienced through the loving commitment of the family. For when the Magisterium speaks of these "issues" – of relationship breakdown and subsequent forms of marriage, of same-sex relationship and its naming as "marriage" in many societies, of cohabiting couples and their families, of methods of reproductive control and so forth – in all these points the church doctrine speaks into the struggles and heart-ache of the vast majority of Catholic families, who experience these realities as shaping relationships within their own close and extended families. Learnings about compassion, living in love with imperfect, even broken down situations, are potentially rich gifts from the ordinary domestic churches that make up our congregations.

The time is ripe to begin to shape a teaching-and-learning church where the wisdom of the Christian household can take its place as an authority on practical loving, mercy and mission. The challenge lies in the reality that this wisdom does not – and should not generally – take the form of neat, entirely rationally worked through accounts of how things are, or should be; nor does it argue from a basis of ontological realities as the most to the fore. Rather, this is a theology embodied in practice, which calls us to new ways of reading, articulating and understanding. In this we should be encouraged as Christians: after all, as Pope Francis has pointed out, "Christian doctrine has a face, a body, flesh; He is called Jesus Christ and it is His life that is offered from generation to generation to all people in all places."[28]

[28] FRANCIS: "Video Message … to Participants in an International Theological Congress".

Clear as a Teacher and Tender as a Mother: The Interface between Doctrine and Pastoral Care

Emmanuel Agius

Clare Watkins' approach to shift the focus of her paper from the thorny debate on which doctrine needs to be developed, or which pastoral practice is unaccept-able in the light of church doctrine, to some major theological themes related to faith-full living of marriage and family today is highly commendable. During the plenary meetings and at the ten *circuli minores* (the different language working groups) of the 2015 October Extraordinary Synod of Bishops on the family as well as during the press briefings on the works of the Synod and interventions by individual bishops and Cardinals to the media, the two areas in the life of the church, namely her teaching and the pastoral practice, continuously featured as the Synod's major bone of contention. Some claim that failure to deal with prob-lems that remain unresolved on a doctrinal level will simply lead to the church's teaching being seen as rigid and lacking sensitivity. Others maintain that, though doctrine and pastoral care refer to two different areas of theology, they cannot contradict each other and for this reason pastoral solutions must be deduced from doctrinal truths. Watkins' theological arguments go beyond the myopic perspec-tive of attempting to strike a "balance" between those who are concerned about a given situation being "in line with the church's teaching" and those who give greater focus to the "individual persons".[1]

At the outset of her paper Watkins rightly remarks that opposing "doctrinal" and "pastoral" is untrue to each. To bring the church's teaching and the pastoral practice into harmony with each other, one needs to go beyond the fake polarity of two churches: the church of mercy and the church dominated by rules which punish the sinner. Since church doctrine and pastoral care should not contradict each other, it is only through a process of re-thinking with "renewed freshness and

1 "The Pastoral Challenges of the Family in the Context of Evangelization", *Relatio synodi*, 2014, 4, http://www.vatican.va/roman_curia/synod/documents/rc_synod_doc_20141018_relatio-synodi-familia_en.html; retrieved 11.11.2015.

enthusiasm"[2] that this thorny issue can be resolved. Watkins' objective is to open a fresh discussion about marriage and the family today by reflecting holistically on theology (doctrinal and pastoral) in order to reconcile the doctrinal vision of marriage with its lived experience.

To overcome the detachment between the doctrinal vision of marriage and its lived experience Watkins refers to the common meaning of *teaching* and *pasturing*. The main concern of both aspects is Christian lives bearing fruits through the education of one's attitudes and dispositions as well as through the cultivation of a good self. The distinctive feature of teaching is not imparting knowledge, but educating one's heart and promoting one's internal growth and health. Pastoral ministry means shepherding, accompanying and motivating others to growth internally and mature in moral virtues. Accordingly, she concludes that in the context of marriage and the family, church doctrine and pastoral ministry are both *pedagogical and missiological* since they are both concerned with how people learn Christian wisdom and practice, rather than simply receiving information about faith. Both share one pedagogical dynamic of the Christian life as a life of discipleship and both have an intrinsic missiological nature since they both serve the salvation of others.

Watkins' approach to harmonize church doctrine on marriage and pastoral ministry to families by attempting to reframe these two areas of concern within a deeper theological context is in tune with Pope Francis' mindset. He explicitly rejects the "church doctrine versus pastoral care" approach and the autonomous and contradictory nature of these two areas of theology. In his concluding address at the October 2014 Synod, he referred to these mindsets as temptations which need to be forcefully resisted. He drew a contrast between the "hostile inflexibility" of those who consider themselves "masters" of the doctrine, those who are closed within the certitude of what they know without allowing themselves to be surprised by God, and a "destructive do-goodery, which in the name of a false mercy bandages wounds without first curing and medicating them".[3] Moreover, he compared these wrong perceptions on truth and mercy to the temptation of those who attempt to transform stones into bread to break the long, heavy, and painful fast; and also to transform the bread into a stone and cast it against the sinners, the weak, and the sick. Furthermore, he referred to the "temptation to neglect the '*depositum fidei*' [the deposit of faith], not thinking of themselves as guardians but as owners or masters [of it]; or, on the other hand, the temptation to neglect

2 Ibid.

3 FRANCIS: "Address for the Conclusion of the Third Extraordinary General Assembly of the Synod of Bishops", 18.10.2014, https://w2.vatican.va/content/francesco/en/speeches/2014/october/documents/papa-francesco_20141018_conclusione-sinodo-dei-vescovi.html; retrieved 11.11.2015.

reality, making use of meticulous language and a language of smoothing to say so many things and to say nothing!"[4]

Pope Francis remarked that he was not surprised by such temptations in the Synod's animated discussions, speeches and interventions which were full of faith, of pastoral and doctrinal zeal, of wisdom, of frankness and of courage, and of *parrhesia.* However, he stressed that the relationship between traditional teaching and today's pastoral challenges of the family "should never be seen as a source of confusion and conflict".[5] Any temptation to foster disharmony between church teaching and pastoral practice needs to be vehemently resisted. It is only through collegiality, synodality and discernment that these two areas of theology find their true meaning and their proper relationship. The collegial path of the bishops and the involvement of all God's people under the guidance of the Holy Spirit is the way forward to discern and reconcile truth and mercy for all.

1 In Search of a Pastoral Method

I concur with Watkins' contention that an adequate theological method is needed to understand appropriately the interface between church teaching and marriage ministry. By incorporating dynamically the integrity of doctrine and the richness of lived experience she hopes to open up a fresh discussion on today's reality of marriage and the family. She claims that the inauthenticity of such a dichotomy is resolved if marriage explained theologically in ontological terms and the practical wisdom gained through today's existential realities of marriage and the family enter into a constructive, dynamic, on-going, open and transparent dialogue. Watkins proposes the conversational method of discernment for mission of the domestic church as the way forward for the evangelisation of the family in today's complex, postmodern and multicultural societies. She innovatively elucidates this method by the theological insights of the conciliar teaching on revelation set out in *Dei verbum.* She moves beyond the standard correlative approaches of practical and contextual theology to an integrative approach, termed as "theology in four voices", by bringing together the valid contribution of Scripture, creeds, church doctrine, theologians and the daily experiences of believers. All voices are heard and responded to, each with its own particular kind of authority since they all contribute to Christian wisdom. Since the gift of God's spirit is present and active within the life of the entire community, theology (doctrinal and pastoral) is essentially a conversational articulation, rather than a monologue. Moreover, the "four voices" have a single purpose of discerning the way forward in faithfulness and practical wisdom.

4 Ibid.
5 Ibid.

Underpinning Watkins' innovative theological method is an ecclesiology which recognises that all baptised persons belong to one *teaching* and *learning* church. Though there are different places held by different people in the church, all participants are disciples or learners and in some sense teachers as well. All baptised persons share a common ministry of *service* to each other since they all partake, through baptism, in Christ's priesthood. Both holy orders and marriage are sacraments at the service of communion. The practical wisdom of the faithful is brought into dynamic and discursive relationship with church teaching, doctrine and the larger tradition as well as with the insights of the academy. Listening to the hidden voices of the practical wisdom of the whole variety of Catholic faithful experiences of living marriage is, according to Watkins, an integral dimension of the teaching and learning ecclesial community.

Though I fully agree with Watkins' conversational method of discernment, however my contention is that her method needs to be reframed and rearticulated from broader and deeper theological and pastoral insights in order to consolidate its somehow fragmented and incomplete theological underpinnings. The ecclesial discernment proposed by Watkins for integrating Scripture, tradition and church doctrine with the practical wisdom of all married couples, including those who are living in complex and broken human lives, needs to be rethought systematically within a pastoral model which takes seriously into account the contemporary empirical situation; a clear vision to broaden its horizon of evaluation and interpretation and hence its projected and desired praxis; and finally sets an ongoing process that leads to the transformation of pastoral practice. The theological model needs to be a dynamic hermeneutical process that accompanies people to move forward to the rich experience of the Gospel core message. It is a process of ecclesial discernment which leads to the respect and acceptance of the whole truth.

Moreover, one of the major shortcomings of Watkins' theological method is its failure to take on board all the theological and pastoral insights inspiring both the October 2014 and 2015 Synodal documents. A pastoral method that creatively integrates the rich, multifaceted, contrasting and novel insights articulated in the synodal documents has the advantage of fine-tuning its theological and pastoral perspective, analysis, objectives and solutions in the light of the Second Vatican Council and the *Magisterium* of Pope Francis. The pontificate of Pope Francis represents a fresh reception of the teaching of Vatican II which is characterized by dialogue with the world, listening to the world, and a critical but sincere openness to human experience.

The *Instrumentum laboris* for the 2014 October Extraordinary General Assembly of the Synod of Bishops, the *Relatio synodi* 2014, the *Lineamenta* and the *Instrumentum laboris* for the 2015 Ordinary General Assembly of the Synod of Bishops follow the same theological method which offers pastoral care to wounded and vulnerable families without however contradicting church doctrine. The key words characterising this paradigm shift in pastoral theology are evangelisation, vocation and mission, listening, mercy and truth, discernment, pastoral accompaniment and conversion. I think that this is the way forward for understanding the church's mission to carry out evangelisation "with the tenderness of a mother and the clarity of a teacher".[6]

Pope Francis' pastoral mindset shaping the Synods' documents does not follow the deductive approach which is based on the application of doctrine to the complex and diverse reality of the family. In fact, the *Lineamenta* (guidelines) on "The Vocation and Mission of the Family in the Church and Contemporary World",[7] released in preparation for the 2015 Synod of Bishops on the Family, encourages the ecclesial community to avoid formulating pastoral care of the family which is simply a deduction from Catholic doctrine. A deductive pastoral method based on the belief that a set of clear and unchangeable principles are considered as a "one-size-fits-all" solution to all the complexities of today's family issues seems to be untenable. The insufficiency of such a deductive approach is due to the fact that praxis is not valued as much as it should and that today's marital relationships have become much more complex and diverse than before, due to socio-economic, political and cultural realities. For this reason, the deductive method leads quite often to wrong pastoral decisions and actions.

Nor is the pastoral approach adopted by the Synodal documents based merely on a type of inductive approach which makes human experience and empirical studies, adopted pragmatically and uncritically, the main determining factors of pastoral strategy. Moreover, it seems that Pope Francis goes beyond the "see, judge, act" method which is used by several documents of the church on social Catholic doctrine.[8] This method takes the situation of the human person, society or human activity as its starting point, followed by judgement and then leading to action. Though this method rightly underlines the need of pastoral reflection on experience, however it has been used at times as a reactive method – reacting

6 *Relatio synodi*, 2014, 29.

7 See http://www.vatican.va/roman_curia/synod/documents/rc_synod_doc_20141209_lineamenta-xiv-assembly_en.html (English version); retrieved 11.11.2015.

8 See R. BIORD CASTILLO: "Ponderación teológica del método ver-juzgar-actuar", conference given in the XXII Jornadas de Teología y Reflexión, "Criterios para efectuar un discernimiento cristiano de una situación histórica", 23.03.2004, http://raulbiordcastillo.com/wp-content/uploads/2011/11/Articulo-Iter-Ponderacion-teologica-del-metodo-ver.pdf; retrieved 11.11.2015. There are other methods which include very similar elements – such as the Pastoral Circle Method, having as phases: Insertion/experience; social analysis; theological reflection; pastoral action – see F. WIJSEN/P. HENRIOT: *The Pastoral Circle Revisited: A Critical Quest for Truth and Transformation,* Maryknoll, NY: Orbis, 2005.

to the particular situation and formulating a pastoral strategy which is a specific response to that situation – and not as a proactive method.

The paradigm shift in pastoral theology which, to my mind, enriches and consolidates Watkins' conversational method by its broader theological and pastoral perspective as well as by its empirical and hermeneutical approach is termed the "empirical-critical-theological" method (or a variant of it). This method articulates more convincingly and adequately the interface between church teaching on marriage and the pastoral care of families in their daily existential experiences. The method is empirical since its starting point is the empirical experience and its aim is the renewal of praxis; it is critical and hermeneutical since it seeks to judge and evaluate human experience with the specific aim of its renewal; it is theological since in all the phases there is an explicit reference to the criteria or horizon of faith. Basically, this method includes the following three aspects: 1) an evaluative analysis and interpretation of the present situation; 2) a vision and a desired praxis; 3) a transformative process from the present situation towards the desired situation. All these three phases include different moments which are not separated but linked to each other.[9]

One may note that the *Lineamenta* for the October 2015 Ordinary Synod of Bishops has three main sections which are in line with this method: (i) *Listening: the Context and the Challenges of the Family;* (ii) *Looking at Christ: the Gospel of the Family;* (iii) *Confronting the Situation: Pastoral Perspectives.* Moreover, the *Instrumentum laboris* for the same Synod follows also the same pattern of thought: (1) *Considering the Challenges of the Family:* (2) *The Discernment of the Family Vocation;* and (3) *The Mission of the Family Today.*

The "empirical-critical-theological" method articulates more systematically and cogently the four consequences which emerge from Watkins' pedagogical and missiological reflections on marriage and the family. Firstly, its evaluative analysis and interpretation of the present situation gives a privileged and key role to the practical wisdom of all Christian households which are envisaged as a rich theological source for contemporary evangelisation. Secondly, the unarticulated practical way of holiness lived by the domestic church is appraised from a theological vision which discerns hidden values, positive elements and signs of hope even in paradoxical situations seemingly riddled only with negative factors. Thirdly, the cultural context experienced by families is described, evaluated and interpreted with the help of human sciences and faith in order to discern adequately the signs

9 Mario Midali has developed this method in M. MIDALI: *Practical Theology: Historical Development of its Foundational and Scientific Character*, Roma: LAS, 1999. He calls the three phases: (i) *kairologica*; (ii) *progettuale*; (iii) *strategica*. See also Don S. Browning's phases in D.S. BROWNING: *A Fundamental Practical Theology: Descriptive and Strategic Proposals*, Minneapolis, MN: Augsburg Fortress, 1996: descriptive and historical, systematic, strategic.

of the times that the Holy Spirit provokes to the community of believers in a specific historical context. Fourthly, the vision of the church as a "field hospital" and as a "guiding torch" recognises the imperfections and vulnerability experienced by so many wounded families as a challenge for the "pastorality of doctrine" and for a richer theology of mercy, justice, compassion and accompaniment.

Similar to Watkins' conversational method, discernment is central to the "empirical-critical-theological" method. In fact, the common thread that unites the three phases is ecclesial discernment[10] which Pope Francis draws strongly on his Jesuit training, particularly the rules for spiritual discernment taught by St Ignatius of Loyola. Discernment is the way we come to the knowledge of God's will. So it is not just common sense, or taking prudent decisions, although these are important elements. Discernment has as its first premise the belief that God's Spirit will show us the direction we are called to take. It assumes our capacity to be enlightened by that Spirit and it requires of us the discipline to be open to what the Spirit is saying to us. Such discipline is not always easy, particularly when it means we have to let go our cherished way of looking at things or reverse a long-held opinion. Discernment is ultimately about our desire to make right judgments in accord with God's hopes for the world.

In ecclesial discernment, what is sought is always that which the Spirit of God is suggesting to the church and the way that the Spirit is indicating. This is possible through a special gift of the Spirit, the gift of counsel. Through this gift, God guides the church by the advice which comes from Him, in the midst of a myriad of opinions and interpretations. Through the Spirit, one definitely realises the limits of human effort and one understands that one is unable to dominate all events that happen and to make a clear prediction, or form the outline, of future events. Being open to the Spirit means that the decisions taken would have the character of a collaborative response.

So basically it is a question of a pastoral-theological method, and that which links all different phases of the method is ecclesial discernment. The following sections of this article continue to discuss in detail the "empirical-critical-theological" method.

2 Evaluative Analysis and Interpretation of the Present Situation

In the first phase, one is expected to analyse, describe, interpret and evaluate a specific situation and praxis with the help of human sciences and faith. The specific aim of this approach is to understand correctly and discern adequately the signs

[10] See S. LANZA: "A proposito di discernimento", in: *Convertire Giona: Pastorale come progetto*, Roma: Edizioni OCD, 2005, 119–131.

of the times that the Holy Spirit provokes to the community of believers in a specific historical context.[11] This approach has its profile in the Argentine variant of liberation theology, which is not focused on a Marxist evaluation of the economic and political situation of the poor and oppressed, but is "a theology of the people", one which takes the experience, wisdom and piety of all Catholics seriously.[12]

The actual situation is analysed against the horizon of past data and its impact on the present. The analysis of the situation does not stop at a descriptive level since it is not simply a sheer acceptance of the *status quo*. The task is that of critically interpreting and evaluating the situation in the light of the Gospel and in response to human aspirations. It is an attempt to see God's presence in today's world, even though human experience is not perfect. Accordingly, theology and human sciences do not only play a descriptive but also a hermeneutical role.[13] At this stage one is even expected to put into question certain historical forms of religious and ecclesial practice.

Moreover, the analysis and the interpretation of the situation are not carried out haphazardly or arbitrarily but on the basis of specific values and criteria inspired by faith and reason. These criteria include doctrinal principles, moral norms, and deep human aspirations. The difference from the deductive (application) method lies here: these criteria are not to be *applied* to the situation, but used to analyse, describe and interpret it. As a result of this analysis and interpretation, one can arrive at values which ought to be preserved, aspects to be excluded or abandoned, aspirations that should be met, problems to be resolved, new values and cultural expressions, and events to denounce or reject. The present historical reality is interpreted as the *kairòs,* a special historical moment and opportunity for creative renewal.

Pope Francis' approach, which takes as its starting point the data of experience, is inspired by his belief that the lived experience of people is a theological source and a place of theological reflection. When we discuss marriage and family we have to listen to what people who are living this reality have to say. Here the church needs to discern the *sensus fidelium*. Accordingly, rather than starting from above, from a doctrine or theory and taking an ideal model of the family and imposing it on reality, this approach starts with open-minded reflections on

---

11 See M. KIRWAN: "Reading the Signs of the Times", in: J. SWEENEY/G. SIMONDS/D. LONSDALE (eds.): *Keeping Faith in Practice: Aspects of Catholic Pastoral Theology*, London: SCM Press, 2010, 49–63.

12 See J.C. SCANNONE: "El papa Francisco y la teología del pueblo", 2014, http://www.amerindiaenlared.org/upload/libros/1407169642_attach37.pdf; retrieved 11.11.2015.

13 See G. HEITINK: *Practical Theology: History, Theory, Action Domains*, Grand Rapids, MI: Eerdmans, 1999, particularly "The Hermeneutical Perspective", 178–200. See also J.-G. NADEAU: "Une méthodologie empirico-herméneutique", in: G. ROUTHIER/M. VIAU (eds.): *Précis de théologie pratique*, Bruxelles: Lumen Vitae, 2007, 221–234.

reality. This method of theological reflection, which starts with the discernment of the concrete daily experiences of married people, is in sharp contrast to an approach which deduces pastoral practice from general, sometimes idealised notions of God, humanity or marriage.

In the run-up to October 2014 synodal meetings, Pope Francis initiated this first phase of pastoral method by launching an unprecedented worldwide survey of Catholic experience of family life today, distributed in October 2013.[14] The questionnaire touched on the whole gamut of issues related to sex and marriage, including matters that had previously been regarded as taboo. The questions were addressed to bishops, asking them to describe the opinions and practices of the people as well as their catechetical initiatives. Laypeople who responded to these surveys knew that they were given a chance to participate actively by making their views heard. For the second time in two years, Pope Francis has asked in December 2014 national bishops' conferences around the world to seek input from Catholics at "all levels" about how the church should respond to sometimes difficult questions of modern family life.

It is interesting to note that Pope Francis' pastoral method is in line with the explanation of Gospel discernment proposed by John Paul II in his apostolic exhortation *Pastores dabo vobis*:

> Knowledge of the situation is important. However, simply to provide data is not enough; what is needed is a 'scientific' inquiry in order to sketch a precise and concrete picture of today's socio-cultural and ecclesial circumstances. Even more important is an interpretation of the situation. Such an interpretation is required because of the ambivalence and at times contradictions, which are characteristic of the present situation where there is a mixture of difficulties and potentialities, negative elements and reasons for hope, obstacles and alternatives, as in the field mentioned in the Gospel where good seed and weeds are both sown and 'co-exist' (cf. Mt. 13:24 ff).[15]

John Paul II then explains how critical such an analysis and interpretation should be, and underlines the fact that even negative factors can have hidden values which need to be affirmed:

> It is not always easy to give an interpretative reading capable of distinguishing good from evil or signs of hope from threats ... it is not sufficient simply to welcome the positive factors and to counteract the negative ones. The positive factors themselves need to be

---

[14] See the "Preparatory Document for the III Extraordinary General Assembly of the Synod of Bishops", 2013, particularly the questions in Part III, http://www.vatican.va/roman_curia/synod/documents/rc_synod_doc_20131105_iii-assemblea-sinodo-vescovi_en.html; retrieved 11.11.2015.

[15] JOHN PAUL II: Apostolic Exhortation *Pastores dabo vobis*, 1992, 10, http://w2.vatican.va/content/john-paul-ii/en/apost_exhortations/documents/hf_jp-ii_exh_25031992_pastores-dabo-vobis.html; retrieved 11.11.2015.

subjected to a careful work of discernment, so that they do not become isolated and contradict one another, becoming absolutes and at odds with one another. The same is true for the negative factors, which are not to be rejected *en bloc* and without distinction, because in each one there may lie hidden some value which awaits liberation and restoration to its full truth.[16]

One should here recall that in line with the explanation of Gospel discernment and the pastoral approach of *Pastores dabo vobis,* the *Relatio post disceptationem* had referred to the importance of recognising the "positive elements even in the imperfect forms that may be found outside this nuptial situation", such as common-law marriage and cohabitation.[17] Indeed, when common-law marriages "reach a notable level of stability" and are "characterized by deep affection" and responsibility toward offspring, they "may be seen as a germ to be accompanied in development towards the sacrament of marriage".[18] As far as cohabitation is concerned, the *Relatio post disceptationem* affirmed that there is a growing number of cases in which cohabiting couples eventually decide to marry if they receive the right accompaniment and help. It cited situations of couples who choose to live together without marriage for economic or cultural reasons, or those in Africa who enter into traditional marriages in "stages", and said that in response the church must keep its "doors always wide open … In such unions, it is possible to grasp authentic family values or at least the wish for them. Pastoral accompaniment should always start from these positive aspects."[19] These statements did not eventually feature in the *Relatio synodi*, but they are in line with the pastoral approach indicated by *Pastores dabo vobis.*

Pastores dabo vobis maintains that for "a believer the interpretation of the historical situation finds its principle for understanding and its criterion for making practical choices in a new and unique reality, that is, in Gospel discernment. This interpretation is a work which is done in the light and strength provided by the true and living Gospel, which is Jesus Christ, and in virtue of the gift of the Holy Spirit."[20] The Gospel discernment is not simply the gathering and recording of the events and circumstances of a particular historical situation but a task, a challenge and a call from God articulated in a particular historical situation.

Accordingly, today's trends in marriage structures and family patterns are a challenge and a call to the ecclesial community to renew its trust in the power

---

[16] Ibid.

[17] See the *Relatio post disceptationem* of the General Rapporteur, Card. Péter Erdő, 13.10.2014, 18, http://press.vatican.va/content/salastampa/en/bollettino/pubblico/2014/10/13/0751/03037.html; retrieved 11.11.2015.

[18] Ibid. 22.

[19] Ibid. 37.

[20] JOHN PAUL II: *Pastores dabo vobis*, 10.

of the Holy Spirit, who is the source of wisdom, counsel and knowledge "all of which are at the centre of making wise choices, of staying on a discerned course, of cutting through extraneous information and getting to the heart of issues so that judgments or decisions are based on the truth of things rather than on opinion, hearsay, appearances, partial information, and, above all, fear of change".[21] The Holy Spirit enriches the church with the special gift of fortitude which enables her to hold fast to true wisdom to discern the signs of the times and to creatively respond to these new challenges by novel pastoral strategies on how to proclaim the truth and beauty of the family and God's unfailing love and mercy to all wounded families.

3 The Vision and Desired Praxis

After taking as starting point the current situation as experienced by people, groups, whole communities or local churches, and reflecting critically on all its dimensions and complexities, one should then raise the question concerning which vision is to be adopted and what kind of praxis is to be desired. The primary objective of the second phase of the "empirical-critical-theological method" is therefore the identification of a vision and long term goals which can be a source of motivation and inspiration for a renewed and more authentic praxis.

One is expected to make explicit the underlying vision firstly concerning marriage and the family. What is the Christian vision of marriage and the family? How is this vision a source of inspiration for contemporary culture? However, this phase seeks to broaden the theological perspective because the vision of marriage and the family has to be contextualised within the wider horizon of evangelisation today. So here one has to raise questions such as: which Christ do we want to announce? What is the core message of the Gospels? Which vision of the Spirit and of his work do we have in mind? Which experience of church do we want to promote? Which models of community do we want to adopt? Which service to people, in the present situation, do we want to offer? Which changes in society do we want to encourage according to the Gospel's primary message?

The Second Vatican Council, papal pronouncements, documents of Episcopal Conferences and local churches, the contribution of theologians and other scholars are all important sources in this reflection. The criteria do not follow the personal or group preferences, but they are spelt out in connection to the Jesus event and the ecclesial community, in dialogue with human sciences such as psychology, sociology, pedagogy, etc. It is not a static but rather a developing and dynamic reflection which introduces new horizons of meaning.

---

21 M.G. LAWLER/T.A. SALZMAN/E. BURKE-SULLIVAN: *The Church in the Modern World: Gaudium et Spes Then and Now*, Collegeville, MN: Liturgical Press, 2014, 57.

Which vision is the Synod under the influence of Pope Francis projecting? Pope Francis is inviting the ecclesial community to broaden its pastoral vision, priorities and perspectives to become empowered to rethink, re-evaluate and re-assess the complex situations in today's family relations from a new horizon of theological meaning and significance which takes into account all the different facets and dimensions of human experience. This pastoral approach does not require a change in church doctrine on the indissolubility and unity of marriage, faithfulness and openness for life, or the theology of Eucharist and Reconciliation.

Pope Francis' vision of the renewal of the church's pastoral ministry is motivated primarily by "the joy of the Gospel".[22] It is a return to the Gospel that has motivated all reform movements within the Christian community from the development of monasticism to the reforms of St Francis of Assisi and St Dominic. Pope Francis does not represent a liberal position, but a radical one – one which goes back to the roots of the Christian faith which is the Gospel listened to, meditated upon, lived, celebrated and witnessed. While building a bridge back to our origins, he is encouraging the ecclesial community to come to a broader consensus in constructing a bridge to the future.

3.1 A Wider Perspective from the Periphery

A main characteristic of Pope Francis' theological and pastoral vision is his innovative concept of periphery. This perspective suggests that it is possible to get a wider perspective of the current state of the world looking from the *edge* rather than from the *centre*. It is a new way of outlining an alternative worldview consisting of rethinking the present state of affairs of the world starting from the periphery rather than from the "headquarters" of church doctrine. As Pope Francis says,

> I am convinced of one thing: the great changes in history were realised when reality was seen not from the centre but rather from the periphery. It is a hermeneutical question: reality is understood only if it is looked at from the periphery, and not when our viewpoint is equidistant from everything. Truly to understand reality we need to move away from the central position of calmness and peacefulness and direct ourselves to the peripheral areas. Being at the periphery helps to see and to understand better, to analyse reality more correctly, to shun centralism and ideological approaches ... [23]

[22] We shall focus especially on the Apostolic Exhortation *Evangelii gaudium* (24 November 2013) which explains the pastoral vision of Pope Francis.

[23] A. SPADARO: "Wake up the World: Conversation with Pope Francis about Religious Life", in: *La Civiltà Cattolica* I (2014), 3–17. English translation of the original text in Italian by Donald Maldari S.J., 3–4.

It is a clear preference for an interpretation of the family life that is decentralised and non- idealised. Beyond the curtains of an idealised picture of the family, there is an alternative existential reality that is often neglected and marginalised that is worth exploring to truly understand the unfolding historical process of family relationship. More fundamentally, Pope Francis intends to anchor his reflections on the family on the direct experience of the true life of and in the periphery:

> This is really very important to me: the need to become acquainted with reality by experience, to spend time walking on the periphery in order really to become acquainted with the reality and life-experiences of people. If this does not happen we then run the risk of being abstract ideologists or fundamentalists, which is not healthy.[24]

3.2 The Church as a Pilgrim People of God

Antonio Spadaro, the chief-editor of *Civiltà Cattolica*, remarked that different church models emerged during the Synod: "At the end of the Extraordinary Synod, we believe it is necessary for the entire church to reflect not just on specific questions, but thanks to these, also on the ecclesiological model it embodies. This allows us to understand the church's mission in the world and its relationship with history."[25] The divergent positions on the thorny issue on the interface between church doctrine and pastoral care are ultimately the result of divergent approaches and interpretations of the church.

Pope Francis' ecclesiological vision is rooted in the metaphor of the church as the pilgrim people of God. He calls for a missionary church. Though he refers to the language of the new evangelisation so central to both John Paul II and Benedict XVI, he however introduces a subtle nuance to his predecessors' theology of mission. Pope Francis uses the term to highlight the fundamentally centrifugal thrust of the church's activity and the need for Christians to enter into a deeper and more profound solidarity with the world. It is for this reason that he frequently refers to one of his favourite expressions, the "smell of the sheep".[26] An evangelising community wants to get involved in the world and in people's daily lives, it bridges distances, it is willing to abase itself if necessary and it embraces human life, touching the suffering flesh of Christ in others. An evangelising community

---

24 P. JENKINS: "A Peripheral Vision", 21.02.2014, http://www.patheos.com/blogs/anxiousbench/2014/02/a-peripheral-vision/; retrieved 11.11.2015.

25 See "The Synod According to Jesuit Periodical La Civiltà Cattolica", 30.10.2014, http://www.lastampa.it/2014/10/30/esteri/vatican-insider/en/the-synod-according-to-jesuit-periodical-la-civilt-cattolica-zW9z0FQbICt7JJsQtxjjAO/pagina.html; retrieved 11.11.2015.

26 See, for example, Pope Francis' homily at the Chrism Mass in St Peter's Basilica, Holy Thursday, 28 March 2013, http://w2.vatican.va/content/francesco/en/homilies/2013/documents/papa-francesco_20130328_messa-crismale.html; retrieved 11.11.2015.

is also supportive, standing by people at every step of the way, no matter how difficult or lengthy this may prove to be.[27]

For Pope Francis, the church's mission does not begin with the language of condemnation but with a humble openness to "a peaceful and multifaceted culture of encounter"[28] which, in the end, is an encounter with Christ. The centrifugal orientation of the church requires that it goes "forth to everyone without exception".[29] He writes: "I prefer a Church which is bruised, hurting and dirty because it has been out on the streets, rather than a Church which is unhealthy from being confined and from clinging to its own security."[30] We need, he insists, a church "that knows how to open her arms and welcome everyone".[31] In his interview, Pope Francis goes further: "Instead of being just a Church that welcomes and receives by keeping the doors open, let us try also to be a Church that finds new roads, that is able to step outside itself ... to those who have quit or are indifferent."[32]

This new ecclesial mindset of Pope Francis which is evident in his evocative image of the church as a "field hospital" that goes out to meet the wounded on the battlefield of life to heal them and to warm their hearts, understands the missionary role of the church not simply in terms of merely addressing the needs of the poor and the marginalised, but also in terms of a learning process from them, from their participation in the *sensus fidei* in which they teach us the suffering Christ. We need to listen to them, to speak for them and to embrace the mysterious wisdom which God wishes to share with us through them.[33] This image is the opposite image of a fortress under siege.

How then can the church, as a field hospital, be present to the world? The *Relatio post disceptationem*,[34] the *Relatio synodi* 2014,[35] and the "Message" together provide an answer. They unanimously speak about the church as a "Guiding Torch" in relation to a church as a "Beacon". The church, in fact, is a *lumen* – a light – because upon its face the Church reflects the light of Christ, who is in turn the *Lumen gentium*.[36] Yet this light can be understood in at least two different

[27] See FRANCIS: Apostolic Exhortation *Evangelii gaudium*, 2013, 24, http://w2.vatican.va/content/francesco/en/apost_exhortations/documents/papa-francesco_esortazione-ap_20131124_evangelii-gaudium.html; retrieved 11.11.2015.

[28] *Evangelii gaudium,* 220.

[29] Ibid. 48.

[30] Ibid. 49.

[31] A. SPADARO: "A Big Heart Open to God: The Exclusive Interview with Pope Francis", in: *America* (30.09.2013), http://americamagazine.org/pope-interview; retrieved 11.11.2015.

[32] Ibid.

[33] See *Evangelii gaudium,* 198.

[34] *Relatio post disceptationem*, 23.

[35] *Relatio synodi*, 2014, 28.

[36] See *Lumen gentium,* 1, http://www.vatican.va/archive/hist_councils/ii_vatican_council/documents/vat-ii_const_19641121_lumen-gentium_en.html; retrieved 11.11.2015

ways, which are not however mutually exclusive. The church can first be understood as a "beacon". This beacon sheds light, but it is also statically fixed on solid foundations. Yet we can also understand the church as a "torch". What is the difference between the beacon and the torch? The beacon stays put. It is visible, but it doesn't move. The torch, instead, sheds its light on the way, as it walks amongst humanity. It illuminates those human beings that are closest, shining upon their hopes, but also upon their sadnesses and fears.[37] The church as guiding torch is called to accompany human persons along their journey, to be in contact with their actual experience. Instead of blinding humankind with an unbearable light, the church illuminates their journey step by step.[38]

Pope Francis emphasises this "missionary option" which should inspire all the church's life, as follows:

> … a missionary impulse capable of transforming everything, so that the Church's customs, ways of doing things, times and schedules, language and structures can be suitably channelled for the evangelisation of today's world rather than for her self-preservation. The renewal of structures demanded by pastoral conversion can only be understood in this light: as part of an effort to make them more mission-oriented, to make ordinary pastoral activity on every level more inclusive and open, to inspire in pastoral workers a constant desire to go forth and in this way to elicit a positive response from all those whom Jesus summons to friendship with himself.[39]

This commitment to a missionary church has led the Pope to criticise a more bureaucratic way of dealing with pastoral issues.[40] He has complained that "the Church sometimes has locked itself up in small things, in small-minded rules".[41]

3.3 Listening Church

Another feature of Pope Francis' ecclesiological vision is his call for a "listening church". He speaks positively about a church that is committed to honest dialogue, listening, and even disagreement. In his interview, "A Big Heart Open to God" he reflects on the meaning of *sentire cum ecclesia*. It means thinking with the *whole* church and not just the ones who count ecclesiastically. It means daring to enter into a "complex web of relationships" and living in receptive solidarity with all God's people. It means recalling not only the infallibility of the church's teachers but also, as the Council taught, the infallibility of the believing church.

37 See *Gaudium et spes*, 1, http://www.vatican.va/archive/hist_councils/ii_vatican_council/documents/vat-ii_const_19651207_gaudium-et-spes_en.html; retrieved 11.11.2015.

38 See A. SPADARO: "The Church in a Synodal Journey", in: *America* (07.11.2014), http://americamagazine.org/church-synodal-journey; retrieved 11.11.2015.

39 *Evangelii gaudium*, 27.

40 See ibid. 63.

41 See A. SPADARO: "A Big Heart Open to God".

In a genuine listening and disarming church, Pope Francis wants to include those who are in ecclesial exile of one kind or another.[42]

3.4 The "Pastorality of Doctrine"

Pope Francis' understanding of church doctrine is firmly rooted in the Council's commitment to what Christoph Theobald has termed as "the pastorality of doctrine".[43] This approach to church doctrine has its origin in Pope John XXIII's influential opening address at the Council, *Gaudet Mater Ecclesia*.[44] Pope John called for a *Magisterium* that is fundamentally pastoral in character. His vision was not simply to have a Council that offers a mere repetition of previous doctrinal formulations, but rather a genuine effort to rethink church doctrine in view of the pressing questions of the time. The Council followed the Pope's lead and consistently treated doctrine as something to be authentically interpreted and faithfully lived within concrete historical, cultural, and pastoral contexts.

Pope Francis has a particular interest and commitment to the pastorality of doctrine as he insists that doctrine must be interpreted in relation to the core Christian *kerygma* and in the light of the particular pastoral context. In his address at the plenary session of the Congregation for the Doctrine of the Faith, Pope Francis expressed his understanding of doctrine in one sentence: "In reality, doctrine has the sole purpose of serving the life of the People of God and it seeks to assure our faith of a sure foundation."[45] Moreover, in an open letter to the founder of the Italian newspaper *La Repubblica,* Eugenio Scalfari, the Pope admitted to certain reluctance to speak of "absolute truth", not because he was a "relativist" but because, for Christians, truth is mediated through a relationship with a person, Christ. As such, truth is always encountered in history.[46] Furthermore, in his interview with Antonio Spadaro, Pope Francis states: "The most important thing is the

---

42 See R.R. GAILLARDETZ: "The 'Francis Moment': A New Kairos for Catholic Ecclesiology", in: *Proceedings of the Catholic Theological Society of America* 69 (2014), 63–80 at 72 (http://ejournals.bc.edu/ojs/index.php/ctsa/article/view/5509/4988, 72; retrieved 11.11.2015).

43 See C. THEOBALD: "The Principle of Pastorality at Vatican II: Challenges of a Prospective Interpretation of the Council", 26.09.2013, http://www.bc.edu/content/dam/files/schools/stm_sites/c21online/pdf/legacy-translation.pdf; retrieved 11.11.2015

44 See JOHN XXIII: *Gaudet Mater Ecclesia*, English translation, 11.10.1962, http://conciliaria.com/tag/gaudet-mater-ecclesia/; retrieved 11.11.2015. Original Italian version at http://w2.vatican.va/content/john-xxiii/it/speeches/1962/documents/hf_j-xxiii_spe_19621011_opening-council.html; retrieved 11.11.2015.

45 See FRANCIS: "Address of Pope Francis to Participants in the Plenary Session of the Congregation for the Doctrine of the Faith", 31.01.2014, http://w2.vatican.va/content/francesco/en/speeches/2014/january/documents/papa-francesco_20140131_plenaria-dottrina-fede.html; retrieved 11.11.2015.

46 FRANCIS: "Letter to a Non-Believer", 04.09.2013, http://w2.vatican.va/content/francesco/en/letters/2013/documents/papa-francesco_20130911_eugenio-scalfari.html; retrieved 11.11.2015

first proclamation: Jesus Christ has saved you. And the ministers of the Church must be ministers of mercy above all ... Proclamation in a missionary style focuses on the essentials, on the necessary things: this is also what fascinates and attracts more, what makes the heart burn, as it did for the disciples at Emmaus."[47]

Pope Francis's recontextualisation of doctrine is seen in his retrieval of one of the most neglected themes of the Second Vatican Council, the "hierarchy of truths". In his interview with Antonio Spadaro, he states that "the dogmatic and moral teachings of the Church are not all equivalent".[48] The Council in *Unitatis redintegratio* states that: "When comparing doctrines with one another, they should remember that in Catholic doctrine there exists an order or 'hierarchy' of truths, since they vary in their relation to the foundation of the Christian faith."[49] In this brief passage, the Council introduced a crucial distinction between the content of divine revelation, understood as God's self-communication in Christ by the power of the Spirit, and those church doctrines which, in varying degrees, mediate that content.

Unfortunately, since the Council there have been little references to this statement in magisterial documents. One should also note the reformulation by the Congregation of the Doctrine of the Faith (CDF) which states that "some dogmas are founded on other dogmas which are the principal ones, and are illuminated by these latter".[50] The difference in formulation is significant. Whereas Vatican II introduced a crucial distinction *between* doctrine and the more fundamental Christian *kerygma*, the CDF asserted only that doctrines vary in their relations one to another. The principal consequence of the CDF's reformulation was a severe restriction of the field of application for the hierarchy of truths.[51]

Pope Francis has reminded us of the true meaning of the Council's teaching on the hierarchy of truths in *Evangelii gaudium* when stating that doctrines are not ends in themselves; they serve us when they draw us into life-giving relationship with Christ. He writes:

> All revealed truths derive from the same divine source and are to be believed with the same faith, yet some of them are more important for giving direct expression to the heart of the Gospel. In this basic core, what shines forth is the beauty of the saving love of God made manifest in Jesus Christ who died and rose from the dead. In this sense, the Second

---

47 Quoted in A. SPADARO: "A Big Heart Open to God".

48 Ibid.

49 *Unitatis redintegratio,* 11, http://www.vatican.va/archive/hist_councils/ii_vatican_council/documents/vat-ii_decree_19641121_unitatis-redintegratio_en.html; retrieved 11.11.2015.

50 CONGREGATION OF THE DOCTRINE OF THE FAITH: "Declaration in Defense of the Catholic Doctrine on the Church against Certain Errors of the Present Day", 24.06.1973, 4, http://www.vatican.va/roman_curia/congregations/cfaith/documents/rc_con_cfaith_doc_19730705_mysterium-ecclesiae_en.html; retrieved 11.11.2015.

51 See R.R. GAILLARDETZ: "The 'Francis Moment'", 77.

Vatican Council explained, "in Catholic doctrine there exists an order or a 'hierarchy' of truths, since they vary in their relation to the foundation of the Christian faith." This holds true as much for the dogmas of faith as for the whole corpus of the Church's teaching, including her moral teaching.[52]

Pope Francis interprets the Council's teaching on the hierarchy of truths as more than just ranking doctrines; the Council wished to relate doctrine to something more basic, the Christian *kerygma*. He writes:

> Pastoral ministry in a missionary style is not obsessed with the disjointed transmission of a multitude of doctrines to be insistently imposed. When we adopt a pastoral goal and a missionary style which would actually reach everyone without exception or exclusion, the message has to concentrate on the essentials, on what is most beautiful, most grand, most appealing and at the same time most necessary. The message is simplified, while losing none of its depth and truth, and thus becomes all the more forceful and convincing.[53]

This passage from *Evangelii gaudium* shows that Pope Francis is not afraid to affirm church doctrine as basic to Christian identity, but he consistently orients that doctrine toward the basic Christian *kerygma* and situates it within the pastoral life of the church.

In his comments Pope Francis has already given concrete examples of the pastorality of doctrine. It is evident in his openness to a rethinking of the church's teaching on the possibility of communion for the divorced and remarried. He has no wish to reverse church teaching on marital indissolubility, but he is committed to placing it within the field of Christian mercy. In his interview with Antonio Spadaro, Pope Francis referred to Christians who live in situations that from the point of view of the church are irregular or somewhat complex, Christians that, in one way or another, live with open wounds. These are divorced and remarried, same-sex couples and other difficult situations. What kind of pastoral work can we do in these cases? What kinds of tools can we use? The Pope responds: "We need to proclaim the Gospel on every street corner ... preaching the good news of the kingdom and healing, even with our preaching, every kind of disease and wound."[54]

Pope Francis gave us another example in his discussion of Pope Paul VI's teaching on artificial birth regulation in *Humanae vitae*. In a March 5, 2014 interview he responded to a direct question about adherence to this controversial Papal teaching:

> It all depends on how the text of *Humanae Vitae* is interpreted. Paul VI himself, towards

---

52 *Evangelii gaudium,* 36.

53 Ibid. 35.

54 Quoted in A. Spadaro: "A Big Heart Open to God".

the end, recommended to confessors much mercy and attention to concrete situations. But his genius was prophetic, as he had the courage to go against the majority, to defend moral discipline, to apply a cultural brake, to oppose present and future neo-Malthusianism. The object is not to change the doctrine, but it is a matter of going into the issue in depth and to ensure that the pastoral ministry takes into account the situations of each person and what that person can do. This will also be discussed on the path to the Synod.[55]

This statement by Pope Francis resonates John XXIII's call for a deeper penetration of church doctrine and its more pastoral realisation. This does not reflect a pastoral compromise on the demands of church teaching, but an authentic interpretation of the doctrine apprehended within a specific cultural and pastoral context.[56]

Pope Francis is not concerned with either a simple reaffirmation or reversal of the church's official teaching but rather with a deep reconsideration of what John Langan calls the church's "stance". For Langan, "stance" is distinct from a specific doctrinal formulation. To consider the church's "stance" on an issue is a matter of "critical reflection on the tradition to clarify what strengths are to be preserved and what continuities are to be affirmed even while searching for the sources of limitations in the teaching and acknowledging the development of new questions and problems".[57]

A change in stance may or may not bring about a development in church doctrine. What it does allow for is a consideration of hitherto neglected factors and insights. However, some continue to press whether such a change in "stance" would inevitably lead the Pope to reverse this or that controversial church teaching. Such a question can be answered by looking at the way doctrine develops in the church. There is a common misconception that doctrinal development occurs primarily by ecclesiastical decision. On the contrary, history shows that doctrine develops when pastoral contexts shift and new insights emerge such that particular doctrinal formulations no longer mediate the saving message of God's transforming love. The gradual shift in the church's condemnation of usury offers us a classic example of what is meant here. That teaching was not reversed in a single papal decree. Rather, there was a gradual and halting pastoral discernment that the teaching, in its classical formulation, no longer served the central values it was intended to

[55] Quoted in A.F. ROUCH: "Pope Sees Scope for Pastoral Response to Contraception Ban", in: *The Tablet* (05.03.2014), http://www.thetablet.co.uk/news/494/41/-pope-sees-scope-for-pastoral-response-to-contraception-ban; retrieved 11.11.2015, reporting interview of Francis with Ferruccio de Bortoli, editor-in-chief of *Corriere della Sera* published on 5 March 2014, http://www.corriere.it/cronache/14_marzo_04/vi-racconto-mio-primo-anno-papa-90f8a1c4-a3eb-11e3-b352--9ec6f8a34ecc.shtml; retrieved 11.11.2015.

[56] See R.R. GAILLARDETZ: "The 'Francis Moment'", 78–79.

[57] See J. LANGAN: "Understanding Pope Francis' Statements on Homosexuality", in: *America* (10.03.2014), http://americamagazine.org/issue/see-person; retrieved 11.11.2015.

protect, namely the welfare of the poor. A similar development is observed in the church's teaching on capital punishment and on religious freedom.

Beyond doubt, church leaders may contribute to the development of doctrine. However, they could only do that when they do what Pope Francis has been insisting upon so far. They need to move from the centre to the periphery and see, in specific pastoral contexts, how doctrine actually "works", that is, how it contributes to bringing people into a saving encounter with God's abundant love and mercy.[58]

3.5 A Church of Mercy and Justice

Pope Francis' doctrinal and pastoral approach is rooted in a vision of a missionary church that is tirelessly engaged in the world to show the face of God's mercy which is at the centre of the Gospel. In *Evangelii gaudium,* he says: "An evangelising community knows that the Lord has taken the initiative, he has loved us first (cf. 1 Jn 4:19), and therefore we can move forward, boldly take the initiative, go out to others, seek those who have fallen away, stand at the crossroads and welcome the outcast. Such a community has an endless desire to show mercy, the fruit of its own experience of the power of the Father's infinite mercy."[59]

He emphasises this point in several instances. For Pope Francis, "The Church must be a place of mercy freely given, where everyone can feel welcomed, loved, forgiven and encouraged to live the good life of the Gospel."[60] We need "a Church that is again capable of restoring citizenship to so many of its children that walk as if in exodus".[61] Christian citizenship is above all the result of God's mercy.

This approach is not a betrayal of church teaching, but rather the centre of its identity as a sign and sacrament of God's love in the world. The Pope's teaching on mercy shows that, as St Thomas Aquinas said, God is not bound by our rules of justice. God is love and because he is true to himself, he is merciful. John Paul II had already underlined the centrality of mercy in his Encyclical *Dives in misericordia*, where he says that mercy "constitutes the fundamental content of the messianic message of Christ and the constitutive power of his mission".[62]

Some of the forty-six questions of the *Lineamenta* take the theme of mercy head-on, asking: "How can people be helped to understand that no one is beyond

---

[58] See Richard R.R. GAILLARDETZ: "The 'Francis Moment'", 79–80.

[59] *Evangelii gaudium,* 24.

[60] Ibid. 114.

[61] FRANCIS: "Meeting with the Bishops of Brazil: Address of Pope Francis", 28.07.2013, available at http://w2.vatican.va/content/francesco/en/speeches/2013/july/documents/papa-francesco_20130727_gmg-episcopato-brasile.html; retrieved 11.11.2015.

[62] JOHN PAUL II: *Dives in Misericordia,* 30.11.1980, 6, http://w2.vatican.va/content/john-paul-ii/en/encyclicals/documents/hf_jp-ii_enc_30111980_dives-in-misericordia.html; retrieved 11.11.2015.

the mercy of God and how can this truth be expressed in the Church's pastoral activity towards families, especially those which are wounded and fragile?[63] While avoiding any unjust discrimination, how can such persons receive pastoral care in these situations in light of the Gospel? How can God's will be proposed to them in their situation?"[64] Quoting St Thomas Aquinas, Pope Francis explains the centrality of mercy as follows:

> Thomas thus explains that, as far as external works are concerned, mercy is the greatest of all the virtues: "In itself mercy is the greatest of the virtues, since all the others revolve around it and, more than this, it makes up for their deficiencies. This is particular to the superior virtue, and as such it is proper to God to have mercy, through which his omnipotence is manifested to the greatest degree".[65]

There might be a misunderstanding on what mercy is all about. Some think that mercy is cheap grace or pastoral weakness. However, mercy is a very demanding virtue; it does not soften the commandments of the Lord, nor does it weaken dogmas. But as it is the fundamental virtue according to St Thomas Aquinas, mercy is a hermeneutical key for interpreting the commandments. With his constant focus on mercy and his insistence that the church and its pastors recognize the reality people are living in, Pope Francis hopes to discover new pastoral ways to reach people and bring them closer to Christ. The most important message in pastoral care is the proclamation that Jesus Christ is saviour. The ministers of the church must be dispensers of God's grace and mercy above all.

4 A Transformative Pastoral Process

The third phase of the pastoral method is a journey from the present situation towards a desired state of affairs. A true pastoral strategy for family ministry becomes a journey of transformation when the empirical findings concerning the family today are critically evaluated and interpreted in the light of a theological vision which broadens rather than restricts the horizons of meaning and interpretation. This discernment process is the way forward for the church's ministry for the family since such a process opens up innovative and creative avenues for pastoral care. This is the ripple effect of the theological-pastoral critical reflection which cannot be left simply to the creativity and experience of pastoral workers or to spontaneity. It cannot be satisfied by the attitude: "this is the way it has always been done".[66]

---

63 "The Vocation and Mission of the Family in the Church and Contemporary World: *Lineamenta*", 2014, question 20.

64 *Lineamenta*, 2014, question 40.

65 *Evangelii gaudium,* 37.

66 Ibid. 33.

A transformative pastoral process[67] is the result of a systematic reflection which attempts to identify through discernment, in the light of the desired vision, those steps in pastoral practice, such as a change in attitudes and perspectives, which need to be taken in accordance with the Gospel. Moreover, it aims to identify those attitudes and mindsets that need to be overcome since they are inspired merely by human interests and the eclipse of the whole truth. This dynamic process is not a betrayal of doctrine but rather faithfulness to the whole truth. A change of attitude is required particularly for "those who long for a monolithic body of doctrine guarded by all and leaving no room for nuance. This might appear as undesirable and leading to confusion. But in fact such variety serves to bring out and develop different facets of the inexhaustible riches of the Gospel."[68]

So it is not just a question of reacting to current issues by applying doctrine. It is a much more demanding process of discernment which ultimately does include other important tenets of church teaching which might have been ignored or given less importance. The challenge of the 2015 Synod is to indicate the highlights and steps of this journey of transformation rather than seek to provide "solutions" to all complex issues being discussed.

4.1 Pastoral Conversion

Pastoral conversion is a top priority in the Synod of the family. This renewal does not concern only individuals but the entire church.[69] Change of attitudes is the primary requirement of this pastoral conversion. In his interview with Antonio Spadaro, Pope Francis remarked that the structural and organisational reforms are secondary. The first reform must be the attitude. The ministers of the Gospel must be people who can warm the hearts of the people, who walk through the dark night with them, who know how to dialogue and to enter into their people's night, into the darkness, but without getting lost. The people of God want pastors who care.

The documents of the Synod of Bishops on the family are explicit in their call to the church to support and nourish today's marriages and family life by re-examining its pastoral attitudes, approaches and structures in the light of a pastoral conversion.

Neither a rigorist nor a lax attitude is the right pastoral approach. On the one hand, the rigorist does not see the person but the rule. On the other hand, we cannot be lax when it comes to sin, as if sin does not exist. What is needed is to reach out and to see the person before the rule. As Pope Francis remarked: "The

---

67 See E. GRAHAM: "Practical Theology as Transforming Practice", in: J. WOODWARD/S. PATTISON (eds.): *The Blackwell Reader in Pastoral and Practical Theology*, Oxford: Blackwell, 2000, 104–117.

68 *Evangelii gaudium*, 40.

69 Ibid. 26.

rigorist washes his hands so that he leaves it to the commandment. The loose minister washes his hands by simply saying, 'This is not a sin' or something like that ... "[70] This pastoral conversion, which is the result of one's openness to the whole truth of the Gospel, is crucial for overcoming the temptation of stifling legalism as well as the soft-headed compassion which pretends that sin does not exist.

In *Evangelii gaudium*, Pope Francis states that the church's pastoral and missionary mission needs conversion in order to rediscover and renew its central moral commitment, namely our response to God's love. Under no circumstance can this invitation be obscured! Christian morality "is not a form of stoicism, or self-denial, or merely a practical philosophy or a catalogue of sins and faults".[71] A morality which becomes detached from its core Gospel message risks becoming an ideology that enslaves rather than liberates:

> All of the virtues are at the service of this response of love. If this invitation does not radiate forcefully and attractively, the edifice of the Church's moral teaching risks becoming a house of cards, and this is our greatest risk. It would mean that it is not the Gospel which is being preached, but certain doctrinal or moral points based on specific ideological options. The message will run the risk of losing its freshness and will cease to have "the fragrance of the Gospel".[72]

Moreover, Pope Francis warns the church to resist the temptation of rendering religion a form of servitude. Precepts and rules are important and indispensable. However, these should be contextualised within a broader perspective of the Gospel message. Pastoral conversion is needed to avoid a rush attitude of deductive reasoning leading to the application of moral principles to particular complex situations without searching for a prudential moral judgment which takes seriously into consideration the faith journey of persons involved:

> At the same time, the Church has rules or precepts which may have been quite effective in their time, but no longer have the same usefulness for directing and shaping people's lives. Saint Thomas Aquinas pointed out that the precepts which Christ and the apostles gave to the people of God "are very few". Citing Saint Augustine, he noted that the precepts subsequently enjoined by the Church should be insisted upon with moderation "so as not to burden the lives of the faithful" and make our religion a form of servitude, whereas "God's mercy has willed that we should be free". This warning, issued many centuries ago, is most timely today. It ought to be one of the criteria to be taken into account in considering a reform of the Church and her preaching which would enable it to reach everyone.[73]

---

[70] Quoted in A. SPADARO: "A Big Heart Open to God".

[71] *Evangelii gaudium,* 39.

[72] Ibid.

[73] Ibid. 43.

The pastoral care of families needs conversion from a legalist attitude since this is a symptom of doctrinal insecurity and a sign of narrow, static and inward-looking perspective. Pope Francis states that: "If the Christian is a restorationist, a legalist, if he wants everything clear and safe, then he will find nothing. Tradition and memory of the past must help us to have the courage to open up new areas to God. Those who today always look for disciplinarian solutions, those who long for an exaggerated doctrinal 'security,' those who stubbornly try to recover a past that no longer exists – they have a static and inward-directed view of things. In this way, faith becomes an ideology among other ideologies. I have a dogmatic certainty: God is in every person's life. God is in everyone's life. Even if the life of a person has been a disaster, even if it is destroyed by vices, drugs or anything else – God is in this person's life. You can, you must try to seek God in every human life. Although the life of a person is a land full of thorns and weeds, there is always a space in which the good seed can grow. You have to trust God."[74]

4.2 Pastoral Accompaniment

Pope Francis, in *Evangelii gaudium*, emphasises that "accompaniment" is crucial to this transformative pastoral process. He refers to this pastoral approach as the "art of accompaniment" which "teaches us to remove our sandals before the sacred ground of the other (cf. Ex 3:5). The pace of this accompaniment must be steady and reassuring, reflecting our closeness and our compassionate gaze which also heals, liberates and encourages growth in the Christian life."[75] Moreover, in his interview with Spadaro, Pope Francis states that "[t]he Church's ministers must be merciful, take responsibility for the people and accompany them like the good Samaritan, who washes, cleans and raises up his neighbour. This is pure Gospel. God is greater than sin."[76]

The issue of pastoral accompaniment was at the foreground of the 2014 October Synod discussions. The *Lineamenta,* quoting *Evangelii gaudium*, indicates that this issue shall once more be discussed at the 2015 October Synod since it needs further reflections: "Synod discussion highlighted the need for a pastoral line based on *the art of accompaniment* ... "[77] Christ wanted his Church to be a house with doors always open to welcome everyone, without leaving anyone out. Hence bishops are called to accompany couples and families and care for their personal and social wounds.

In the Pope's ecclesiological vision, pastoral accompaniment is rooted in the Emmaus story. Similar to Jesus who accompanied the two disciples who were sad

---

74 Quoted in A. SPADARO: "A Big Heart Open to God".
75 *Evangelii gaudium,* 169.
76 Quoted in A. SPADARO: "A Big Heart Open to God".
77 *Lineamenta*, 2014, Introduction to section on "Caring for Wounded Families" (44–54).

and disappointed on their way to Emmaus, the church needs to overcome fear of encountering people on their way. "We need a Church capable of entering into people's conversation. We need a Church able to dialogue, as Jesus did with those two disciples who, having left Jerusalem behind, were wandering aimlessly, alone, with their own disappointment, disillusioned by a Christianity now considered barren, fruitless soil, incapable of generating meaning. We need a Church capable of warming hearts; a Church capable of leading people back to Jerusalem."[78]

The art of accompanying others starts with a non-judgmental attitude towards others. Pope Francis stated many times that the church needs to be less judgmental and more open in accordance with the Gospel spirit. Compassionate language must replace the language of condemnation. When Pope Francis told reporters the frequently misunderstood statement "Who am I to judge?", he wanted to express the church's mission of accompaniment. He did not criticise the church's teaching on homosexuality. However, what he meant is that the doctrine makes sense within the broader understanding of the Gospel message and the art of accompaniment.

In his interview with Spadaro, Pope Francis remarked that "a person once asked me, in a provocative manner, if I approved of homosexuality. I replied with another question: 'Tell me: when God looks at a gay person, does he endorse the existence of this person with love, or reject and condemn this person?' We must always consider the person. Here we enter into the mystery of the human being. In life, God accompanies persons, and we must accompany them, starting from their situation. It is necessary to accompany them with mercy. When that happens, the Holy Spirit inspires the priest to say the right thing."[79] His non-judgmental attitude towards persons who are not living according to the church's moral standards is articulated in *Evangelii gaudium* as follows:

> One who accompanies others has to realize that each person's situation before God and their life in grace are mysteries which no one can fully know from without. The Gospel tells us to correct others and to help them to grow on the basis of a recognition of the objective evil of their actions (cf. Mt 18:15), but without making judgments about their responsibility and culpability (cf. Mt 7:1; Lk 6:37). Someone good at such accompaniment does not give in to frustrations or fears. He or she invites others to let themselves be healed, to take up their mat, embrace the cross, leave all behind and go forth ever anew to proclaim the Gospel. Our personal experience of being accompanied and assisted, and of openness to those who accompany us, will teach us to be patient and compassionate with others, and to find the right way to gain their trust, their openness and their readiness to grow.[80]

Again in *Evangelii gaudium,* Pope Francis invokes traditional moral reasoning

[78] FRANCIS: "Meeting with the Bishops of Brazil".

[79] Quoted in A. SPADARO "A Big Heart Open to God".

[80] *Evangelii gaudium,* 172.

and basic Christian values to underpin his pastoral vision. Accompaniment with compassion and care must replace condemnation and exclusion. He says that it is only in this way that we can "enter on the paths of true growth and awaken a yearning for the Christian ideal: the desire to respond fully to God's love and to bring to fruition what he has sown in our lives. But this always demands the patience of one who knows full well what Saint Thomas Aquinas tells us: that anyone can have grace and charity, and yet falter in the exercise of the virtues because of persistent 'contrary inclinations'. In other words, the organic unity of the virtues always and necessarily exists *in habitu*, even though forms of conditioning can hinder the operations of those virtuous habits." Here the Pope emphasises the need for "a pedagogy which will introduce people step by step to the full appropriation of the mystery. Reaching a level of maturity where individuals can make truly free and responsible decisions calls for much time and patience."[81]

This leads us to the "law of graduality" which is the other side of the coin of pastoral accompaniment.

4.3 The "Law of Graduality"

In Christian life, pastoral accompaniment is the step-by-step guidance which families need in their search for improvement in moral behaviour. "Graduality" (sometimes termed also "gradualness") can be considered as a pastoral attitude which takes into consideration the difficulties that can separate real families and persons from the Christian ideal. Many of the Synod fathers spoke of the "law of graduality" – a concept that at one level observes that there are gradations of virtues and vices, and that living situations need not be either completely good or completely evil.

In his opening address of the 2014 Synod of Bishops, Cardinal Péter Erdő of Hungary said that *Humanae vitae* should be read in light of graduality.[82] Cardinal Reinhard Marx of Munich also invoked graduality as a key to helping the church develop a new way of talking about sex.[83] Cardinal Vincent Nichols explained it as "a law of pastoral moral theology which permits and encourages people ... to take one step at a time in our search for holiness".[84] Even if someone's situation is far from perfect, this does not mean it has no moral value. It is better to encour-

[81] Ibid. 171.

[82] See the *Relatio ante disceptationem*, 06.10.2014, http://press.vatican.va/content/salastampa/en/bollettino/pubblico/2014/10/06/0712/03003.html; retrieved 11.11.2015.

[83] See F.X. ROCCA: "On Sexual and Medical Ethics, Synod Fathers Speak of 'Graduality'", 07.10.2014, http://www.catholicnews.com/services/englishnews/2014/on-sexual-and-medical-ethics-synod-fathers-speak-of-graduality.cfm; retrieved 11.11.2015.

[84] Ibid.

age the positive elements in people's life rather than to castigate them for their mistakes.

This is, in fact, an anthropological principle. It considers the human person not as an ethical test-taker, getting some questions right and others wrong, but as a pilgrim, journeying through peaks and valleys towards goodness.[85]

In fact, the *Relatio post disceptationem* refers to the "law of gradualness" as "the fruit of discernment applied on a case-by-case basis ... that takes into consideration the distinction between state of sin, state of grace and the attenuating circumstances".[86] As a pastoral strategy, graduality can be an effective, even necessary approach in order to lead people more deeply into the moral and spiritual life of the church.

Some theologians have mistakenly made of this concept the basis for a permissive attitude to moral norms, treating them merely as ideals. Pope John Paul II, in his Apostolic Exhortation *Familiaris consortio*, cautioned about this misinterpretation when stating that "what is known as 'the law of gradualness' cannot be identified with 'gradualness of the law'".[87] And in guidelines for confessors in 1997, the Pontifical Council for the Family stated that they should not be led by the law of gradualness to give people the impression that repentance does not require a decisive break with sin.[88]

In his *Familiaris consortio*, Pope John Paul II declared: "What is needed is a continuous, permanent conversion" that "is brought about concretely in steps which lead us ever forward. Thus a dynamic process develops, one which advances gradually." He added that man "day by day builds himself up through his many free decisions; and so he knows, loves and accomplishes moral good by stages of growth".[89]

One can here recall what Pope Benedict XVI said in an interview with a German journalist that if a male prostitute uses a condom to try to avoid infecting people with HIV/AIDS, it can be "a first step in the direction of a moralization, a first assumption of responsibility, on the way towards recovering an awareness

---

85 See N. COLLURA: "Graduality", in: *National Catholic Reporter* (14.10.2014), http://ncronline.org/blogs/ncr-today/graduality; retrieved 11.11.2015.

86 *Relatio post disceptationem*, 2014, 47.

87 JOHN PAUL II: *Familiaris consortio*, 1981, 34, http://w2.vatican.va/content/john-paul-ii/en/apost_exhortations/documents/hf_jp-ii_exh_19811122_familiaris-consortio.html; retrieved 11.11.2015.

88 See PONTIFICAL COUNCIL FOR THE FAMILY: *Vademecum for Confessors Concerning Some Aspects of the Morality of Conjugal Life,* 1997, 9, http://www.vatican.va/roman_curia/pontifical_councils/family/documents/rc_pc_family_doc_12021997_vademecum_en.html; retrieved 11.11.2015.

89 JOHN PAUL II: *Familiaris consortio*, 34.

that not everything is allowed and that one cannot do whatever one wants".[90] Benedict was not questioning the church's teaching, but he was saying that concern for others could be a step in a gradual movement of change.

Pope Francis explains how important this awareness of graduality is when pastors and lay people accompany others in their journey, and particularly in the sacrament of confession. Even small steps should be appreciated and encouraged:

> Moreover, pastors and the lay faithful who accompany their brothers and sisters in faith or on a journey of openness to God must always remember what the *Catechism of the Catholic Church* teaches quite clearly: 'Imputability and responsibility for an action can be diminished or even nullified by ignorance, inadvertence, duress, fear, habit, inordinate attachments, and other psychological or social factors'. Consequently, without detracting from the evangelical ideal, they need to accompany with mercy and patience the eventual stages of personal growth as these progressively occur. I want to remind priests that the confessional must not be a torture chamber but rather an encounter with the Lord's mercy which spurs us on to do our best. A small step, in the midst of great human limitations, can be more pleasing to God than a life which appears outwardly in order but moves through the day without confronting great difficulties. Everyone needs to be touched by the comfort and attraction of God's saving love, which is mysteriously at work in each person, above and beyond their faults and failings.[91]

5 Concluding Reflections

The main focus in this article is to identify a theological and pastoral method which enriches, deepens and consolidates rather than replaces, challenges or discredits Watkins' innovative conversational method of discernment. The "empirical-critical-theological method" discussed in the previous sections incorporates all the theological insights expounded by Watkins, but at the same time offers a broader and richer theological and pastoral underpinnings in the light of the synodal documents on the family and Pope Francis' fresh and innovative mindset. It is a method that takes into account the spirit and message of the Gospel; the tradition of the Christian people; today's culture as an important source for theologizing; and the emerging social changes in contemporary culture.

Moreover, the "empirical-critical-theological method" seems to be more adequate than Watkins' conversational method of discernment to articulate the harmonization of church doctrine and pastoral practice. It takes the contemporary empirical situation as its starting point; then moves on to elaborate the vision which broadens the horizon of evaluation and interpretation and hence the projected and

---

90 BENEDICT XVI: *Light of the World: The Pope, the Church and the Signs of the Times: A Conversation with Peter Seewald*, San Francisco: Ignatius Press, 2010, 119.

91 *Evangelii gaudium*, 44

desired praxis; and finally sets the process that leads to the transformation of pastoral practice. It is a dynamic hermeneutical process that accompanies people to move forward to the rich experience of the Gospel core message. It is a process of ecclesial discernment which leads to the respect and acceptance of the whole truth.

One might raise the question about the advantages of this approach to the issue of the interface between church doctrine and pastoral care over the traditional approaches such as casuistry, the distinction between objective and subjective order, etc.

Whereas the traditional approaches are constrained by their deductive method of moral reasoning by simply applying church doctrine to concrete situations, the approach I am proposing focuses on the person who is on a journey of spiritual and moral growth. It sets the roadmap, but it is more concerned with the person and the journey than the roadmap itself.[92]

How should we move forward on this pastoral journey? Pope Francis has repeatedly insisted that, if we truly are on our way, the road will open step by step. We must proceed with the guidance of consolation. That is to say, we must proceed by our interior perception of the presence of God, and a complete trust in him, rather than letting ourselves be guided by our fear or our anxieties.

Ultimately it is an adventurous journey inspired by an open vision, rather than cutting short our voyage and opting to remain in a secure and comfortable place in the shadow of a partial vision of the truth.

---

92 Ibid. 82.

Part II

AN ETHICS OF MERCY

"The Sacred Ground of the Other": Landmarks for a Christian Ethics of Gradualness as an Ethics of Mercy

Roger Burggraeve

Introduction

The idea, or rather the de facto necessity, of a growth-ethics came about in my educational-pastoral work with young people aged sixteen years and older, from 1968 up to 2005, in the Salesian youth pastoral Centre "Eigentijdse Jeugd" ("Youth Today") in Dilbeek (Brussels). This engagement ran parallel with my academic assignment in moral theology at the Catholic University of Leuven. Hence the cross-fertilisation between practice and reflection. In my dealings with young people at the end of the 1960s and the beginning of the 1970s, I quickly discovered that in their discoveries and explorations of relationships and sexuality, young people no longer followed the path laid out by Catholic teaching (which I in my own upbringing had accepted as self-evident). In our educational-pastoral work we asked ourselves how we could "assist" and guide them to grow in the direction of what Catholics consider as the ideal of human sexuality and love, notwithstanding – or perhaps even by means of – the digressions that young people made, influenced as they were by increasing "emancipatory" trends within a society that was growing more secular. It was certainly a struggle, with ups and downs, to avoid ending up in two extremes: either into deductive rigourism or into inductive laxity or situationism. This is the reason why John Paul II's idea on the ethical "law of gradualness" was a true discovery for me,[1] and offered a possibility

[1] Remarkably, this idea has not been the object of broad and frequent study and critical discussion. The first monograph on the "law of gradualness" is a Master's thesis written under the direction of Philippe Delhaye (UCL): A. YOU: *La loi de la gradualité: Une nouveauté en morale?*, Paris: Lethielleux, 1991. In 1993, in Ars (France), a theological and pastoral session was devoted to: "Gradualité de la Loi et Loi de la gradualité". A more recent monograph is the doctoral dissertation of B. ATANGA: *De la gradualité de la norme morale à la croissance dans les vertus: Le débat théologico-moral à partir de "Familiaris Consortio"*, Rome: Pontificia Università Lateranense, 2009 (Excerpta theseos ad Doctoratum in S. Theologia). See also

for developing an "ethics of the achievable for young people on the way", without renouncing the Christian view of what is "desirable", or abandoning young people (and all people) "on the way".[2]

1 "Law of Gradualness": A Dynamic View on Moral Life

Let us thus begin by reflecting on John Paul II's idea of the "law of gradualness". We shall then investigate the ways in which his idea can help us today with the double Synod on marriage and the family (2014–2015) in developing an ethics of growth in education and pastoral work. This ethics should express – both in practice and in reflection – the "mercy" called for by Pope Francis.

The concept of the "law of gradualness" was introduced by John Paul II in the Apostolic Exhortation on the family *Familiaris consortio* (1981). The Synodal document interprets the "law of gradualness" (FC 34, par. 4) as the "step by step and unceasing progress" of married couples in their moral life, namely in substantiating better and better their relational and familial vocation in and through their concrete choices regarding responsible parenthood and birth control. The concept of gradualness is based on the conviction that the human person is an historical being: "Man, who has been called to live God's wise and loving design in a responsible manner, is an historical being who day by day builds himself up through his many free decisions; and so he knows, loves and accomplishes moral good by stages of growth" (FC 34, par. 3). From the beginning of *Familiaris consortio,* a dynamic vision on growth is promulgated, as in the paragraph "Gradualness and Conversion": "What is needed is a continuous, permanent conversion which, while requiring an interior detachment from every evil and an adherence to good in its fullness, is brought about concretely in steps which lead us ever forward. Thus a dynamic process develops, one which advances gradually with the progressive integration of the gifts of God and the demands of His definitive and absolute love in the entire personal and social life of man. Therefore an educational growth process is necessary, in order that individual believers, families and peoples, even

---

the recent contributions by J. SAUTERMEISTER: "Das Prozesshafte in der Lebensführung", in: *Herder Korrespondenz* 69 (2015/5), 229–233; and D. BOGNER: "Was meint und wobei hilft 'Gradualität'? Eine Begriffsklärung zur Familiensynode 2015", in: *Stimmen der Zeit* (2015/7), 446–454.

2 A warning is not out of place here: The idea of growth-ethics is only one of the possible responses to the pastoral and ethical problem that arises with what in traditional church language is called "irregular" behaviour. An equally important tool is *epikeia* and its accompanying judgment of conscience. There is, after all, not only "deviant" behaviour, in the sense of behaviour that de facto deviates from the church's ethical norms. Deviant behaviour often presents itself as "heterodox" behaviour, in the sense that those who practise this behaviour hold a "deviant conviction" and believe they must follow that conviction in good conscience.

civilization itself, by beginning from what they have already received of the mystery of Christ, may patiently be led forward, arriving at a richer understanding and a fuller integration of this mystery in their lives" (FC 9, par. 2).

This approach recognizes and affirms the by now well-known insights from the human sciences that help us to understand dynamically the person. By applying the concept of "dynamism" to the human person, the ideas of existential time and narrativity are introduced. We can call this "the parameter of time", or rather "the parameter of temporality": it is not about objective and matter-of-fact time, but about the personal and existential perception of time (cf. Bergson, Heidegger).[3] In a person's past, we encounter already existing elements that should be understood not only as conditioning factors (that can possibly limit one's freedom and responsibility) but also as potentialities and challenges. A person always has a story about that which has already happened, about experiences that characterise one's here and now – and also one's future. Some of those experiences are easily recountable, others have disappeared into the past, although they remain slumbering. They return by means of certain events and we have to relate to them. By recalling and recounting those previous experiences, we express who we are, *and* we discover meanings that are interesting for the future as well. This finds an echo in Paul Ricœur's idea of dynamic narrative identity.[4] We need to integrate new events into our life story, whereby they also create new meaning and "inducements" for the future. Not only does the future flow forth from the past, it is also active in the present as new possibilities, dreams, plans, wishes, hope *and* fear – which incite choices and commitment. In that "planning", responsibility plays an important role, in the sense that my existence is for me to take up as a project, both as source and goal of meaning. Responsibility is a form of freedom that authenticates itself, or rather that can only authenticate itself in and through time. I am what I am, *and* I am not yet what I am and can be. Hence, the idea of "trial and error" is essentially linked to the temporality of the life project. The unfolding of one's own project of meaning – in relation to oneself, the individual and social others, and (possibly) the transcendent Other – is a growth process in and through all the vicissitudes of life. The transformation of the person usually does not run along a straight line, but according to different steps and phases that do not follow each other harmoniously. Blockages, relapses, and displacements are possible, with all the overlaps, tensions, inhibitions and hindrances that accompany them. At times, the steps taken are premature or partial, and they bring about

---

3 A. FUMAGALLI: "The Parameter of Temporality and its Importance for Moral Theology", in: A. MANENTI/S. GUARINELLI/H. ZOLLNER (eds.): *Formation and the Person: Essays on Theory and Practice*, Leuven: Peeters, 2007, 141–156.

4 P. RICOEUR: *Soi-même comme un autre*, Paris: Seuil, 1990, 167–198.

a one-sided development of the person. At other times, they make true progress and human flourishing possible.

I would like to end this first part by referring to the remarkable link Pope Francis makes in his exhortation *Evangelii gaudium* (2013) between the idea of deculpabilisation and the idea of growth: "Pastors and the lay faithful who accompany their brothers and sisters in faith or on a journey of openness to God must always remember what the *Catechism of the Catholic Church* teaches quite clearly: 'Imputability and responsibility for an action can be diminished or even nullified by ignorance, inadvertence, duress, fear, habit, inordinate attachments, and other psychological or social factors' [cf. CCC 1735]. Consequently, without detracting from the evangelical ideal, they need to accompany with mercy and patience the eventual stages of personal growth as these progressively occur. I want to remind priests that the confessional must not be a torture chamber but rather an encounter with the Lord's mercy which spurs us on to do our best. A small step, in the midst of great human limitations, can be more pleasing to God than a life which appears outwardly in order but moves through the day without confronting great difficulties. Everyone needs to be touched by the comfort and attraction of God's saving love, which is mysteriously at work in each person, above and beyond their faults and failings" (EG 44) Now the question is how the concept of deculpabilisation can be an impetus for a growth-approach of vulnerable and broken persons in difficult life circumstances and relationships. For a true growth-ethics, more is needed than just deculpabilisation. While the paradigm of deculpabilisation puts the emphasis on the ethical fragilities and "impossibilities", and thus on the reduced or even non-existent freedom of the person, a growth-ethics looks for "seeds of growth" in that person and her or his live story, in the stubborn belief that these seeds – despite all the vulnerabilities, insufficiencies and "defects" – are still present.

Therefore, with an eye to a dynamic and progressive interpretation of moral fragility, we suggest the linking of two categories that are presupposed by the traditional paradigm of deculpabilisation, namely "circumstances" and "reduced freedom". *First*, there is the idea of the conditions or circumstances (*circumstantiae*). In traditional moral theology, attention was always given to the historical circumstances of ethical acting. This historicity was, however, never interpreted in a "life-historical" or "biographical" way, i.e., in accordance with age and developmental stages or life phases (Erikson) and the different stages in moral development (Piaget, Kohlberg, Gilligan). The ethical feeling, judging, and acting of persons is inevitably marked by the fact that they are "on the road". A second possibility offered by classical moral theology, in the context of deculpabilisation, is the idea of decreased human freedom and a lowered capability of value-estimation (*impedimenta libertatis*). It is an important task for a realistic ethics, directed towards a growth-promoting guidance, to distinguish as best as possible between what is the fruit of a bad or sinful will and what is the expression of human imperfection. However, an important perspective of this idea of "reduced freedom" has not been sufficiently explored by traditional moral theory. Therefore, the idea of "phases of life" has to be integrated into the reflection on "subjective deculpabilisation". We must regard freedom as that which it is, namely, a freedom that has to be explored and conquered, rather than a mature and balanced freedom one already possesses and controls.

In the end, every person has his or her own history of somatic, psychic, relational, ethical and spiritual development. Indeed, every person *is* a story, namely, a self-reflexive and narrative identity, which means an understanding-interpreting identity and a narrating-explaining identity. When someone experiences something, or does something, through which his or her existence is disrupted and disturbed, some work of interpretation and reinterpretation is needed (Ricœur). What is remarkable is that this (re)interpretation usually takes place in and through the telling of the event like a narrative to someone else, whereby one also tries to create a "sensible" or "meaningful" narrative for oneself, without this being an endpoint, since one gradually realises that at times, even a radical "change" or "conversion" is necessary.

2 "Without Gradualness of the Law": A "Pro-Vocative" Horizon for Growth

Up to this point we have reached the easiest part of the idea of ethical gradualness, namely the subjective dimension of growth, where we pay attention to the elements in the subject that hinder growth and especially make it possible, in spite of these difficulties. The objective dimension of growth, namely its goal, is much more difficult and delicate, however. Certainly in Western societies, where a liberal interpretation of the emancipation of the moral subject leads people to no longer accept a normative perspective, people want to be themselves the moral authors of their own existence, and to define by themselves the goal, without external patronising and certainly without the patronising of any religious or church authority.

2.1 On the Way to Perfection: Meaningful Living and Loving

Christian thought, as it has grown out of the gospel, does not shy away from speaking about the task – the task that is at the same time a vocation – to strive for perfection. We already find this in the Didache: "See that no one leads you astray from the way of this teaching [*the Way of Life, in contrast to the Way of Death*], since all other teachings train you without God. For if you are able to bear the entire yoke of the Lord, you will be perfect; but if you are not able, then at least do what you can." (6,1–2) It is remarkable how this early text implies the idea of "attainability" without however annulling the normative goal, namely the striving for perfection. On the contrary, the idea of attainability is possible only in the context of a literally "pro-gressive" thought on perfection!

Against this background, we can understand entirely how John Paul II's affirmation of the law of gradualness is followed immediately by a warning: "What is known as 'the law of gradualness' or step-by-step advance cannot be identified with 'gradualness of the law,' as if there were different degrees or forms of precept in God's law for different individuals and situations" (FC 34, par. 4). Here, the pope cites a sentence from his homily at the closing of the Synod on the Family on 25 October 1980. Undoubtedly, the Pope wants to prevent the idea of gradualness and growth from ending up in ethical relativism and laxity, or in a subjectivist situationism. Although it is accepted that people, conditioned by concrete circumstances in time and space, and in personal, social and cultural contexts, do not succeed in realising the moral norm effectively, as a consequence of their internal (personal) or external (contextual) conditions, they are nevertheless faced with the task of striving at least for the realisation of the law or the "moral good".

Although John Paul II applies his position – that there can be no mention of any gradualness of the law – directly to the moral law of birth control, as it is expressed in *Humanae vitae* (FC 34, par. 4), the idea of the law should not be reduced to this, or to an "act-oriented" view of human behaviour. In the Christian tradition, the goal of the moral law finds its highest expression in "agape": the gift of divine love, which for believers consists in the task of loving God and neighbour, and to which the striving for perfection is unequivocally oriented. We can call this the great Christian "core commandment". Inspired by John Paul II's notion of "the good in its fullness" (FC 9, par 2), we interpret the idea of "moral law" in a dynamic, qualitative and "holistic" way. This is why we plead for superseding an act-orientated view on human behaviour by the concept of "life form" (*Lebensform*), wherein the distinct options, acts, behaviours and styles of interaction are integrated, and from which they derive their meaning and value as well.

On the level of sexuality and intimate relationships, we would like to qualify the "life form" of "meaningful" living as "integral love". We are challenged by the Gospel commandment of love to understand intimate love adequately and integrally (cf. *Gaudium et spes* 51) as "covenantal love", based on free and informed consent, exclusiveness and reciprocity, equality-in-difference, authentic intimacy as "expressive perfection" of the covenantal love (cf. GS 49), creative fidelity as a path to "indissolubility from within", generous and responsible openness for children, and *last but not least,* socially confirmed (and – for the faithful – sacramentally celebrated). This is the "core" of what the Christian tradition calls the conjugal covenant as the basis for the family.

2.2 *"Lesser Good" (minus bonum)*

When Christians live out this integral or covenantal love as the core and horizon of sexuality and intimate relationship, and thus consider it as the specific incarnation of the *vere bonum*, the question arises of what this means for the "law of gradualness" as we elaborated it in our first part.

It implies, in our opinion, an ethically qualified interpretation of growth-ethics, in the sense that it is both about an "ethics of the achievable" and about a "pro-vocative" ethics that calls people – *and* assists them – to go along the way towards the good, namely, meaningful living and loving. To make this concrete, we would like to make use of a paradoxical idea, namely the concept of *minus bonum* – the lesser or partial good. This concept aims at maintaining the middle point between, on the one hand, the "lack of good" (implying the idea of "lesser evil" or *minus malum*, namely the duty to prevent as much evil as possible) and, on the other hand, the "full good" or the meaningful (*vere bonum*). In certain situations, where behaviour does not correspond to the norm or to that which is desirable, the meaningful, namely, the fullness of love, one appeals to the concept of the "lesser evil" in order to guarantee, in case of an "ethical deviation", at least a minimum of humaneness, for example preventing HIV-infection or other sexually transmitted diseases, or undesirable and unwanted pregnancies. We can consider this as an "ethical minimum" that especially ensues from a sense of reality and respect of life. One takes the reality of concrete people just as it is and not as it should be, as the starting point for a first (and sometimes seriously) limited humanization of the situation by, of course, preventing the unacceptable consequences. However necessary it may be, this emphasis on the ethical minimum cannot suffice. It is, after all, not sufficient that people "avoid misfortune"; they also need to grow towards the direction of the meaningful, *in casu* the perfection of integral love. This is precisely what we mean by "growth-ethics". There are, as I have already mentioned, many situations where people are not yet capable (and perhaps never will be capable) of attaining meaningful loving. In guidance that is directed towards flourishing, it is not enough to achieve the ethical minimum of the least evil so that the gravest negative results are avoided. Rather, one is faced with the challenge of developing realistic growth-perspectives that are suited to them, not only in keeping with their limitations, but also in keeping with their real, albeit, reduced possibilities. In this way, they can reach an attainable quality in a certain domain of life. This growth-perspective demonstrates the "lesser good": it is not the integrally meaningful, but it is no less the complete minimum of the least evil. The attainable quality moves in between as a "lesser good", that at times is a *larger* "lesser good" insofar as it more closely approaches the meaningful, and sometimes a *smaller* "lesser good" insofar as it retreats from the meaningful or integral love.[5] Taking the image of the glass, the "least evil" can be considered as the empty glass, while the full glass depicts the meaningful, and the partially-filled glass, the lesser good, namely, partially-filled to the attainable level, conditioned by the subjective and contextual "circumstances" of persons. By speaking of the "lesser" or "partial" good we avoid a relativising laxity or situationism that treats axiologically all behaviours as equal. At the same time, we avoid a mere deductive rigourism that – without regard for persons and without mercy – imposes unbearable ethical burdens upon injured and vulnerable people, under which they are in danger of breaking.

2.3 The Lesser Good and Necessary Boundary Rules

How can we now concretely ensure that the idea of the "smaller good", notwithstanding its noble pastoral intention, does not end up in a "gradualness of the law", against which John Paul II warns us? For this purpose, we would like to formulate a paradoxical statement, namely that a realistic *and* at the same time qualitatively oriented growth-ethics is more in need of negatively formulated boundary rules or prohibitions, rather than of positive behavioural rules that normatively prescribe a certain action. Such a set of prohibitions are found in the second table of the Ten Commandments, to which John Paul II also refers in the second chapter of his encyclical *Veritatis splendor* (1983) with his commentary on the Gospel narrative of

[5] See "Gegen das Süssholzraspeln: ein Gespräch mit Kardinal Christoph Schönborn über die Familiensynoden", in: *Herder Korrespondenz* 68 (2014/12), 613–617, at 614–615: "Ich habe vorgeschlagen, das bekannte Prinzip der Gradualität auch bei den Ehefragen anzuwenden. Es hat mich gewundert, wie vielen dies Sorge bereitet hat. Unser Leben ist ein graduelles Verwirklichen von etwas, was wir gewiss anstreben, aber nicht immer voll erreicht haben, sondern in das wir hineinwachsen müssen. Ich habe die Analogie zur Kirche gezogen, wo wir das *Prinzip der Gradualität* kennen, und das hat eine große Debatte ausgelöst. Doch ich bleibe dabei, dass diese Herangehensweise hilfreich ist. Sei bedeutet ja nicht, dass, wenn ich nur einen Teil verwirkliche, dann alles in Ordnung ist. Wenn wir sagen, dass es in anderen Religionen auch Elemente der Wahrheit und der Heiligung gibt, dann sagen wir ja auch nicht, dass wir alles gutheißen. Das ist ja gerade das Wesen des Prinzips. Aber wir erkennen die Suche, den Weg, das Prozesshafte an." ["I have suggested that the well-known principle of graduality should also be applied in questions concerning marriage. I was surprised to see how many people found this worrying. Our life is a gradual realizing of something towards which we must indeed strive, but which we have never fully attained – something into which we must grow. I have drawn the analogy on the church, where we are familiar with the *principle of graduality,* and this gave rise to a great debate. But I remain convinced that this approach is helpful. It does not mean that if I realize only one part, everything is ok. When we say that there are elements of truth and of sanctification in other religions too, we are not saying that we approve of everything. This is precisely the nature of the principle involved. But we acknowledge the search, the path, the processual." (English translation: B. McNeil)]

the rich young man (Mt 19; Mk 10; Lk 18). The encyclical calls the prohibitions of the second table the "basic prerequisites" for the love of neighbour (VS 13). In order to be sure that growth proceeds in the direction of the humane, boundaries must be respected. The "lesser good", presented or accepted as an attainable project, should never be based on any form of killing and violence or power abuse ("you shall not kill"), on untruth and inauthentic communication ("you shall not lie"), on theft and the abrogation of the difference between mine and thine ("you shall not steal"), on sexual (and other forms of) infidelity ("you shall not commit adultery"), and last but not least on possessive and abusive desire ("you shall not covet ... anything that belongs to your neighbour"). These prohibitions indicate the fundamental condition or the "bottom line" for every form of humane love; they are the first necessary step on the journey towards freedom and love. Or, paraphrasing Augustine, we can affirm, in line with John Paul II, that by realising the prohibitions of the second tablet of the Decalogue one begins to lift up one's head towards freedom and love. But this is only the beginning of freedom and love, not perfect freedom and love (VS 13).

These boundary rules are applicable to all human forms of love, even intimate love: both to the conjugal covenant and to other – so called "irregular" and "heterodox" – intimate relationships, both to heterosexual and to homosexual marital, pre-, non- and post-marital forms of cohabitation. We can call this a "consistent relational and sexual ethics" in the sense that all who, on the basis of personal conviction or as a consequence of certain external or internal circumstances, enter into one or other form of intimate relationship are called to develop this relationship as humanly as possible. For that purpose, the five prohibitions of the second table of the Ten Commandments offer an inspiring framework. Indeed, this consistent relational and sexual ethics should in no way lead to the axiological equalization (or levelling) of all intimate relational and cohabitation life forms with the marital covenant.[6] But notwithstanding this acknowledgement of the essential difference, a Christian growth ethics that wants to be pastoral is also faced with the challenge of developing guidelines not only for those who take up the vocation of integral love in marriage and family life, but likewise for those who enter into a different form of intimate, enduring partnership, and even for those who enter into temporary relationships or experiment with sexuality and intimacy (as is often the case among young people, even though most of them long for "love forever" ...). Surprisingly, it is the ancient text of the Decalogue that inspires us to draw out the new from the old (see Mt 13,52).

---

6 An important theme in this critique of axiological equalization is the constitutive meaning of the sexual body for marriage and family. See R. BURGGRAEVE: "Recovering the Meaning of the Sexual Body for Marriage", in: *INTAMS Review* 8/1 (2002), 4–20.

3 "Marriage-in-becoming" (*matrimonium in fieri*) Revisited

We conclude our attempt to sketch the hallmarks of an "ethics of gradualness" by illustrating on the basis of one case study how such a growth-ethics can work. We focus on the phenomenon of premarital cohabitation, one of the forms of unmarried living together. It is a theme that has also been taken up by the double Synod on the Family (2014–2015) in the awareness that it is an increasingly widespread phenomenon that challenges the church's view and pastoral work on marriage and the family. In the texts of the first session in 2014[7] as well as in the *Instrumentum laboris* in preparation for the second session in October 2015,[8] mention is made of "living together on an experimental basis", "de facto unions", "concubinage", and "trial marriage". A distinction is thereby made between "unions which have not been religiously or civilly recognised nor officially registered in any way" and "cohabitation before marriage".

We now focus further on this premarital cohabitation, precisely because, ethically and pastorally, it can be an important and extensive field of application of the "ethics of gradualness and growth". In order to embed reflexively such a pastoral, growth-ethics approach, we suggest a revisiting of the old (traditional) concept of *matrimonium in fieri*[9] – "marriage-in-becoming" – and to enrich and broaden it. Marriage arises by means of the free "yes", but it is not thereby consummated (*matrimonium initiatum*). Marriage is only factual (*in facto esse*) when it is sexually consummated (*ratum et consummatum*). This is the juridical approach to marriage-in-becoming that has been valid in the Church for centuries. Actually, though, this is a narrowing down of a broader interpretation of the "beginning" of marriage at the engagement or betrothal (*sponsalia*). Different authors[10] argue

---

7 "The Pastoral Challenges of the Family in the Context of Evangelisation", *Instrumentum laboris*, 2014, http://www.vatican.va/roman_curia/synod/documents/rc_synod_doc_20140626_instrumentum-laboris-familia_en.html; retrieved 06.11.2015; *Relatio post disceptationem*, 13.10.2014, http://press.vatican.va/content/salastampa/en/bollettino/pubblico/2014/10/13/0751/03037.html; retrieved 06.11.2015; "The Vocation and Mission of the Family in the Church and Contemporary World", *Lineamenta*, 2014, http://www.vatican.va/roman_curia/synod/documents/rc_synod_doc_20141209_lineamenta-xiv-assembly_en.html; retrieved 06.11.2015.

8 "The Vocation and Mission of the Family in the Church and Contemporary World": *Instrumentum laboris*, 23.06.2015, http://www.vatican.va/roman_curia/synod/documents/rc_synod_doc_20150623_instrumentum-xiv-assembly_en.html; retrieved 06.11.2015. Cf. 28.

9 For a correct understanding of this traditional meaning, according to canon law, see T. KNIEPS-PORT LE ROI: "Die Ehe als Prozess aus sakramentologischer Perspektive", in: *Zeitschrift für Katholische Theologie* 132 (2010), 273–292, particularly at 277–281.

10 C.J. SNOEK: "Marriage and the Institutionalisation of Sexual Relations", in: *Concilium* 56 (1970), 111–122; H. WINDISCH: "*Ehe-Wege*", in: *INTAMS Review* 6 (2000), 101–105; A. GUINDON: "Case for a "Consummated" Sexual Bond before a "Ratified" Marriage", in: *Église et Théologie* 8 (1977), 137–181; M. KNAPP: *Glaube – Liebe – Ehe: Ein theologischer Versuch in schwieriger Zeit,* Würzburg: Echter Verlag, 1999; A. THATCHER: *Living Together and*

today for a broadening of the idea of "marriage-in-becoming", based on a processual understanding of marriage, both in its beginning – before marriage – as well as in its development after the contracting of marriage. In such a dynamic view, love-as-dynamism then comes to take a central position. Certainly, in our Western societies where marriage no longer primarily concerns the family, but rather the couple itself – as "a most individual expression of a most individual emotion" – love begins with attraction and infatuation, which then develops (or better, can develop or endeavours to develop) through different stages into a stable and lasting love.

For this growth concept we find points of contact in the sociological research[11] of writers such as Thérèse Jacobs,[12] building on the work of Anthony Giddens.[13] In their investigations into the diversity of, and the shifts in, the concepts of love in our Western (American and Western European) societies, they make a distinction between "pure love" and "romantic love". With "pure love" they mean a "function-free relationship", a relationship that can be entered into only for the sake of the relationship itself and that is thus not laden with "external", namely economic or social reasons: "just for love". Here, actual intensity is more important than a possible future goal of permanence. And if mention is made of permanence, it can only follow from the experience of love itself, without it being the intention or normative goal from the outset. Hence, "pure love" is in principle monogamous but not permanent, that is to say, a "serial monogamy": the relationship is exclusive as long as it lasts. The sociologists find a quite different concept of love in what they call – with a surprising term – "romantic love" (whereby they seem to suppose that "pure love" is more realistic than "romantic love", which according to them strives for a "lofty dream" and thus a less achievable ideal). That ideal is strongly similar, in their opinion, to the traditional (Christian) relationship model of monogamy and permanence. The relationship is experienced as a "we" of reciprocity that not only prefers faithfulness (exclusivity) but also strives for a stable future; and this implies that divorce is seen as failure. At the same time, a

Christian Ethics, Cambridge: Cambridge University Press, 2002; H. SANDERS: *Huwelijk-in-(ver)wording? Ongehuwd samenwonen als maatschappelijk ethos: Sociologische verkenning en ethisch-theologische reflectie*, unpublished doctoral dissertation, Leuven, Faculty of Theology and Religious Studies, 2009, 170–172.

11 Cf. H. SANDERS: "Ongehuwd samenwonen: Huwelijk op (de) tocht", in: *Collationes* 33/4 (2003), 342–362; ID.: "Cohabitation – An Obstacle or an Obeisance to Marriage?", in: *INTAMS Review* 13/1 (2007), 19–32.

12 T. JACOBS: *Gezinsontbinding in Vlaanderen,* I: *Persoonlijke relaties in beweging*, Antwerpen: Universiteit Antwerpen, 2000. See also K. VAN DEN BRANDE: *Ongehuwd samenwonen: Betekenis van de relatie en de leefvorm*, Leuven-Apeldoorn: Garant, 1996 .

13 A. GIDDENS: *The Transformation of Intimacy: Sexuality, Love and Eroticism in Modern Societies*, Cambridge: Polity Press, 1992.

broader anchoring plays an important role in this concept of love, namely the embedding in an environment of like minds, common friends, family, children, social networks of the neighbourhood and associations. According to Jacobs' research, there would be – in Belgian society, and thus in secular Western society, to which her research is directed – an almost fifty-fifty proportion between both concepts of love: 46,6 % give preference to "pure love" and 48,9 % to "romantic love" (4,7 % of the respondents gave preference to a "polygamous love" that deems relationships with multiple partners simultaneously to be enriching). In contrast to the clear distinction made between "pure love" and "romantic love", and in contrast to the sociological finding (or thesis) that in secular societies a shift from a traditional to a more liberal concept of love is taking place, we direct our attention especially to the transition from pure to romantic love. We see how this transition in the non-married cohabitation of young adults can take place, and even does take place on a regular basis (animated by the underlying desire for a lasting love).

Precisely for that reason, and likewise with an eye to a pastoral, growth-ethics approach in a Christian perspective, it is interesting to make a distinction in the socially normal – or rather in what has de facto become normative – phenomenon of the heterosexual cohabitation of young adults between "premarital cohabitation" and "pre-conjugal" or "prenuptial cohabitation". Premarital cohabitation functions as a descriptive term, in the sense that it refers to all possible forms of unmarried cohabitation (*inter alia* in the age bracket between 20 and 30 years), some of which come to an end, while others persevere, and eventually end up in marriage. Some of those relationships are transformed into a form of "non-marital cohabitation", whether or not as an alternative for marriage and whether or not in order to start a family. We qualify premarital cohabitation as pre-conjugal or prenuptial cohabitation when it is directed intentionally at marriage as a life covenant and as a basis for building a family. The distinction between premarital and prenuptial cohabitation therefore rests on the nature and the quality of the commitment of the cohabitants. There are cohabitants who in no way whatsoever desire to commit for the future. We can call this a form of "unattached cohabitation": it lasts as long as it lasts, until the desired satisfaction on the relational, sexual or practical levels no longer obtains. In addition, we can distinguish a form of "temporarily committed cohabitation", in the sense that the partners place the emphasis on the temporariness of their relationship, without excluding the possible outcome of commitment for the future ("you never know that it works"). The "trial marriage" in the strict sense of the word implies the conscious intention to try out whether the partners can remain together. This form can directly be called pre-conjugal while the form of "temporarily committed cohabitation" can be called an indirect pre-conjugal cohabitation: one then perhaps dreams of a permanent relationship but in fact one leaves that aside for the time being.

This differentiation in cohabitation can give the impression that the different forms are clearly distinct from each other, but a closer inspection shows that evolutions and transitions from one to the other form are possible, and likewise take place in reality. We can state concretely that premarital cohabitation, certainly among young adults, often begins as a form of "pure love" but in the course of time – motivated by the desire for lasting love and through the experience itself of cohabitation – evolves into a form of so-called "romantic love", i.e. towards prenuptial cohabitation with an eye to a conjugal life covenant and building a family. In this regard, married cohabitation displays a dynamic and progressive character and it is not only sociologically, but experientially, a form of "partnership transition",[14] literally the transition from a dreamed-of towards a real "lasting relationship" that bears within it the chance for success and strength for the future. We can call this a form of a greater "lesser good" vis-à-vis "pure living together" precisely because the "seeds of growth" are clearly present leading to the fullness – the *vere bonum* – of the marital bond. At the same time, it is important to acknowledge pastorally that even the cohabitation in "pure love", notwithstanding its ambiguities and fragilities, is not without qualitative potential and thus can also be a form of "lesser good", albeit a smaller "lesser good" than pre-conjugal cohabitation. The couple get to know each other and explore each other, and bodily closeness grows and usually leads to sexual intimacy. After again some – shorter or longer – time, the couple decide to live together with the intention of making their love both more comprehensive and more real. It is thus not non-committal but committed, although still in tentativeness (i.e. a form of "temporarily committed cohabitation", as qualified above). The couple would like to test and discover whether the relationship truly has a future. In and through that experience, premarital cohabitation can then move on to a pre-conjugal cohabitation, which upon closer inspection can be called a new form of the former engagement. And when both professionally have permanent jobs and income,[15] they can decide to start a family and thereby also get married, civilly and possibly in church. It goes without saying that this description of the phases should not be taken normatively. After all, it is a sociologically tinted description. The steps can be arranged in a different order. In any case, those who choose to get married experience their meeting, getting acquainted and first courtship, their growth in intimacy towards

---

[14] In sociology, "partnership transition" is understood as a transition in the way that men and women become couples and partners. Cf. K. KIERNAN: "Cohabitation in Western Europe: Trends, Issues and Implications", in: A. BOOTH/C. CROUTER (eds.): *Just Living Together: Implications of Cohabitation on Families, Children and Social Policy*, Mahwah, NJ: Erlbaum, 2002, 3–32.

[15] See also *Instrumentum laboris*, 2015, 100: "Simply to live together ... can also be done while awaiting more security in life (a steady job and steady income)."

a steady relationship, and certainly their living together, as a dynamic progression that leads them to an adult and responsible choice of marriage as an expression of their choice to start a family. We can call this the actual "marriage in becoming" in the Western context. In other words, the choice of two people to bind themselves together unconditionally by means of a marital bond no longer takes place all at once in today's Western societies.[16] It takes place via all sorts of stages and phases, in and through every couple's individual process, with all the ups and downs that form a part of this learning and growth process. We can indeed speak of a gradual or progressive development of the relationship and of cohabitation, with the intention – or rather with the hope – of ending up in the life commitment of marriage. Precisely because one experiences in one's own family and in the world around so many broken relationships and divorces, one does not want to tread on thin ice, but rather take to heart in a responsible manner the chances for success of one's own relationship-with-a-future. Here we hit upon a paradox, namely, that the confrontation with the fragility of partnerships and marriages can lead to "fear of commitment" and "fear of failure".[17] On the other hand, that confrontation can lead to a greater sense of responsibility in entering into and in shaping relationships. Then cohabitation also becomes an expression of and a school for increasing responsibility in the dynamic and progressive road to a mature and lasting commitment of marriage.

The Christian concept of the covenant of marriage, whose main lines we have sketched briefly above, challenges us not only to emphasise the importance of lasting love but also to develop a growth-ethics approach that searches for elements in the experience of intimate love itself that promote permanence. In other words, in a pastoral context we do not need the proclamation of an external norm,

---

[16] This likewise implies what sociologists call the "de-institutionalisation" of the lifecycle. In the past, marriage also meant the standardised and decisive entrance into adulthood, as leaving the home, getting married and having children. It happened in that order, and shortly one after the other. In contrast, the transition to adulthood today takes place via multiple steps. One such "marking step" is premarital cohabitation (initially, usually not yet pre-conjugal in intention), besides the choice of a profession and building a family with one's life partner. And the choices are more spread out in time than before. See J. SELTZER: "Families Formed Outside of Marriage", in: *Journal of Marriage and the Family*, 62 (2000), 1247–1268.

[17] See *Instrumentum laboris*, 2015, 65: "When considering the prospect of marriage, many young people are afraid of failure, which is also a result of their witnessing, in these times, many marriage break-ups. Consequently, more attention needs to be given to discerning the underlying reasons for their renunciation and discouragement. Indeed, some think that, in many cases, the reasons might have to do precisely with an awareness of a goal which — while appreciated and no less desired – seems incommensurable in reasonably evaluating one's strengths or might arise from a grave doubt about the constancy of one's feelings. As for fidelity and stability in a loving relationship, which, nevertheless, still remain desirable, some young people feel an anxiety – or even anguish – at not being able to ensure fidelity and stability in love, which often causes them to renounce marrying."

but rather a phenomenological, humanely recognisable description of the growth of intimate love towards authentic permanence. In short, we need a "pedagogy of lasting love from the inside out", and this in a realistic manner. The available texts of the double Synod on the Family 2014–2015 point to the need for a mature view on love, paying attention to the factors that promote stability and authentic affectivity, and especially to developing the capacity to withstand difficulties. Thanks to the "art of accompaniment, which teaches us to remove our sandals before the sacred ground of the other (cf. Ex 3:5)",[18] this entails "a prudent and merciful discernment process"[19] whereby one arrives at the acknowledgement of the seeds of growth in the direction of the sacrament of marriage.[20] We read in the *Instrumentum laboris* (2015): "Therefore, even in cases where the decision of persons living together ... to proceed to a sacramental marriage is still in a virtual state or in its initial stage or in a gradual approach, the Church is asked not to shy away from the task of encouraging and supporting such a development. At the same time, something good can be done by showing, in a friendly manner, an appreciation for the commitment already made and acknowledging adherence to those elements proper to the divine plan arising from the relation of the person created by God and God the Creator."[21] With this realistic and at the same time "constructive approach",[22] the Synod wants to mark a distance vis-à-vis the excessively romantic views on love that often circulate in public opinion and in the media (note how here an understanding of "romantic love" is used that, as a consequence of the perspective taken, is radically opposed to the semantics of the sociologists above).

On the basis of this qualitative view of "adult intimate love" one is able to do justice to the potentialities and qualities that are effectively present in premarital cohabitation, in particular in pre-conjugal or prenuptial cohabitation, at times even more than in certain marriages that present only a meagre reflection of the

18 *Instrumentum laboris*, 2015, 109, quoting *Evangelii gaudium*, 169.

19 Ibid. 107. Cf. also numbers 3, 63, 81, 84, 98, 112, 120.

20 Ibid. 102: "The choice of civil marriage or, in some cases, simply 'living together' is very often not a result of prejudice or an aversion to sacramental union but instead linked to cultural or contingent situations. In many circumstances, the decision to live together is a sign of a relationship which wants to be built and opened to the prospects of personal fulfilment. The determination of a couple, which becomes translated into an enduring bond, stable and open to life, can be considered a condition for embarking on a journey of growth which can perhaps lead to a sacramental marriage – a possible good which ought to be proclaimed as a gift to enrich and strengthen married life and the family, instead of as a difficult ideal to achieve."

21 *Instrumentum laboris*, 2015, 57, par. 2. See also ibid. 99: "The Church also ought to accompany ... those living together in a gradual discovery of the 'seeds of the Word' which lie hidden, so as to value them until the fullness of union in the Sacrament [of marriage] might be achieved."

22 Ibid. 98, 101, 112, 127.

marriage covenant as a "meaning-full" life project.[23] In that way, the guidance of couples in their transition from pure to covenantal love can be linked to the broadened interpretation of "marriage-in-becoming" (*matrimonium in fieri*) that we suggested.[24] Then, pre-conjugal cohabitation can be acknowledged *de facto* as a decisive step along the way to the marital vows, whereby the sacrament of marriage can come to be[25] – thus without detracting from that which is meaningful and desirable in conjugal love in all its multifaceted fullness:[26] "The determination of a couple, which becomes translated into an enduring bond, stable and open to life, can be considered a condition for embarking on a journey of growth which can perhaps lead to a sacramental marriage – a possible good which ought to be proclaimed as a gift to enrich and strengthen married life and the family, instead of as a difficult ideal to achieve".[27]

4 Conclusion: Growth Ethics as Ethics of Mercy and Redemption

Let me conclude by pointing to the theological foundation of the ethics of growth and gradualness, as we have presented it briefly. Central to the Gospel message is the proclamation of God's mercy, and from that flows forth the forgiveness of sins. People are not angels, but vulnerable and often injured creatures, prone to failure and sin, successful in many things except in complying with the "measure of Christ", that is, with the ethical demands of evangelical radicalism. We are called to discipleship in Christ and thus to meaningful living and loving. But we often fall short, not only through incapacity, inadequacy and failure, but also

---

23 An analogous pastoral-ethical approach is desirable in the case of non-marital cohabitation, i.e. of Christians who – because of circumstances or on the basis of their personal conviction – decide not to marry but still live together in a covenant spirit and likewise, on that basis, make the transition to family building. Although their relationship is marked by gaps, it still possesses positive aspects especially when it is based on stability and faithfulness. In this regard, it can be considered as a *minus bonum* that invites us to be near and to value these couples and possibly guide them to the choice of a sacramental marriage. The *Instrumentum laboris* 2015 therefore pleads for an accompanying "method which, inspired by grace and in a respectful manner, might foster the gradual opening of minds and hearts to the fullness of God's plan" (103).

24 This transition can perhaps also be marked in a ritual, namely by a "parental blessing". See H. SANDERS: "Parental Blessing at a 'Marriage-in-Becoming': A Pastoral Proposal", in: *INTAMS Review* 16/1 (2010), 13–26.

25 On the analogy of the "baptism of desire", we can in particular circumstances even speak of a "marriage of desire". Some couples want to marry but unfortunately cannot do so, because of particular familial, social, economic, or cultural circumstances. In that case, their pre-conjugal cohabitation becomes a form of "marriage of desire", in the sense that their cohabitation is an expression of their desire for marriage, a desire that cannot (or cannot yet) be effectively realised because of contextual factors.

26 *Instrumentum laboris*, 2015, 37–68 ("The Discernment of the Family Vocation").

27 Ibid. 102.

through negligence, guilty omission, pride, and lazy or bad will. Not only are we finite beings, who fail or commit mistakes, but we are also "poor sinners". That is why we are in need of mercy and forgiveness in order to find once again "the way towards the light" after our failures and sins. But more is needed. Mercy is needed not only "after" ethics, but also "in" ethics itself. For this reason, the growth-ethics just sketched seeks to be an "ethics of mercy", in line with what Pope Francis in *Evangelii gaudium* proffers as the "gospel of mercy", which "understands, assists and promotes" people on their way (179). Without ceasing to be a "pro-vocative" prophetic ethics, this ethics of mercy intends at the same time to be a form of redemption, as an expression of the "divine pedagogy".[28] An "ethics of redemption" that desires to be near people in their imperfection and brokenness, so that they are healed of their alienations. This makes it possible to appeal to the "seeds of growth" in them, also improving some positive elements in their life circumstances. That these "seeds of growth", as sensitivity to meaningful living and loving, are always present, however precarious and injured people may be, is a form of "hope against all hope" that is anchored in the faith and conviction that Jesus is our Redeemer. To be redeemed means that freedom is again gifted back to itself. Redemption is the rebirth of freedom into a real freedom so that human persons are again capable of, or are enabled to grow towards, the ethical good and the meaningful, *in casu* integral love.

---

[28] Ibid. 39, referring to the law of gradualness: "In the Christian life ... the believer ... thus beginning a 'dynamic process [which] develops, one which advances gradually with the progressive integration of the gifts of God' (FC, 9), in on ongoing conversion to a love that saves us from sin and gives us fullness of life." See also ibid. 62: "In considering a pastoral approach towards people ... simply living together, the Church has the responsibility of helping them understand the divine pedagogy of grace in their lives and offering them assistance so that they can reach the fullness of God's plan for them ... The Church turns with love to those who participate in her life in an incomplete manner, recognizing that the grace of God works also in their lives."

Discernment of Biographies and the Moral Development of Identities: Perspectives of a Christian Ethics Approach to Deviance, Failure, and New Beginnings[1]

Jochen Sautermeister

1 Biography and Identity as Constitutive Elements of a Theology of Marriage and the Family

"Marriage is a reality that is concerned in a very special way with the daily life of the world. Indeed, it is often hidden in ordinariness and inconspicuousness. This unadorned experience of marriage and the family signifies *per se* an indirect criticism of every excessively vehement theological reflection on marriage."[2] In these words, Karl Lehmann points to the particular dangers that can be linked to a theological reflection on marriage. In marriage, normative aspects, on the one hand – that is to say, the Christian ideal of marriage,[3] its function as a guiding principle, and its concretion in specific individual norms – are united, on the other hand, to descriptive aspects such as the historical, sociocultural, legal, economic, societal, and biographical factors, which also determine the concrete living of marriage and the family. The contemporary challenge is to form an appropriate theological understanding of marriage and the family, and to shape a pastoral care that does not define its claim to help and to give support exclusively on the basis of an ideal, but derives this claim also (and above all) from the concrete needs of the persons concerned, and from their experiences which are interpreted in the light of the Gospel. It is obvious that these challenges are extremely demanding, because it is necessary both to get to grips with the variegated conditions in which people

1 I am very grateful to Brian McNeil and Richard Mathieu for the translation of the text and of the quotations.

2 K. LEHMANN: "Die christliche Ehe als Sakrament", in: *Communio* 8 (1979), 385–392, at 385.

3 According to the Pastoral Constitution *Gaudium et spes* of the Second Vatican Council (GS 47–52), the following elements are essential to the Christian ideal of marriage: love, fidelity and the mutual gift of self, fruitfulness and creativity, and sacramentality. On this, see also M.M. LINTNER: "The Spirituality of Marriage after the Second Vatican Council", in: *Melita Theologica* 65 (2015), 97–119.

live their specific lives and to avoid downgrading the contextually conditioned differences as accidental, as accessories that can be ignored. On the contrary, these differences must be recognized as the concrete possibilities for the realization of marriage and the family. This, however, entails looking not only at the various sociocultural and economic factors,[4] but also at the biographical factors involved in the beginning and in the development, in crises and in success, but also in the breakdown of particular forms of life. The only appropriate way to understand people's life stories is to take account of the first-person perspective, that is to say, of their self-interpretations, their self-perceptions and self-evaluations, the self-concept that guides their behavior, and their identity. All this must be integrated into the theological and pastoral endeavor to understand concrete biographies and the stories of couples or families.

The acknowledgment of the partners as subjects of their conduct of life and of the shaping of their relationship is linked to the Christian ideal of marriage and the family. These subjects must be given support and empowered; they must be protected from external and internal dangers. And this implies the acknowledgment of people's identity and life histories as a constitutive element of the theological discourse about marriage and the family. It is consistent with such an approach that we also look at those forms of life that do not correspond to this ideal; a value-oriented perspective can certainly see in them elements of the Christian guiding principle of marriage and family. A sensitivity to biography and to context is necessary, if theological perception and reflection are to be open to the everyday character and the "unprettiness" of marital and family reality.

This perception was a central issue in the context of the Fourteenth Ordinary Assembly of the Synod of Bishops in Rome in October 2015 on the theme of "The Vocation and Mission of the Family in the Church and Contemporary World." The reference by various participants to the principle of graduality,[5] as a source of

---

4 In a global perspective that embraces the world church, these are extremely numerous and varied. This is why they demand a contextual approach in pastoral care.

5 The intention was to employ the principle of graduality to take into account the process-character in the moral-religious self-formation and conduct of life. This is appropriate to a historical-biographical understanding of the human being and of his or her dignity – understood as the possibility of a free and conscious acknowledgment of that which is recognized to be morally and religiously valuable. The idea is that the principle of graduality should acknowledge processes of growth and maturing, the approach by stages to the realization of ethical values and to the moral ideal, as well as the endeavor to practice conversion, reconciliation, and a new beginning – in other words, life in its character as a path, with its searching for that which is good and right. This would do justice to the reality of people's lives and to their moral-religious endeavor, while at the same time holding fast to the validity and decisiveness of the ethical-religious ideal of marriage and the family. On this, see J. SAUTERMEISTER: "Das Prozesshafte in der Lebensführung: Zum Prinzip der Gradualität im Kontext der Familiensynode", in: *Herder Korrespondenz* 69 (2015), 229–233; D. BOGNER: "Was meint und wobei hilft 'Gradualität'?

theoretical tools that would permit an orientation of Christian ethics and pastoral care to mercy, was not something completely new. It is one consequence of the acknowledgment of the conduct of human life as a historical-dynamic process of free subjects who – in Christian terms – are both seekers and answerers in the encounter with God, when they lead their lives (or want to lead them) more or less consciously in the context of faith. For a Christian ethics of gradualness as an ethics of mercy, therefore, personal biography and identity are important theoretical and practical references, because these categories focus on the real life of individuals within their sociocultural contexts.[6] These categories will be vital for the following deliberations, which incorporate a view of marriages that have been irreparably damaged or have definitively failed.[7]

The following reflections seek to elaborate the theological-ethical significance of the biography and the formation of identity for a Christian ethics that is particularly concerned with questions of deviating, of breakdown, and of a new beginning in the context of partnership, marriage, and the family. We begin with the question of the extent to which the moral-theological concept of the *minus bonum* can adequately make sense of frictions and experiences of the breakdown of marriage and the family (2). We shall then examine the fundamental challenge posed to Christian ethics by the experience of failure (3). The categories of failure and of guilt are then employed to differentiate two theological-ethical interpretations of deviations from ideals and guiding models that can further develop a theological ethics and a pastoral care that are sensitive to biography and to context (4). In order to do justice to the lived reality of human beings, the special character of Christian

Eine Begriffsklärung zur Familiensynode 2015", in: *Stimmen der Zeit* 233 (2015), 446–454; E. AGIUS/J.G. CURMI: "Family Ministry: The Interface between Church Doctrine and Pastoral Care", in: *Melita Theologica* 65 (2015), 11–41.

6 See K. HILPERT: "Moraldoktrin oder Moral als Wahrnehmung 'im Kontext der Evangelisierung'? Bemerkungen zur bevorstehenden Familiensynode", in: *Stimmen der Zeit* 232 (2014), 448–457.

7 According to a recently published empirical study by the Universities of Münster and Berlin, a consistent majority of believers in over forty countries have spoken in favor of a modification of the present official teaching and practice of the church regarding divorced and remarried persons (see S. DELERE/A. ROTH/T. ROTH: "Neue Formen des Hörens in der katholischen Kirche: Ergebnisse eines länderübergreifenden, empirischen Forschungsprojekts zur Familiensynode 2015", in: *Stimmen der Zeit* 233 [2015], 599–610, at 604). Many find it inappropriate to describe these relationships in general terms as "irregular". Even some authorities in the church, such as Cardinal Walter Kasper (see *Das Evangelium von der Familie: Die Rede vor dem Konsistorium,* Freiburg i.Br.: Herder, 2014; "Nochmals: Zulassung von wiederverheiratet Geschiedenen zu den Sakramenten? Ein dorniges und komplexes Problem", in: *Stimmen der Zeit* 233 [2015]: 435–445) and Johan Bonny, Bishop of Antwerp (see the English translation of the Dutch text: http://archief.kerknet.be/admin/files/assets/subsites/4/documenten/SYNOD_ON_FAMILY_ENG.pdf; retrieved 31.10.2015), have argued in favor of a greater sensitivity towards these relationships and of compassion in dealing with those concerned.

ethics as an ethics of mercy will be explained (5); against this background, we shall set out the significance of the conscience and of the societal recognition of a value-oriented conduct of life by persons who deviate on the concrete level of norms from specific ideals and models that are promulgated by the magisterium. We shall also make explicit the need for a perceptive ability that is empirically informed (6). This requires a differentiated way of speaking about moral responsibility, which takes up, not only the category of guilt, but also the categories of liability and regret (7). After sketching perspectives for the understanding of a Christian ethics of mercy that operates with the principle of graduality (8), this essay concludes with summarizing reflections (9).

2 Frictions and Experiences of the Breakdown of Marriage and the Family

Failure, as a radical and definitive experience of breakdown, is one of the fundamental existential experiences of the human being. The definitive collapse of a perspective in one's job, the definitive end of a familiar and close relationship, the shattering of an existential life project, of one's self-image, or of the image of God that had hitherto given support, belong to the existential experiences that can make the human being profoundly insecure and bring him or her to the limits of the livable. These somber and difficult aspects of the reality with which one is confronted generate feelings of helplessness and being overwhelmed, of impotence and despair, of shame, but sometimes also of rage.

Experiences of the breakdown of partnership, marriage, and the family are not foreign to the church. Marriage counseling, family counseling, and life counseling offered by the Catholic Church often experience couples in different situations: crises, reconciliations, separation and divorce, or new partnerships, patchwork families, or single parents. These are prominent realities in the German-speaking world.[8] Many of these women and men had experienced in their marriage something that they had neither expected nor hoped for beforehand. Unlike younger couples, they have experience of life, and they are able to find a reality in their new partnerships that they experience as acknowledged by God, even when they are in a form of life that the official magisterium regards as "irregular" and that can no longer be brought back or transposed intact into a regular form. In the case of premarital cohabitation, this is in principle possible, but this option is excluded in the case of marriages that have broken down. To use a metaphor: these situations involve, not so much the early growth and ripening of a young plant, but rather

[8] See J. SAUTERMEISTER: "Ehe-, Familien- und Lebensberatung als kirchliches Handlungsfeld," in: K. HILPERT/B. LAUX (eds.): *Leitbild am Ende? Der Streit um Ehe und Familie,* Freiburg i.Br.: Herder, 2014, 267–280.

a tree trunk that has been cut down, while a new, stable and promising sapling is forming and growing.

Marriage is a companionship of life and love in which the partners usually experience in themselves and with their partner something that would not have been possible in the same way with another person.[9] The psychological insight that something arises in the concrete dynamics of a couple that cannot be merely predicted in an additive fashion on the basis of two biographies explains why the partners are able to call forth, to "love forth", the best sides of each other, but also to provoke the dark and uncomfortable sides that neither knew about themselves, or that they would have preferred to have left behind (or at least, not to have induced).[10] It is the intensity of love and the energetic dynamic of intimacy that can lead partners to hurt each other – even unintentionally – in such a way that nothing of their love remains perceptible; its blaze can go out. This can produce constellations so shattered that it is humanly impossible to take up this marriage again.[11]

There are several approaches in moral theology that attempt to grasp exactly the specific character of such existential situations and to do justice to them in a perspective that – measured against the ideal of marriage – is graduated. In the context of the idea of graduality, the concept of the so-called *minus bonum* is also discussed. This refers to a good that is indeed lesser than the ideal itself, but is nevertheless valuable to a certain extent: it is not worthless.[12]

The concept of *minus bonum* appears to offer a promising perspective with regard to the possible growth processes in young people. For here, the biographical possibility of realizing the ideal of Christian marriage in one's life still remains open. We can, however, ask whether this concept is equally applicable to all situations and phases of life. What effect could it possibly have on persons whose marriage is irreparably damaged, and who gratefully live in a stable new partner-

---

9 On one way of looking at marriage in terms of biography and process, see also E.-M. FABER: "Geschenk des eigenen Lebens: Überlegungen zu einer Theologie der Biographie," in: H. LANGENDÖRFER/O. RIBADEAU DUMAS/E. TANNER (eds.): *Theologie der Liebe: Zur aktuellen Debatte um Ehe und Familie,* Freiburg i.Br.: Herder, 2015, 64–84; A. BRENNINKMEIJER-WERHAHN/K. DEMMER (eds.): *Close to our Hearts: Personal Reflections on Marriage*, Münster: LIT, 2013 (Symposion; 12); and T. KNIEPS-PORT LE ROI: "Die Ehe als Prozess aus sakramententheologischer Perspektive", in: *Zeitschrift für katholische Theologie* 132 (2010), 273–292.

10 See J. WILLI: *Psychologie der Liebe: Persönliche Entwicklung durch Partnerbeziehungen*, Stuttgart: Klett-Cotta, ^{5}2002; H. JELLOUSCHEK: *Die Kunst als Paar zu leben*, Freiburg i.Br.: Herder, ^{22}2011.

11 See T. RUSTER/H. RUSTER: *Bis dass der Tod euch scheidet? Die Unauflöslichkeit der Ehe und die wiederverheiratet Geschiedenen: Ein Lösungsvorschlag,* Munich: Kösel, 2013.

12 See R. BURGGRAEVE: "The Sacred Ground of the Other: Landmarks for a Christian Ethics of Gradualness as an Ethics of Mercy", in this book.

ship that is sustained by love, faithfulness, and responsibility – a partnership that they would like to enshrine institutionally?

Is it morally justified, in the light of their biography, to speak of a *minus bonum*? For many people who have divorced and then remarried, it is (for whatever reason) simply impossible to resuscitate their original marriage. They may also have entered moral obligations and taken on responsibilities that cannot be ignored without incurring fresh guilt. For these persons, their second relationship is not a *minus bonum* measured against the indissolubility of marriage, but rather, in a biological perspective, a *vere bonum*, that is to say, that which is possible and good in the light of their biography. This moral-theological assessment is possible only if the biography and the identity of the persons concerned are taken into account. And this means refusing to rely on an ideal of humanity or on a misinterpreted Christian ideal that is detached from the discernment of biography and personal identity. If they are regarded in this way, however, the frictions within concrete life histories and the histories of couples and of families would not have the meaning that they do in fact possess for those who are involved and for the further conduct of their lives. One would fail to take seriously *failure* as a liminal experience in life, both as an existential challenge to people's lives and as a theological challenge to a Christian ethics. This is why the concept of the *minus bonum* has only a limited scope.

3 Failure as a Challenge to Christian Ethics

Christian ethics and pastoral care are honest and credible when they get involved with a realistic perception in human beings' experiences of failure, without either downplaying or dramatizing the existential significance of the radicality of the breakdown of decisions taken about one's life and of choices that one had earlier made about one's life project – and still less, without penalizing such breakdowns. This makes it possible to discover paths for a realistic new beginning that still hangs onto responsibilities that one had entered into earlier on. This promotes the further development of the work on one's personal identity and the chances of finding a trustful relationship or a viable perspective on one's life. It is precisely this that is necessary in view of the experience of failure, if the person is to regain trust in life. This trust can be shaken to such an extent that one doubts its (religious) meaningfulness, since the experience of being overwhelmed and of hopelessness in a breakdown that one does not fully understand, and the superior power of external or ego-dystonic experiences, form a contrast to the experience of trust in existence and in life, of self-efficacy, of the ability to act, of creativity, and of the discovery of meaning.

To speak of coping and coming to terms with failure does however imply the possibility of dealing constructively with failure in a way that permits a recovery of the ability to act, of trust in existence, and of existential meaning. This may sound contradictory; and if spoken at the wrong moment, such words may even signify making an inappropriate demand of those concerned. But a theoretical examination of the phenomenon of failure against the background of a theology of marriage and the family must remain conscious of this dialectical intertwining of failure and coping with failure. Otherwise, there would be the risk of an individual and societal or ecclesial suppression of breakdown, because radical experiences of a breach could be seen as too threatening or unbearable, or else they could be trivialized.

Since failure poses an existential challenge, it also becomes a challenge to faith, spirituality, and theology, involving the question of the meaning of a fragmentary identity and a fragile existence, or of the question mark that is posed against this meaning in the failure. These issues must be taken seriously; they cannot be "tamed" simply and cheaply by a reference to the ultimate salvific activity of God himself, or to the essential and exclusive responsibility that one has for one's own failure. That would be merely a problematic theological suppression of failure, as if the only way to make faith and failure compatible would be to make the individual essentially responsible for his or her failure. Such a reaction would entail the risk of an inhuman and discriminatory praxis both vis-à-vis one's own self and in action together with others. And this risk would in turn be the expression of a spiritual and theological inability to deal with failure, an inability that transposes the burden of a finite and endangered existence onto the question of anthropodicy,[13] in order not to confuse the image of God, and indeed in order to protect God himself from the distress and the accusation that are linked to failure. It would, however, be a problematic theological stabilizing reaction that had recourse to such a "hedging strategy". It would tone down the radicality of experiences of definitive failure, in order to protect God at the expense of the human being. A theological exonerating strategy of this kind is scarcely compatible with the biblical-Christian treasury of experience.[14] For, according to the testimony of the Bible, one may not dissolve the vexing question of theodicy – the question of how the God who loves human beings can be compatible with a reality that is full of suffering – at the expense either of the human being or of God.

The question of theodicy that accompanies the breakdown of marriage and the

---

[13] In contradistinction to the question of theodicy, in the question of anthropodicy the moral causality and responsibility for suffering, failure, and evil are attributed to the human person himself.

[14] See O. FUCHS: *Der zerrissene Gott: Das trinitarische Gottesbild in den Brüchen der Welt,* Ostfildern: Grünewald, 2014, and M. STRIET: *Gottes Schweigen, Auferweckungssehnsucht – und Skepsis,* Ostfildern: Grünewald, 2015.

family poses a central challenge to theology, for lived spirituality, and also for the church's praxis and pastoral care. In the context of the Christian faith and of its message of the God who suffers with us, the God whose justice is perfectly realized in his mercy,[15] talk about God can be maintained only in union with human failure. "God *and* the failure of the human person: they must be mentioned in the same breath, they must be kept together. But the failure cannot be theologically (ontologically) derived from God or traced back to him."[16] From a biblical and Christian perspective, God allows himself to be touched by the human person's failure – although this does not in itself supply a satisfactory answer to the question of why one has experienced failure. It is only a post-Easter theology that is capable of confessing in faith and in hope that the failure of Jesus on the cross has not the final word over the course of time.[17] In contradistinction to a religiously or psychologically motivated suppression of failure, therefore, theology must hold fast to the dialectic of failure and coping with failure. Theology must not be too quick to employ the category of "guilt" in order to make failure manageable and thereby prevent the existing picture of God and the world from being disturbed. Similarly, theology must not exonerate the person who has experienced failure by factoring it out, trivializing it, or delegating it to other persons.

Failure is often associated with guilt, especially when – as in the context of marriage – religious, societal, or ecclesial expectations with regard to continuity are breached. In moral terms, one could speak (depending on the circumstances) of a violation of fidelity, of a deviant disobedience, or also of disloyalty, when the rupture of biographies is usually attributed to the person who acts. This would mean that he himself has incurred a substantial responsibility for the breach, or that he himself is regarded as the cause of his own misfortune.[18]

4 Failure and Guilt as Theological-Ethical Aids to Interpret the Deviation from Ideals and Guiding Models

With the aid of the ethical category of guilt, some deviations from ideals and models are not described merely as matters of fate (that is to say, as events or experiences that could neither be influenced nor foreseen); nor are they understood as a clear deviation from societal norms. On the contrary, when morality

15 See W. KASPER: *Barmherzigkeit: Grundbegriff des Evangeliums – Schlüsselbegriff des christlichen Lebens,* Freiburg-Basel-Wien: Herder, 2012, 76 and 121–125.

16 G. FUCHS/J. WERBICK: *Scheitern und Glauben: Vom christlichen Umgang mit Niederlagen,* Freiburg-Basel-Wien: Herder, 1991, 30.

17 "Without the resurrection, the cross of Christ would merely set the seal on his failure" (W. KASPER: *Barmherzigkeit,* 82); on this, see also O. FUCHS: *Wer's glaubt wird selig ... Wer's nicht glaubt, kommt auch in den Himmel,* Würzburg: Echter, 2012, 40–44.

18 See J. WERBICK: art. "Scheitern", in: *Lexikon für Theologie und Kirche,* 9 (^{3}2000), 121.

lays claim to the category of guilt, or ethics makes this category its point of reference, this denotes the sphere of responsibility that is attributed to the individual or that can be expected of him. The individual finds himself located in this sphere *nolens volens,* and good reasons must be presented, if he is to be dispensed from it. Consequently, the theological discourse about guilt is motivated by the invariably concrete claim posited by that which is morally ideal – a claim that *can* be lived in personal and situational terms, but a claim that has not in fact been lived by the individual concerned.

This means that the theological-ethical discourse about guilt in concrete terms, when it is a question of a deviation from ideals and models about the conduct of life, is subject to the demand that one speak responsibly, if one is to do justice to the persons concerned. In terms of its own self-understanding, Christian ethics must take as its point of reference human beings with their behavioral dispositions, with what they want and what they can do, with their life stories, and their identity,[19] if its normative discourse is to be honest.[20] Depending on the circumstances, all of these aspects can appear as factors that make action possible or as factors that paralyze action with regard to the shaping of forms of life and life projects. The empirical and biographical conditionings will then be regarded as elements of moral accountability or of exculpation when we ask whether or not personal guilt is involved in a case of deviation from normative claims, values, and models. We should not assume that an instance of failure means that something essentially guilty has happened.

Failure is an existentially weighty event in which we see an unbridgeable difference that has been experienced and suffered vis-à-vis ideas about a successful life and fulfilled relationships. One who diagnoses failure as failure always does so against one particular horizon of successful identity or one particular understanding of the biographical success of ideals and models of specific forms of life and life projects. The increasing pluralization of recognized forms of life, together with the loss of significance of societally shared normal biographies, means that the biographical deviation from ideas of normality need not necessarily be characterized and experienced as a failure. At the same time, however, there is a risk that the individual has fewer points of orientation in the claim he makes to an authentic conduct of life and the shaping of relationships; and this means that it still remains relevant, and indeed urgent, to ask about value orientation and about positive models of partnership, marriage, and family.

---

[19] On this, see J. SAUTERMEISTER: *Identität und Authentizität: Studien zur normativen Logik personaler Orientierung,* Freiburg i.Ue.-Freiburg i.Br.: Fribourg Academic Press-Herder, 2013.

[20] On the concept of honesty, see G.W. HUNOLD: "Redlichkeit – zur Geschäftsgrundlage des Ethiktreibens", in: J. SAUTERMEISTER (ed.): *Verantwortung und Integrität heute: Theologische Ethik unter dem Anspruch der Redlichkeit,* Freiburg-Basel-Wien: Herder, 2013, 23–37.

Failure allows one to experience the authenticity of the evaluative and normative demands a person makes of himself. It is not always easy to draw a distinction between the feelings of guilt and of shame that are associated with these demands, since such feelings cannot be ascribed to simple causes. The illusion that one has power over the success or failure of life projects can also provoke feelings of shame and of guilt, but this fact, taken in isolation, does not give us adequate information about the quality of personal guilt in the moral or religious-ethical sense. On the contrary, a premature moralizing can cover over the existential depth that lies in the failure; and this blocks the personal look at the individual and at his identity – the look that is the genuine concern of Christian ethics and pastoral care. This is why a fundamental task of theological reflection, pastoral action, and spiritual praxis, also in the context of partnership, marriage, and the family, is "to give a central place in our conscious expanded perception to real failure, that is to say, to the events in which one unintentionally misses one's goal, the effect of unsuccessful projects, the underlying negative aspect of successes that are pushed through, the losses that lie hidden in victory, and the experience of one's own personal failure and of the failure of others".[21]

Besides this, an inappropriate moralizing of failure can seek to make the "ultimate impenetrability of the 'why'"[22] bearable by identifying in the guilty person an author, one who has caused the failure and is responsible for it. This strategy is meant to make it possible to control something that is threateningly incalculable: namely, the uncertainty that lies in the failure and that eludes complete control. It is obvious that such a strategy for coping with contingencies is not always automatically justified in moral terms. The ability to perceive failure as failure and to endure it presupposes that one can live with this remainder that is not at one's disposal. This also requires the ability to cope existentially with uncertainties and partial experiences of powerlessness, and to integrate them productively into one's own conduct of life and into a collective ethos, and to give all this a place in one's moral judgment and ethical reflection. The ability to perceive failure as failure also means the ability to get to work on individual and communal failure and to accept this.

It thus makes sense, in the framework of the Synodal process that examines questions related to a pastoral care of marriage and the family in accordance with the Gospel,[23] that one should also take up the question of an appropriate under-

---

[21] R. GEISEN: "Ethik des Misslingens: Variationen über das Scheitern", in: *Ethica* 7 (1999), 355–381, at 364.

[22] D. MIETH: "Vom Ethos des Scheiterns und des Wiederbeginns: Eine vergessene theologisch-ethische Perspektive", in: *Concilium* 26 (1990), 385–393, at 387.

[23] On this, see also G. AUGUSTIN/I. PROFT (eds.): *Ehe und Familie: Wege zum Gelingen aus katholischer Perspektive,* Freiburg i.Br.: Herder, 2014.

standing of persons who deviate from the ecclesial ideal of marriage and the family, or who have failed to live up to this ideal, such as persons who have divorced and have entered a second, civil marriage. How can we deal with such persons in a manner that accords with the Gospel?[24] Behind this question lies the further question of the relationship between guilt and failure, both in general and in concrete terms. And the question arises of how failure or deviation can have its full place in the heart of the church.

A theological reflection on radical experiences of rupture and fragmentation is thus not automatically required to trivialize experiences of failure, or to interpret them in moral terms.[25] On the contrary, it can look with empathy and realism at the abysses and despairs of human life. In practice, its task of theoretical reflection takes the form of a spiritual and pastoral task: to accompany "people who have failed in their life"[26] in such a way, and to allow them to experience the gospel of God's unconditional love in such a way, that they can "accept themselves because they are loved by God, not *despite* their failure, but also *because of* their failure and *in* their failure".[27]

In classical terminology, one can also employ the concept of mercy to describe such a way of looking at things.

5 Christian Ethics as an Ethics of Mercy

For a Christian ethics, mercy means striving for a praxis based on a judgment that is appropriate to the persons concerned and to their situation.[28] This implies

---

[24] On this, see E. SCHOCKENHOFF: *Chancen zur Versöhnung? Die Kirche und die wiederverheirateten Geschiedenen,* Freiburg i.Br.: Herder, 2011, and the thematic fascicle on "Umgang mit Scheitern" ("Dealing with Failure"): *Concilium* 26 (1990), fasc. 5; and "Sakramente für wiederverheiratete Geschiedene – seit 25 Jahren umstritten", in: *Theologische Quartalschrift* 175 (1995), fasc. 2, or T. SCHNEIDER (ed.): *Geschieden, wiederverheiratet, abgewiesen? Antworten der Theologie*, Freiburg-Basel-Wien: Herder 1995 (Quaestiones disputatae; 157), and M. GRAULICH/M. SEIDNADER (eds.): *Zwischen Jesu Wort und Norm: Kirchliches Handeln angesichts von Scheidung und Wiederheirat,* Freiburg-Basel-Wien: Herder, 2014 (Quaestiones disputatae; 264).

[25] On the anthropological dimension of failure, see also J. WERBICK: "Gelingen und Scheitern – Kennzeichen menschlicher Freiheitserfahrung: Fundamentaltheologische Vorüberlegungen zu einem kontextuellen Freiheitsverständnis", in: H.-G. GRUBER/B. HINTERSBERGER (eds.): *Das Wagnis der Freiheit: Theologische Ethik im interdisziplinären Gespräch,* Würzburg: Echter, 1999, 88–103.

[26] E. SCHOCKENHOFF: *Chancen zur Versöhnung?*, 121.

[27] Ibid. 121.

empathy for people and for what happens to them, and a fundamental acknowledgement of their life histories. Biography thus becomes an important element of moral-theological reflection and of pastoral deliberations.[29]

The theological-ethical term "mercy" is aligned with the mercy of God, which, according to the biblical testimony, can be perceived as divine justice:[30] God's unconditional love, as a benchmark of action, does not "finish off" – it justifies, and it promises to make a future possible. This does not mean cheaply ignoring what someone is responsible for, and where he or she has incurred guilt. But it pledges that guilt, transgressions, distress, and grief do not have the final say.

Precisely because we create realities in the world by means of our "thoughts, words, and deeds", realities that can never be taken back and that severely harm others, it is not possible for anyone to make up entirely for everything that has come about through one's own fault. We all rely on the courtesy of others. The request for mercy and the praxis of mercy are rationally possible only if this is subordinate to God's unconditional promise that there is a future, if we are willing to accept it and to make it possible for others to experience it in our actions.

This means looking closely, discerning the distress that has been experienced and caused, and asking what help is necessary and what compensations are possible. For some, this may be an imposition: for those who want to ignore guilt altogether, but also for the moral rigorisms that have lost sight of the individual and his or her biography, fixating him or her in a specific image and conduct. The moral attitude of mercy links "care and effort".[31]

Christianity's sensitivity to mercy consolidates the insight that people and their biographies are something individual that cannot be entirely subsumed under general notions. This, however, does not mean that it is impossible to speak in moral and Christian-ethical terms. On the contrary, it means that theological-ethical judging and speaking must meet the requirements of people's lived realities, biographies, and life-contexts, and must provide them with perspectives for the future.[32]

From a theological perspective, God's unconditional promise, which requires no efforts on the part of human beings, stands at the beginning of ethics. It is *this* that enables the human being to become a moral subject in the first place, because:

---

[28] See J. SAUTERMEISTER: "Das Gegenteil von Barmherzigkeit: Ein theologisch-ethischer Blick auf das Phänomen Skandalisierung", in: *Herder Korrespondenz* 68 (2014), 187–192.

[29] See J. SAUTERMEISTER: "Lebenswirklichkeiten gerecht werden: Anforderungen einer evangeliumsgemäßen Ehe- und Familienpastoral", in: *Herder Korrespondenz Spezial* (2014), fasc. 2, 25–29. See W. KASPER: *Barmherzigkeit.*

[30] See W. KASPER: *Barmherzigkeit.*

[31] W. DIRKS: *Barmherzigkeit: Ermutigung zu einer unzeitgemäßen Tugend,* Mainz: Grünewald, 1992, 165.

[32] See J. SAUTERMEISTER: *Identität und Authentizität.*

"For those who have not experienced what encounter and liberating grace are, it will be difficult to rejoice in their own lives and to share joy with others."[33] Only the experience of unconditional acceptance enables us to grant others a future, even if they appear not to deserve it.

From a Christian perspective, mercy does not mean a condescending help or "putting mercy before justice". It is a special form of perception and dedication under the premise that the door to life – as seen from God's side – is never entirely and definitively closed.[34]

6 The Decision of Conscience, the Social Recognition of a Value-Oriented Conduct of Life, and Perceptive Competence

For Christian ethics as a specifically Christian approach, this could mean, with regard to the meaning of the principle of gradualness, that this basic principle challenges us to ask how it is possible for people in their concrete biographies to implement the core values of the Christian concept of marriage and family in their own situations, even when these deviate from the guiding model. A gradual moral scale should be added to the necessary boundary rules,[35] which focus on prohibitions in order to save life and fundamental goods. The question would then be: How can I live the core values of love, trust, reliability, responsibility, intimacy, care, solidarity, and affectionateness in the context of my life and its form, in partnership, marriage, and so on? And: To what extent can a partnership based on love, faithfulness, and responsibility be interpreted and acknowledged as a shared religious path in the presence of God and with God? Especially when taking into account biographies and the circumstances of people's lives, we must pay attention to a person's conscience, which (if properly educated and formed) indicates the *veritas vitae* (the truth of one's life).[36] This indicates a theological-

---

33 M. SCHEUER: "Selig die Barmherzigen, denn sie werden Erbarmen finden", in: *Theologisch-praktische Quartalschrift* 141 (1993), 180–185, at 181.

34 See Pope FRANCIS: *Evangelii gaudium,* 47; W. KASPER: *Papst Franziskus – Revolution der Zärtlichkeit und der Liebe,* Stuttgart: Katholisches Bibelwerk, 2015; T. LAUBACH: "Der Papst und die Moral: Vom Vorrang des Evangeliums und seiner Praxis", in: *Stimmen der Zeit* 233 (2015), 523–534.

35 See R. BURGGRAEVE: "'The Sacred Ground of the Other'", in this book.

36 On this, see J. RÖMELT: "Zweite Ehe und Kommunionempfang: Aspekte einer Gewissensentscheidung," in: U. RUH/M. WIJLENS (eds.): *Zerreißprobe Ehe: Das Ringen der katholischen Kirche um die Familie,* Freiburg i.Br.: Herder, 2015, 225–243; A. BRENNINKMEIJER-WERHAHN: "*Sensus Fidei* and *Sensus Fidelium in a Marriage Debate*", in: *Melita Theologica* 65 (2015), 61–74, at 69; and the fundamental remarks by E. SCHOCKENHOFF: *Wie gewiss ist das Gewissen? Eine ethische Orientierung,* Freiburg i.Br.: Herder, 2003, 196–203.

ethical understanding of the conscience, which can be described as the guardian of the personal integrity of a person.

The current search for an appropriate and theologically-ethically legitimate pastoral care of marriage and the family can be viewed as a struggle for the recognition of the convictions of a person's conscience. If, after diligently consulting the conscience, someone is partly or totally unable to agree with external moral interpretations, and wishes to preserve his or her own normative self-understanding and ecclesial relatedness, this leads to a struggle for recognition – as we can observe in the church today. This struggle for the recognition of the normative self-interpretation of the persons concerned and of their life before God can be understood, from the perspective of moral psychology, as a struggle for the recognition both of one's own interpretation of life and of one's full communal belonging.[37] As the expression of decisions of conscience, such decisions about one's life, and the consequent endeavors to lead a life that is value-oriented and responsible, also seek social recognition.[38] Simple categorizations that do not fully take into account the concrete realities of life misunderstand the complexity of the processes of self-realization in the constellations of couples and families with their own specific momentum; these can be adequately understood only through empirical approaches.

In addition to the experiential sciences (or, more precisely, the human, social, and cultural sciences), this finds advocates in all those who reflect on their experiences in the extremely varied activities they carry out in the broad sector of the pastoral care of marriage and the family, for example, in the parishes, in special courses offered by the diocesan departments for marriage and the family, in church educational institutions and retreat houses, as well as in church counseling centers for marriage and the family. To these we must add those who are active in the wide spectrum of the pedagogical, psychosocial, psychotherapeutic, and medical sectors. These persons are characterized *inter alia* by a capacity for resonance that has been formed through self-experience, supervision, and continuing education. This reduces as far as possible the distorting elements that they bring to the encounter with other persons, and makes them sensitive to factors that potentially exercise an influence. Both in the experiential sciences and in the practical areas of experience, therefore, the perception and interpretation of existential realities become reflexive: that is to say, one is conscious of them as perception and

---

37 See J. SAUTERMEISTER: "Zur Bedeutung der Moralpsychologie für die theologische Ethik – am Beispiel von Scham- und Schuldgefühlen", in: *Münchener Theologische Zeitschrift* 66 (2015), 229–242.

38 On this, see A. THOMASSET: "Berücksichtigung der Geschichte und der biografischen Entwicklungen in Ethik und Pastoral der Familie", in: H. LANGENDÖRFER/O. RIBADEAU DUMAS/E. TANNER (eds.): *Theologie der Liebe*, 54–63, at 62f.

interpretation, which are also conditioned in their genesis by the structures of perception and interpretation of the subjects involved. Thanks to this self-reflectivity in the process whereby experience is formed, the possibility of fallibility in oneself and in others is recognized, and it becomes possible to open oneself to the dynamic realities of life – something that is necessary for the complex field of partnership, marriage, and family. This ability to call oneself into question, or to ask questions about one's own perspective and interpretation, is an important presupposition, if one is to come closer to realities, to do justice to human beings, and to enter into a genuine encounter with them, at least if we grant that, in the modern period, self-contained interpretations of the world, of life, and of conduct are no longer possible. To put it more simply: perceptive competence is also characterized by the ability to recognize and to monitor the structures of one's own prejudices in the encounter with other people.

7 Moral Liability and Regret as Personal Expressions of Responsibility

Despite what some people fear, an experience-based view of this kind does *not* mean reducing the human responsibilities that have come into being. Nor does it mean eliminating the question of personal responsibility of guilt. But this way of looking at things is opposed to an abstract and ahistorical attribution of responsibility and guilt, which (understandably enough) can lead to defensive reactions that prevent, instead of encouraging, a personal moral reappraisal. These reactions block personal growth and the moral development of the identity. A Christian ethic is typified by its sensitivity to the dynamic that is inherent in life stories, and thus to a gradual understanding of practical freedom, guilt, and personal responsibility, as well as of the interweaving of failure and guilt in life stories.[39]

It is beyond doubt that, in the course of the breakdown of a marriage and afterwards, consequences can arise that cannot simply be blamed on the individual as morally culpable, although the individual may have caused them or contributed to them. How can we speak appropriately about moral responsibility for actions and their consequences in the context of a Christian ethics of gradualness, if they originate only partly in human intentionality? This question is important, because what happens in the process of marriage breakdown can be grasped more appropriately through the acknowledgment of gradual voluntariness and partial control than through simplified categories of pure guiltiness in regard to the violation of the objective marriage bond.

[39] On this, see A. THOMASSET: "Berücksichtigung der Geschichte".

With regard to theological ethics and pastoral care, the categories of moral liability and regret can be helpful.[40] Both of these refer to the role of the persons involved as agents insofar as they are causally responsible, but not necessarily responsible in terms of intentionality. It is thus possible to take on responsibility for unintentional effects. And one can regret the unintended effects of one's actions, such as those entailed by adjustments in life such as divorce and remarriage. "The issue of a possible adjustment in life always concerns the consensus of more than one person. Being bound by decisions is always a discretionary judgment. However, this judgment cannot just be disconnected from the responsibility one has for those who are affected by such an adjustment."[41] What this means in practice in the specific constellation must be explored. This needs pastoral sensitivity and sound judgment, taking into account the psychological, social, material, and cultural resources of the persons concerned.

On the basis of the concepts of liability and regret, therefore, we can propose a complement from the perspective of moral psychology to the exclusive principle of guilt, which has dominated up to now: "Moral liability ranges over the complex and dynamic relational structure of an agent in social life, who must take responsibility for unintentional effects; it is dependent on the persons concerned."[42]

This distinction could offer a perspective for a theologically candid and pastorally appropriate behavior towards divorced and remarried persons in the church. The responsibilities resulting from the breakdown of a marriage, on the one hand, and entering into a new partnership on the basis of regained hope, on the other, would thus not necessarily need to be perceived as opposites. Such a value-oriented perspective would be more able to appreciate the moral efforts of people who intend to conduct their lives in a responsible way, bearing in mind their specific biographical conditions and situations.

8 Perspectives of a Christian Ethics of Gradualness as an Ethics of Mercy

I would now like to offer three suggestions about how to deepen theologically the principle of gradualness, which focuses on the discernment of biographies, personal growth, and the moral education of identities in the context of theological reflection and pastoral practice.

---

40 See M.-S. LOTTER: *Scham, Schuld, Verantwortung: Über die kulturellen Grundlagen der Moral,* Berlin: Suhrkamp, 2012, 123–180.

41 G.W. HUNOLD: "Lebensentscheidungen als Teil der Biografie: Zeilen aus einer theoretisch vernachlässigten Anthropologie: Ein Zwischenruf", in: K. HILPERT (ed.): *Zukunftshorizonte katholischer Sexualethik,* Freiburg i.Br.: Herder, 2011, 134–145, at 144.

42 M.-S. LOTTER: *Scham, Schuld, Verantwortung*, 141.

First, if evangelization aims at making present the kingdom of God for everyone, the pastoral program for marriage and families based on gradualness must make sure that discriminations (as well as unrealistic idealizations or relativizations) do not occur. Discrimination posits something that cannot be identified or overcome exclusively in objective terms, since this depends on the persons against whom the discrimination is potentially directed, or has been directed in the past. The subjective acknowledgement by those concerned that they are not (or no longer) subject to discrimination becomes a crucial criterion for whether or not discriminating practices exist – unless one were to suggest that such persons are easily offended and unrealistically sensitive, and hence incapable of an exact perception. If we abstain from grave general accusations of this kind and from a generalizing cultural pessimism, and if the personal integrity and the responsible formation of the consciences of the persons concerned are acknowledged, it still remains difficult to achieve the intention of a differentiated appreciation of people whose way of life is different, and of removing discrimination of such persons. It is only against this background that we can understand the struggle for the church's acknowledgment of the judgments made by mature Christians – spouses, couples, and partners – in their consciences before God. The inherent logic of the principle of gradualness is related not only to a moral ideal, but also to the personal conscience. This must be spelled out in the context of the pastoral care of partnership, marriage, the family, and single or unmarried persons, in accordance with the Gospel.

Secondly, the principle of gradualness implies the knowledge of the permanent fragmentariness of lifestyles. From a theological perspective, this is not to be seen merely as a deficit. On the contrary, it can be seen as an expression of openness and dependence on a perfection that is outside the control of human self-empowerment because it belongs to an eschatological perspective. It is precisely the theological insight into human imperfection, which unmasks every perfectionist ambition as a self-misunderstanding, that opens up the potential for conversion and new beginnings that is characteristic of the Christian faith. This also holds good in light of the Christian hope that the irreversibility of failure does not have the last word, even if it is no longer possible biographically to fulfill the moral ideal of marriage and the family. In fact, within the understanding of evangelization, every biography is open to traces of the presence of God. Pastoral narratives that are sensitive to context and biography could be developed, detecting these traces hermeneutically and explicating them. These would then be useful for religious (self-)education as both a testimony and a motivation.

Thirdly, in this way, the principle of gradualness could be part of a sacramental thinking or pattern of thought whereby, regardless of the particular form of life, God's love is perceived as being present in a biography and in specific actions and attitudes. This suggests that biographical realizations of moral convictions can be viewed as signs that are transparent to the kingdom of God. From a sacramental perspective of this kind, all those partnerships and expressions of family in which people struggle for the realization of values like faithfulness, reliability, solidarity, solicitousness, affectionateness, reciprocal respect of equality, responsibility vis-à-vis existing commitments, parental care, responsibility for life and creativity – even in the recognition of existential vulnerability, biographical brokenness, and in light of the reality of moral imperfection – could be theologically appreciated without discrimination.

9 Conclusion

What theological-ethical and pastoral consequences are to be drawn from these reflections? In negative terms, one could say that we must prevent the discrimination of those who are unable to live the moral and religious ideal of marital love. This is required (to use secular language) by respect for human dignity; but it is also prefigured in the praxis of Jesus himself, as the Gospels record it. In positive terms, it means recognizing the struggle for a realization of moral values in the lives of those for whom it is impossible to live the religious and moral ideal of marital love. Such a recognition must not be equated with a trivialization of all forms of living, because that would be a failure to appreciate individuals in their moral struggle; it would mean judging people merely on the basis of general and abstract forms of living, regardless of their concrete way of life, regardless of their particular biography, and regardless of their bodily determined identities. From the perspective of a Christian ethics that is concerned with the promotion of authentically human existence as a means of being authentically Christian, and with moral and religious education against the horizon of the Christian faith, those concerned are to be taken into consideration in moral and pastoral discourse. Interpretations of life are to be appreciated in terms of their relationship with God.

A Christian ethics of gradualness, as an ethics of mercy, is therefore aware of its responsibility in ethical and moral discourse. Its perspective is one of education and assistance, of personal development and of conscience, as well as of promotion of the ability to deal with reality and moral ability. This indicates some central aspects of the moral psychological elements that are essential to living integral love.

Part III

INDISSOLUBILITY AND THE THEOLOGY OF MARRIAGE

"Individua coniunctio": What Does Indissoluble Marriage Mean in Times of Individual Freedom?

Andrea Grillo

> *Cum igitur instinctus naturalis sit in specie humana ad hoc quod coniunctio maris et feminae sit individua, et quod sit una unius, oportuit hoc lege humana ordinatum esse*
> (St. Thomas Aquinas, *Summa contra gentiles, III, 123, 7).*
>
> *Ubi gratia largienda est, Christus adest; ubi exercenda severitas, soli adsunt ministri, deest Iesus*
> (St. Ambrose, *De Abraham, I, 6, 50).*

The title of my paper wishes to bring out *the* question that lies beneath the current debate, that is to say, the conflict – which I do not believe to be insuperable – between two readings of "human identity" and of its relationship to the Gospel. These readings belong to two different epochs and two diverse conceptions of what Christian culture is. The Gospel can be translated in the first conception or in the second. The principle of authority (*individua coniunctio*), which is typical of the traditional, "closed" society, contrasts with the principle of freedom (*individua libertas*), which is characteristic of late-modern, "open" society. I am convinced that the claim to trace back the doctrine of matrimony directly to the Gospel risks all the time confusing a *legitimate (but variable) social and cultural need* with the *indisputable truth of the Word of God.* This claim is therefore incapable of mediating the "cultural difference" that is necessary, if we are to have a non-fundamentalist access both to the Gospel and to the experience of human beings.[1] The fact that the matrimonial *coniunctio* is *individua* is a cultural experience as old as the human person. The safeguard of the "married partner" and that of the "third parties" (the children) has an evidential social and cultural character

[1] In the present phase of civil and ecclesial development, some sectors of the church are tempted to make "matrimonial" questions a "barricade" against the open society – a place, so to speak, where a decisively anti-modern model of faith and of the church can mount its resistance.

that cannot be denied, even today, and despite everything. *What has changed in the course of history is the way in which this need is protected by the institutions.* It is on this level that we must interpret the late-modern novelty of a "legislation" that provides for the new forms of "extended families" in which absolute indissolubility is left behind and a new formal – and egalitarian – principle of relative dissolubility is introduced. That which could not be dissolved by means of a justified meta-individual authority can now be dissolved. And the authority in question here is the individual, although this does not take place without specific and binding conditions. Today, "individual" becomes *the predicate above all of the single human being, not of the matrimonial communion.*[2]

This cultural transition cannot be judged in a unilateral manner. The authority of matrimony is contrasted today with the authority of the conscience, of the freedom, and of the self-determination of the individual, as well as with the history of these delicate relationships. New balances come into being, but the "communitarian" authority is not simply cancelled in favor of the "individual" authority. This phenomenon entails a slow work of *giving matrimony a new theological meaning,* in which we must distinguish clearly the levels of experience, of praxis, and of theory. Even in theology, from the late modern period onwards, there is never "knowledge without a subject". In this field, every illusion is unfailingly counterproductive. What I shall now do is in fact a work of drawing distinctions and of discernment. This is useful, if we are not to take the wrong direction when we ask our questions and make our replies about the term "indissoluble" in connection with matrimony. I shall investigate the "meaning" of the term (1); its classical and late-modern reception (2), and then focus on the importance of *Dignitatis humanae* in the recent history of this reception (3). This will be followed by a rapid presentation of today's debate on this topic (4). I shall then formulate some "fundamental theses" to guide our rethinking (5), indicating the principal perspectives for an effective and efficacious solution to the contemporary impasse (6). I shall conclude by formulating a hypothesis of a systematic and disciplinary rethinking of the *individua coniunctio* (7).

1 On What Level Are We Talking about "Indissolubility"?

The history of the application to marriage of the word – that is to say, the adjective *indissolubilis* or *individuus* or *indivisibilis* – originates with Augustine, but it was developed above all in the juridical and systematic reflection of scholasticism. It does not, however, depend directly on "religious history" or on the "Christian

[2] On the other hand, to affirm the existence of God is not to deny the free subject and the history of the conscience. To identify God with the absence of freedom and the lack of history is a typical commonplace of anti-modernism.

theological tradition" in the strict sense. We find a sufficiently clear reflection of this situation in the thinking of Saint Thomas Aquinas. We could synthesize the more surprising insights of one of his great texts in the *Summa contra gentiles* (III, 123) as follows: in the traditional context, the "justification" of indissolubility is *anthropological, rather than theological.* This led the tradition step by step to propose a "physical" and "ontological" concept of indissolubility, with an evidential character that is antecedent to the Gospel and almost makes it redundant, since the Gospel would be merely the repeating of an evidential character that came to maturity on a philosophical-anthropological terrain that was exempt from history, from tradition, and from culture. Again and again, we find the affirmation that Christ "elevates matrimony to a sacrament" – often without a genuine comprehension of the "difference" that this sacrament makes manifest in the context of Christian experience. This is probably due to the exclusive juridical competence that the Catholic Church enjoyed in questions of matrimony until 1804, which has weighed heavily on the way of thinking about marriage and of exercising discipline in this field.

Let me make the same point in different terms: We must recognize that the mediaeval model of understanding indissoluble matrimony lived on, via the "canonical form" of Trent, down to the codification of canon law in 1917. We can discern here a progressive hardening of the "objectifying" paradigm that has its starting point in "cultural" and "traditional" motivations that were completely uncontested in the pre-modern world, and that has increasingly taken over institutional needs and apologetic motifs and transcribed these into its own register. The "resilience of an exclusive juridical competence of the Church with regard to matrimony" has almost given the impression of the survival of a "temporal power", of a *societas perfecta,* of a possibility of determining directly the life of society and culture in "obedience" to the Gospel. All this must be considered the "proximate context" of the way in which "indissolubility" is defined. As an abstract term – not only as an "adjective" of *coniunctio* or of *vinculum* – it is a typical "negation of negations" on which the late-modern Church has taken its defensive stand against what has become newly obvious in the liberal epoch. What happens to "indissolubility" is a phenomenon similar to what happens to "infallibility" and "inerrancy". On these "negations of negations", a barricade has been erected against the modern corrosion of conduct and of consciences that makes it very difficult today to attain to the truth of the experience of human subjects and of the Word of God. *Our theological history prevents us from coming to terms with reality: this "ideal world" defiles our relationship with reality – and it should be recognized that the priority belongs to reality.*

2 How Have We Received this Discourse in the Last Two Hundred Years? From the "Opposition" to Modernity at the Second Vatican Council down to *Familiaris consortio*

Thanks to an ancient tradition, the Gospel of matrimony is based and flourishes on evidence about "what is convenient" – but this can change in the course of history. The transformation in the last two hundred years has been structural. If we look at it in perspective, we can observe a series of highly important shifts that concern the definition of the subject in relation to his or her own actions. The "conscience", understood no longer only as a "judgment", but as a *habitus,* is profoundly transformed by these changes.

In the historical development, we cannot fail to admire the freedom and the strength which the Church over the centuries has intervened with its own doctrine and its own discipline to "regulate", "govern", and "structure" the matrimonial relationship between men and women. And it is obvious that the accuracy and subtlety of the ecclesial intelligence have been obliged to take account, precisely in the area of matrimony, of the "complexity of the levels involved". I should like to recall here, with great admiration, the lucidity of what Thomas writes about matrimony in his *Summa contra gentiles*:[3] the space lit up by this flash of lightning appears very rich and finely articulated. Above all, Thomas properly redefines the various levels (natural, civil, ecclesial) on which the *generatio* becomes meaningful and plays its role. This description, formulated many centuries ago, reconciles us with the world that lies before our eyes. In particular, it shows the "autonomy" that matrimony enjoyed in the scholastic conception. It shows how hard it is today, especially for some sectors of the Catholic world, to hear with freedom these mediaeval words. If we free the mediaeval words from the modern (Tridentine) and late-modern (beginning with the *Codex*) projections onto the past, we can find in them a reason for ecclesial prophecy and the principle of a new lucidity. In other words, they contain a "prophetic vision" of the matrimonial question that has been

---

3 "*Considerandum* est autem quod, quando aliquid ad diversos fines ordinatur, indiget habere diversa dirigentia in finem: quia finis est proportionatus agenti. Generatio autem humana ordinatur ad multa: scilicet ad perpetuitatem speciei; et ad perpetuitatem alicuius boni politici, puta ad perpetuitatem populi in aliqua civitate; ordinatur etiam ad perpetuitatem Ecclesiae, quae in fidelium collectione consistit. Unde oportet quod huiusmodi generatio a diversis dirigatur. Inquantum igitur ordinatur ad bonum naturae, quod est perpetuitas speciei, dirigitur in finem a natura inclinante in hunc finem: et sic dicitur esse naturae officium. Inquantum vero ordinatur ad bonum politicum, subiacet ordinationi civilis legis. Inquantum igitur ordinatur ad bonum Ecclesiae, oportet quod subiaceat regimini ecclesiastico. Ea autem quae populo per ministros Ecclesiae dispensatur, sacramenta dicuntur. Matrimonium igitur secundum quod consistit in coniunctione maris et feminae intendentium prolem ad cultum Dei generare et educare est Ecclesiae sacramentum: unde et quaedam benedictio nubentibus per ministros Ecclesiae adhibetur." (*Summa contra gentiles*, IV, 78)

almost completely lost to sight by the theological debate of the last hundred years, which has preferred to shut itself up in theological commonplaces that were far too aseptic and far too isolated from the natural and cultural substratum of the sacrament.[4]

The Second Vatican Council did not fail to seize the opportunity to speak an authoritative word on this matter. This word, however, has remained implicit, so to speak, and on the secondary level in contrast to other fundamental themes of the Council's teaching. The *bonum coniugum* is the "intersubjective" category that appears in *Gaudium et spes* and bears witness to the official beginning of a repositioning of the doctrine about marriage in keeping with a "new perspective". It is the way of looking at things that starts to change, thanks to an act of fidelity to the Gospel and to human experience (GS 16). In the perspective of a "personalistic" evaluation of matrimony, to change one's way of looking *means mediating in a different way the liberty of the subject and the authority of the bond.* Above all, *it means bidding farewell to the logic that simplistically posits an antithesis between objective and subjective, and entering the sphere of intersubjective logic.* This shift creates what I would call the conceptual and experiential space *for translating the doctrine of indissolubility into new terms, creating the conditions for a different discipline.* The cue in the Council's text lay dormant for a long time, but it has inspired two fundamental transitions that we have to take into account here. The first, to which *Familiaris consortio* (1981) bears witness, happened *with the recognition that divorced and remarried persons are not separated from the Church.*[5] The second transition, desired by Pope Francis today, involves an effective proclamation of mercy that is capable of recognizing not only sin, but also illness; not only an end, but also a beginning; *not only a loss of communion, but also the possibility of a new experience of communion.*[6]

All this, as a post-conciliar development, certainly finds its primary presupposition in *Gaudium et spes* 47–52 – that is obvious. But even more radically, it is based on the presupposition of a "discovery" that is in fact profoundly innovatory,

4 This way of doing theology often fails to conceal a substantially "apologetic" intent: it postulates a "Christian differentness" that leads one to understand the sacrament "against" the contract and "against" nature. This tendency clearly leads to a progressive loss of contact, not only with natural and civil reality, but also with the Gospel.

5 "Together with the Synod, I earnestly call on pastors and the whole community of the faithful to help the divorced, and with solicitous care to make sure that *they do not consider themselves as separated from the Church,* for as baptized persons they can, and indeed must, share in her life" (JOHN PAUL II: *Familiaris consortio,* 84).

6 The first transition is the recognition that the condition of those who are "divorced and remarried" is not foreign to ecclesial communion. The second transition, thirty-five years later, is the recognition that this condition possesses a quality of ecclesial communion. This presupposes an aggiornamento of the concept of "indissolubility".

a discovery realized by the Second Vatican Council above all in the Declaration *Dignitatis humanae*. The long-term influence of this text on the theology and the discipline of matrimony deserves a more attentive analysis than it usually receives. In effect, since the sacrament of matrimony is the "hinge" between private and public experience, it feels much more strongly the change of perspective that has been introduced on the public level with the positive reception of the "freedom of conscience", against the background of the Christian revelation.[7]

3 A New Self-Awareness of the Subject and a New Equilibrium between Freedom and Authority: The New Insights of *Dignitatis humanae*

The fathers of the Second Vatican Council may not have thought that acceptance of the "open society" – which happens officially through the text of *Dignitatis humanae* – would have brought such modifications to the sacrament that is the "hinge" between the private and the public and institutes the "forms" of the communion that can be lived between husband and wife. The history of the location of matrimony in the "juridical system" (family law can be located at one time in "private law" and at another time in "public law") would easily have shown them that acceptance of the "freedom of conscience" – a principle that had been so strongly opposed by the magisterium of the Catholic Church for nearly two centuries – would make a profound impact on all the forms of "visible communion", and above all, on marriage and the family.

The grammar of Christian marriage is destined to change profoundly when it is recognized in principle that every subject has an original relationship to freedom. Every subject: the wife and the husband, the child and the father, the legitimate child and the illegitimate child. This new horizon of the "perception" and the "experience" of the world and of the human person, whereby access to freedom is assured "in principle" to every subject, changes not so much the act of matrimony, as the relationship of matrimony. And *it makes this relationship simultaneously more profound and more fragile.*

This is not the appropriate place for an exact analysis of the test of the Declaration *De libertate*.[8] All we can do is to take up some key dimensions of the text

7 The resistance that puts up innumerable obstacles to every variation of the discipline of the sacrament of matrimony is not generated by obvious theological principles, nor by pastoral priorities, but by political imperatives and by ecclesiological resistance to change. This model of the relationship between the church and the world and of an ecclesial concept sees marriage today as a quasi-natural "barricade" ready for the fight against the late-modern spirit. In one sense, marriage becomes the testing ground for resistance to the Council's project of a "translation of the tradition".

8 For an initial in-depth analysis of the "theological", "anthropological", and "institutional" notes

in order to grasp their indirect consequences in the reformulation of the question of the family and of marriage in our own days within an "open society". *It is, unfortunately, a rather bitter experience, when we observe that no small part of the Catholic theology of marriage appears today to want – and almost to need – to turn back the civil and political calendar by at least two hundred years in order to be able to say something meaningful to the men and women of good will.*

The two fundamental data of the Declaration *De libertate* are: (1) the acceptance that one is not free because one is in the truth, but that liberty is the precondition of truth; and (2) that this assumption is not only "tolerated", but is theologically and anthropologically grounded. It must also be protected by juridical means.

This relationship between freedom and truth, which is analyzed so solemnly and is so obviously different from the past, soon makes it necessary to revise profoundly all the "communitarian" experiences and institutions. It redefines in some way the "forms of lived communion". This applies first of all to marriage, although it appeared at first sight that the state and the city (and the Church) were the most typical "places" where freedom is exercised. *Dignitatis humanae* thus has a serious and wise impact on the theology of marriage and on how we think about the "indissoluble" bond that constitutes marriage.

4 What Solutions Are Proposed Today (*"De iure condito"*)?

This history is clear, but today's debate often seems to have forgotten it all, and smooths out the tradition into a "traditionalism of style" that is integralist, maximalist, and fundamentalist. There are many proposals in this debate that sound like "non-solutions", because *they do not accept the cultural and ecclesial paradigm shift that was caused by the irreversible arrival of an "open society"*. It is not surprising that, where society is still characterized by strongly traditional elements, this "open" situation is perceived as dangerous, treacherous, and explosive – in contrast to the tradition. The social and cultural differentiation has long demanded a differentiation in the formulation of the doctrine and the discipline of marriage. As G. Angelini has lucidly stated,[9] the appeal to the "evidential character" of the principle of indissolubility is an objective defect of the prevalent way in which questions of marriage and the family are treated today.

One of the most impressive facts in the civil developments of the last decades is *the increasing discrepancy between marriage and the family. The experience*

---

present in the conciliar text, I refer to the recent study by P. TRIANNI: *Il diritto alla libertà religiosa: Alle fonti di Dignitatis humanae*, Vatican City: Lateran University Press, 2014.

9 See G. ANGELINI: "Indissolubile: in che senso?", in: *Il Regno-attualità* 6 (2015), 413–419.

of "family", in its various forms, no longer necessarily presupposes marriage.[10] Whereas we are enquiring – and rightly so – into the forms of indissolubility, social and cultural development seems to be interested only in "solubility". In some cases, there is a surprising kind of "congruence" (at a distance) between the administrative form that divorce takes in the civil sphere (with the "quick divorce"), which is arriving in Italy too and dispenses with the decision of a judge who is a "third party" in relation to the marriage partners, and the proposals that we hear in church spheres of a "quick annulment" that is to be entrusted *to the discretion of the bishop.*

This "congruence", which certainly is surprising, derives from a changed world, from forms of life, of work, of culture, of self-consciousness, and of dwelling that are no longer traditional. Both secular culture and Catholic culture respond to these with "diverse categories". Here, we need a forward-looking and calm discernment. This will be demanding and complex, but it is urgent and necessary.

Taking our starting point in the "historical inheritance" of the paradigms of which we have spoken, we can sum up by saying that before us lie two paths that offer alternatives so drastic that they seem to pose an impasse that no ecclesial solution can overcome.

In view of the change in the self-consciousness of the subjects and of their relationship to "intimacy", it appears that there are only two alternatives for coping with the crisis of the family communion and with the need to provide for a "reconstruction" after the crisis. *Either we give the subject the possibility of interrupting the bond (by admitting divorce), or else we undertake the official examination of an original defect in the consent or in the consummation (recognizing nullity). The first alternative points us to the sphere of what is available to the subject. The second alternative points us to the institutional collection of objective data.*

This way of doing this must be called into question *on the theoretical level.* Let me put it like this: the fact of reconstructing the relationship between divorce and nullity as a "drastic antithesis" between "subjective remedies" and "objective remedies" is, in reality, a dangerous ideological abstraction. *It means, in fact, both*

[10] A "non-apologetic" interpretation of these developments can be found in a "triad" of books that examine the development of the concept of "intimacy". I refer to A. GIDDENS: *The Transformation of Intimacy: Sexuality, Love, and Eroticism in Modern Societies,* Redwood City: Stanford University Press, 1993. There are also fascinating pages in N. LUHMANN: *Liebe als Passion: Zur Codierung von Intimität,* Berlin: Suhrkamp, 1982. Alongside these two books, we should add a more recent contribution: F. JULLIEN: *De l'intime: Loin du bruyant amour,* Paris: Grasset, 2013. These works are linked by the theme of "intimacy". Although their theses and their methodologies differ, they bring out clearly the "context" in which the discussion of Christian matrimony is taking place today.

that divorce brings objective motives to light, and that nullity puts into words elements that are subjective, and even "arbitrary".[11]

We have now clarified this first point, but I should like to spend some time on an even more radical question. In other words, I wish to deny that it is only on these two "extremes" that one can polarize the ways in which the Church (or the state) permits the subject to "remedy" his or her own error, to "medicate" one's own wound, to give "a new beginning" to the relationship in which one lives. We must track down (or, at the same time, find and invent) "intermediate forms" between the subjective (but not absolute) availability of divorce and the objective indissolubility that admits of only one possibility, namely, identifying an original nullity that may have existed. The subject has the power to make use of the availability of divorce; the indissolubility is suffered as an object. And these two are the antipodes of an "intersubjective" experience in which the "bond" lives in a constitutive manner a *history of freedom that cannot simply be halted at the moment of the official expression of consent.* This, in any case, does not alter the fact that getting hold of the "historicity of the bond", its relationship to the freedom of the subject and to the events that have taken place within the relationship, is neither simple nor straightforward.

I believe, however, that we can identify a "classical category" that permits us to overcome the impasse. This is the category of "sickness or death", which can act as a "mediation" to ensure a meaningful relationship between the ecclesial tradition and contemporary forms of life. We can say that *the bond, which is not at the free disposition of the subject, does not exist as an "unbreakable and impassible object". On the contrary – although it is radically blessed by God – it is not withdrawn from the "passible" history of human beings, from their sins and their crises and their sicknesses.* The western tradition, unlike the eastern tradition, has rather little to say about this consideration, but it deserves to be reclaimed and developed.

4.1 The Non-Solutions (Which Are Part of the Problem)

The classic structure of the response to the question of "indissolubility" is presented clearly in *Familiaris consortio* 83–84, which states that with regard to a union of persons who are divorced and remarried, the possibility of "ecclesial communion" is subject to four alternative conditions:

- giving up the second union (that is to say, separation and return to the person who is one's only marriage partner);

[11] In other words, the president of the civil tribunal who evaluates the conditions of a separation or divorce may be much more "pastoral" than an ecclesiastical tribunal that limits its work to implementing what the parties have already agreed upon among themselves. Besides this, the primacy of God is not guaranteed by adding an extra ecclesial competence.

– giving up the sacrament of the eucharist;
– giving up sexual relations in the second union;
– recognition of the nullity of the original bond.

These "solutions" fail almost entirely to recognize the problem, that is to say, the "breakdown" of a matrimonial relationship and the inauguration of a "second union". This failure means that these "non-solutions" make the problem worse instead of resolving it, adding a no longer tolerable dose of indifference and of fiction to the question that is at stake.[12]

4.2 The Partial Solutions (Which Recognize the Problem without Resolving It)

Alongside this maximalist claim to identify the Gospel with an aseptic historical and cultural given, we find the proposal of a "solution in the *forum internum*". Here, the problem is recognized, but the solution that is offered does not correspond to the "matter" that is involved. Since marriage is a "hinge" between the private and the public, it needs solutions that take account of this double dimension. Solutions that are "only public" or "only private" do not tackle the question. They give satisfaction to the institutions, but not to the persons – or else, they give in to the "desiderata" of the persons, but they cause confusion to the institutions. The solution *in foro interno*, like some proposals of a "penitential itinerary", gives the individual the possibility of receiving sacramental communion, but it does not recognize the living communion of the second union. Communion is declined only "in the singular", leaving unanswered the legitimate request for "dual" and "plural" communion. In other words, such solutions are ineffective because they do not want to take into consideration a different paradigm of the doctrinal and disciplinary comprehension of the "indissoluble bond". They pretend to themselves that they can make an impact on the level of discipline alone.

5 How Can we Conceive of the Ecclesial Future in this Field?

This means that without a comprehensive rethinking of "indissoluble marriage" – avoiding regarding this "question" as a simple question of church discipline – it is impossible to find a way of rethinking "ecclesial communion" in the face of the "breakdown of marriage and new unions". I would like to formulate the essential requisites of such a reflection in the form of the following "fundamental theses".

1. We must assume *the primacy of reality over ideas.* Without a dose of healthy realism, we remain victims of an artificial language that is nourished by an

[12] On this limitation of *Familiaris consortio*, see J.-P. VESCO: *Tout amour véritable est indissoluble: Plaidoyer pour les divorcés-remariés,* Paris: Cerf, 2015, 83ff.

alliance that pulls both theology and canon law downwards. They are always inclined to invent unrealities, provided that this helps them to avoid confronting reality.

2. We must get away from the antithesis between the "objectivity of the bond" and the "subjectivity without bonds". There is a "median zone", a zone "of mediation" between an objective theory of the bond and a subjective dissolution of every bond, and the Church too can and must take care of this zone. *If it remains in the "opposition to the subjective", the Church loses both its relationship to the objectivity of the effects and its relationship to the subjectivity of the emotions.*
3. Only an "intersubjective theory" of the freedom of conscience and of the history of the bond can get to the bottom of complex past experiences and of legitimate expectations of "new beginnings" that are possible and also desirable.
4. The fact that a "history of the bond" is recognized means admitting that, in specific circumstances that are not foreseeable or manageable, *the bond can become sick and even die.* The Church can care for this breakdown only by elaborating new categories that are more flexible and less maximalist, categories that can do justice not only to the experience of the subjects, but also to the Word of God which becomes audible in these subjects. *The contemporary defect is not only a defect in the anthropological analysis, but also a defect in the theological interpretation, which misunderstands the Word of God and forces it into categories that are theologically and culturally inadequate.*

6 Beyond the Paradigm "Mediaeval or Modern": Solutions to a Theology of Matrimony after *Dignitatis humanae*

The elaboration of "another paradigm" of theological and juridical understanding of marriage is pursued today along two paths. On the one hand, in the context of a comprehensive "deinstitutionalization of the family", it takes up anew the older and more elementary idea of "fidelity" and of "indissolubility". This proceeding is suggested today, with great authority, by Bishop Jean-Paul Vesco,[13] and I see it as an interesting path – because it is both classical and new. It means recovering a more elementary meaning of "indissolubility", a term that is referred, neither to the "ecclesial sacrament" nor to the "civil contract", but to the "natural given or relationship", that is, to the "natural society", to the *fact* of living together, to the *relationship of authentic love.* This is an "ancient doctrine", not only ecclesiastical, but also civil and sapiential. Although it has its origin in a world that is so

[13] See ibid.

different from our own, it still retains its power and its persuasiveness. Every true love is forever. We do not need the Gospel in order to experience this truth, which is inherent in every authentic relationship. The question arises when, in a relationship of love – even one that has no formal elements involving third persons, and hence even in the most pure form of living together – an element of crisis arises and the relationship becomes heavy and complicated. It gets blocked and takes the form of hostility, indifference, suffering, incomprehension, pain. And it is precisely at this point that, in one case, "the decision to put an end to the relationship" is taken, while, in another case, every subjective decision is rejected, with the exception of the possibility of identifying an original defect in the marriage.[14]

But the Church's *sollicitudo* does not preclude a "third path" that exists *de facto* but needs a doctrinal and disciplinary formalization. Serious work has been carried out by theologians and canon lawyers for years now on this question.

I believe that a "third path" of this kind can be found in an "intersubjective dimension" that gives life to the "nuptial bond" and that is both *more than subjective and less than objective.* The qualifying point of this "intersubjective identity of the bond", which the ecclesial tradition wants to preserve, consists in the fact that, while *it is not something over which the subject can freely dispose, it cannot simply be treated as the objectivity of an "entity" or a thing.* This is why such a solution does not follow the extreme logic of the availability of divorce; nor is it simply imposed on the couple as an "object". The bond is a living, active, and historical reality that can flourish or wither, that can glow with health, or become sick, or even die. The specific character of a *sollicitudo* that is ancient and modern, civil and ecclesial, is that it *leaves a space for a prudent but urgent consideration of the "history of the bond".* This is what *sollicitudo* with regard to this problem means in humanity.

The Church has always paid attention to this experience, but it has done so by means of paradigms and categories that are "non-historical". In this way, it remains faithful, not to the Gospel, but to these categories that interpret it in the contingency of the present day – but employ inadequate frameworks and concepts. The Church risks thereby being unable to say anything about the matter that is truly important, that is to say, about the "custody of the bond". The bond cannot be put away in a strongbox or a deep-freezer, nor in a museum. It must be accompanied, healed, or put right, depending on the circumstances. Above all, its intersubjective quality must be respected. We must therefore bid farewell to the

---

[14] I do not consider here the degeneration of the two possible models of "remedy" to the crisis. In both cases, ultimately, the subjective judgment (either openly or underhandedly) is always just around the corner. For an ample consideration of the conditions that make possible the very institution of "nullity", see the classic study by G. DOSSETTI: *La violenza nel matrimonio in diritto canonico,* Milan: Vita e Pensiero, 1998 (anastatic reprint of the 1943 original).

logical opposites of subjective and objective, which are also *arbitrary and authoritarian.* There is a social and cultural tendency to "subjectify a relationship". If the Church's only response today were to "objectify it", that would merely make the situation worse.

As I shall go on to say, there are some unequivocal signs of this potential shift in the recent debate. I believe that we must recover here the best of the mediaeval and modern tradition, but we must translate it into the language of the history of the subjects in relationship and the history of the freedom of conscience.[15]

All the forms of "solution" that deserve to be considered here are located, in my view, precisely in the "objective space" that lies *between a purely subjectivist understanding of divorce and an "objectifying" and almost "reifying" hermeneutic of objectivity.* The interplay of forces, in the past and today, always and everywhere tends to "polarize" the positions, to squash on the rock of "divorcism" even the most timid attempt to understand indissolubility anew, and to accuse of obscurantism every limitation placed on the "subjective freedom of self-determination".[16] We must find the courage and the strength to claim for ourselves a legitimate space that is possible and necessary for "intermediate forms". These comply with an ecclesial mission in which the space between God and the human person is the place of christological, ecclesiological, and sacramental mediation. Such mediations cannot ever be reduced to a "juridical norm", although they must be composed and articulated by means of such a norm. Some hypotheses about this mediation are already available to us, in at least three versions, and I should like to say something about these.

6.1 The Path of the "Moral Sickness or Death of the Bond"

One first path proceeds by means of an interesting analogy. If we are to grasp it fully, I must make an introductory remark that I believe to be very important. Saint Thomas said that if we had an "impassible life", the three sacraments of initiation

---

[15] Obviously, this development does not lack ambiguities and traps. For a reflection on the stratification of the concept of freedom, see A. GRILLO: *Genealogia della libertà: Un itinerario tra filosofia e teologia,* Cisinello Balsamo: San Paolo, 2013.

[16] Thus, in the "laicist" camp, there is a tendency to think that every form of "limitation" on the "freedom of divorce" is a form of absolute obscurantism. In the clerical camp, it is often held that if one moves even one millimeter from an "objectifying" interpretation of indissolubility, one is denying the Gospel and turning one's back on the Word of God. The Gospel would be preserved only by the most blind and mechanical application of the antithesis between subjective and objective. But this solution, which solves nothing, is not only repugnant to common sense, but is also alien to the true tradition of the Gospel and of the church. God does not need the lack of human liberty, and the affirmation of the "history of freedom" certainly does not imply the negation of God.

would be sufficient for us.[17] But since we know "crises of life and of faith", we also need the sacraments of healing. It is here, I believe, that ecclesial reflection has got "bogged down" for some time now, since it claims to *understand the two sacraments of healing according to a univocal logic, that is to say, exclusively as the healing of sin.* I, on the other hand, believe that the tradition contains evident traces, which have recently been rediscovered even on the level of the official statements of the magisterium, of a *double logic of the sacraments of healing.*[18] This logic gives a different response to the two causes of the crisis. *There is one crisis by reason of guilt or sin, to which penance responds. And there is a crisis without guilt or sin, to which the anointing of the sick responds.* As we know, this reinterpretation is neither simple nor immediate. The tradition that weighs upon our shoulders is far too long, a tradition that even today leads us to think that anointing too (regarded as "extreme unction") belongs to the logic of the remedy for sin at the moment of death.

Going beyond the limits of the common tradition, I believe that it is truly important today to apply not only penance, but also the anointing, to the complex logic of "wounded families". The juridical language that we have elaborated over the centuries generates a significant distinction between the guilty partner and the innocent partner. But it is difficult to find words to speak of married partners who are suffering, sick, put to the test, and laid low by the "sickness of their bond".

Opening our eyes to the reality of the "sick bond", without following a strict logic of attaching guilt or seeking to pin down responsibility, is a resource with a double effect: (1) It permits a different form of accompanying the subjects, looking at them as persons stricken by a suffering that has the characteristics of an illness, without immediately concentrating our attention on the aspect of "guilt"; (2) it predisposes us to accept the perspective that this "sick" condition can make such an impact on the bond, in specific instances, that it "dies" – quite apart from the guilt of the subjects who are involved.

The oriental tradition, though with many variants in the concrete application, and with its own limitations, still knows this way of interpreting a situation, this attitude, this pastoral and relational style. If we look at "the crises in the family" not primarily as "guilt or sins", but as "sicknesses or deaths", we could develop pastoral and legal processes that would look at the crisis in an "intersubjective" manner. Leaving behind the dry alternatives of a subjective divorce and an objec-

---

17 *Summa theologiae*, III, q. 65, a. 1, *corpus*.

18 [18] I have elaborated a systematic reflection on this decisive difference in A. GRILLO: "L'unzione degli infermi: Salvezza e guarigione. quale efficacia sacramentale?", in A. GRILLO/E. SAPORI (eds.): *Celebrare il sacramento dell'unzione degli infermi: Atti della XXXI Settimana di Studio dell'Associazione Professori di Liturgia, Valdragone, San Marino, 24–29 agosto 2003*), Rome: CLV – Ed. Liturgiche, 2005 (Bibliotheca Ephemerides Liturgicae: Subsidia; 130), 41–59.

tive nullity, the recognition of a "moral sickness or death of the bond" would allow the Church to "mediate" between God and the human person. Man may not put asunder what God has united, but Christ and the Church, who mediate between the divine Father and the human son who squanders his love, can take note, with prudence and lucidity, of the mortal sickness that has left its mark on a bond. This could make possible a new union. And this union – while not forgetting the lived wound of the first union – need not necessarily be regarded as "non-sacramental".

6.2 The Path of the Differentiation between Sacrament and Contract

The mediaeval paradigm, which was the object of reflection at the Council of Trent and was taken into the codification of canon law in the twentieth century, has made more and more rigid an identification that has a primarily institutional function: this means that *every matrimonial contract between baptized persons is* ipso facto *a sacrament.* This "communitarian excess" can be understood as an ecclesial response to the hostility on the part of civil society in the nineteenth century. But we must ask whether it is genuinely compatible with an "open society". A direct superimposition of the civil and the sacramental is certainly comprehensible, on the theological level. But can it make an adequate response to the forms of life and to the phenomena of the family that we know and practice today in the open and free societies of Europe and America?[19] The path taken by some German theologians and canon lawyers[20] is favored by the specific history of the German nation and of its state and church structure. It draws a distinction between the civil level and the sacramental level. This distinction, which corresponds to the mediaeval tradition, does not claim that the *forma canonica* absorbs into itself all the "valid" forms of Christian matrimony. The *forma canonica* continues to be demanded for the sacrament. But baptized persons could nevertheless also have a "civil marriage" recognized as valid. In the case of divorced and remarried persons, this would entail recognizing that, although there is no existing sacramental bond with effects that could be considered and declared non-existent in a form similar to the "ecclesiastical dispensation", the subject could validly take on a new bond. This would

---

[19] If we situate the abstract theology in its own context, it appears to be characterized by a "maximalist acceleration" that no longer succeeds in considering the "portions of good" and the "possible good". By pushing to extremes the relationship between contract and sacrament, it is always at risk of interpreting every sacrament only as a contract, and of mechanically attributing to every contract sacramental logics that are extraneous to it. Here, there is a lack of theological and juridical thinking.

[20] For example, see the theologian E. SCHOCKENHOFF: *Chancen zur Versöhnung? Die Kirche und die wiederverheirateten Geschiedenen,* Freiburg i.Br.: Herder, 2011; and the canon lawyer S. DEMEL: "Unauflöslichkeit der Ehe und Zulassung zu einer Zweitehe: (K)ein Widerspruch?", in: *Herder Korrespondenz* 68/6 (2014), 303–307.

not be sacramental, but its effects would be recognized as valid in the ecclesial sphere too.

This also entails a *"diverse articulation" of the relationship between objectivity and subjectivity.* There is no absolutization of the sacramental objectivity; nor is everything reduced to the purely subjective decision. Rather, intersubjectivity mediates between the Gospel and life, finding a middle path, a "lesser evil" or (better) a "possible good" for the subjects who are involved. We must stop dreaming of a "closed society" that ought to be imposed, with the exclusive goal of salvaging *in extremis* a Tridentine discipline of matrimony!

6.3 The Path of Recognition of Indissolubility as "The Logic of Living Together"

A third path is a kind of "hybrid" between the first two, and could be given a different structure in conjunction with the first or with the second path. It undertakes even more explicitly a surprising mixture of the recovery of the "tradition" and "new hermeneutics".

Bishop Jean-Paul Vesco, in the book already mentioned, explicitly challenges the official position that is expressed in *Familiaris consortio* 83–84. He makes a double assumption: (1) On the one hand, as a good Dominican, he recovers the "classical" meaning of indissolubility, ascribing this characteristic neither to the sacrament nor to civil marriage, but to the "natural society" between man and woman, that is to say, to their living together! Thanks to this first move, Vesco is convincing when he regards as contradictory an ecclesial discipline that demands that the divorced and remarried person must "separate" from the partner in the second marriage before being allowed to receive sacramental communion. The second marriage too is indissoluble, just like the first! (2) On the other hand, the same author suggests a hermeneutic that differs from canon 915 (which was given an authentic interpretation in 2000 by the Pontifical Council for the Interpretation of Legislative Texts – which took the opposite view from Vesco). He draws a distinction between "permanent crimes" and "instantaneous crimes". This allows us to interpret the condition of the divorced and remarried person, not as "continued adultery", but as an original sinful condition, after which the acts of the "second family" must be interpreted in accordance with a different autonomy. Not "for the evil that they perpetuate", but "for the good that they make flourish".

The combination of the first and the second assumptions allows the Bishop of Oran to conceive straightaway of the possibility of a "penitential and eucharistic pastoral care" in keeping with the proposals of Cardinal Kasper, but with a double clarification, both systematic and juridical.

7 Conclusion: Can We Translate "Indissolubility" by "Non-Availability"?

In my book *Indissolubile*,[21] I have attempted to put forward a "different translation" of indissolubility that would be able to break free from the antithesis between an "objective, indissoluble bond" and a "subjective, dissoluble bond". If we let this alternative be imposed upon us dryly, the Church would be forced down a blind alley. It would be compelled to deny the logic of "available divorce" while speaking only the language of the sixteenth century. But this dry alternative is false. *The truth of matrimony, in the "open society", is not truly protected by an "objective theory of the bond".*[22]

We must no longer remain prisoners of the alternative "valid or void". We can look with greater serenity at the hypothesis that the bond itself can die. *A preliminary theoretical assumption is that the bond between the married partners can and must have a history, and that the bond can flourish or die in the course of this history. This assumption leaves a profound and irreversible mark on the difference between the pre-modern translations and the late-modern translations of one and the same Gospel of matrimony.* At any rate, the difference between this logic and the logic of the "availability of the bond", that is to say, of "divorce", seems clear. The bond is not at anyone's disposition. The bond is not "mine". But nor is the bond an "object". The bond is in a "between", in an "*inter*" that is a delicate place of grace and of disgrace. The subject who is involved, and the Church as a community, can register, by means of opportune procedures, that the bond in certain circumstances is "dead". A "moral analogy" between physical death and relational death can lead the Church to make an adequate response to the challenge that it faces.

To proclaim in contemporary categories the beauty of "what God has joined together" means knowing how to resist the temptation of simplistically identifying it with "that which man must not put asunder". But *there is surely no abyss between God and the human person.* The "mediations" of this "salvation-history" genuinely exist and have always been significant: *Christ, the Church, and the sacraments are located precisely in this precious "mediation". The contemporary Church seems to want to abandon this mediation in such a drastic manner that it would appear to be in discontinuity with its own history.* In the name of the tradi-

---

[21] A. GRILLO: *Indissolubile? Contributo al dibattito sui divorziati risposati,* Assisi: Cittadella, 2014.

[22] The proof of this is the fact that, in face of a prevalent theory of this kind, the forms of escape-hatch on the juridical level easily lead to declarations of nullity that are completely subjective, and even arbitrary. *The parties can dispose of their preceding marriage by agreeing on the "grounds for nullity" that they will then consent to uphold before the ecclesiastical tribunal.* Only an "intersubjective theory of the bond" can offer a good solution to "broken marriages".

tion, it risks losing every space of newness, and considering this newness merely as a "concession" to new times.

If all that was at stake in matrimony was an "ontology", we would already have resolved all the questions on the level of a "metaphysical evidential character" even before theology had been able to speak its own, more original word. *Our highest authority would be an "anthropology", but we would no longer be capable of recognizing a good that would not be "the greatest good". In that case, as indeed is always the case, maximalism would be the worst ally of formalism.*[23]

We could, of course, refuse to accept the historical, complex, and opaque logic of the "lesser evil" or the "possible good". We could wish to pursue only the greatest good in its purity, which makes the relationship vacuous, and makes the subject likewise vacuous (but also omnipotent). But then we would end up in an infinite series of contradictions, of legal fictions, of balancing acts, to which we are already condemned thanks to the everyday employment of inadequate categories that prevent experience from being recognized – and that prevent the teaching of the Gospel from being recognizable.

We could also outline a series of "pastoral consequences" of our reasoning here. This is precisely the Church's pastoral task: *to remain in a living continuity with its own tradition.* It must defend this tradition scrupulously, but without being afraid to let the tradition speak with the language that is most persuasive, most profound, and at the same time, most modest and most respectful. To safeguard God's dream for the life of a married couple and for their "forever" does not mean translating the Word of God into the categories of the necessity and the imperturbability of dead things. To say that matrimony is transcribed into the categories of being – in imitation of the theological history of the eucharist – is certainly not intended only to guarantee the quality of the testimony that appeals to the will of God. If God is transcribed into the categories of necessity, he can lose his most characteristic trait, namely, the fact that he is outside, beyond necessity, that he is "more than necessary".

If the formulation of doctrine and the structuring of discipline accepted the logic of this "translation" of indissolubility into non-availability, there would be several important consequences. Let me offer an initial preliminary list of these:

1. To safeguard "indissolubility" [*indissolubilità*] in terms of the "non-

---

[23] In this way, we would be perpetuating the "holy alliance" between the maximalism of the good and the formalism of the institution that permits us to be certain – like so many who raise their voices loudly today – that the validity of a matrimony guarantees the indissolubility of the bond on the part of God, whereas the tiniest defect in the consent or in the consummation – when this is ascribed with formal certainty to the subjects – is still capable of generating the "nullity" that can brush aside not only the history of the couple, but God himself in his plan of incarnate grace.

availability" [*indisponibilità*] of the bond would make it possible to evaluate objectively and sapientially the *conditions subsequent to the consent and the consummation.* We would not necessarily be compelled to "back-date" all the questions. This would, of course, exclude all those cases that openly denied the non-availability of the matrimonial bond. This means that the late-modern ideas of "freedom" and "sexuality" are not reducible to the classical concepts of "consent" and "consummation". This difference must be grasped in both theory and praxis.

2. A proceeding to *"ascertain the moral death of the bond"* could still be entrusted to the ecclesiastical tribunals, but it would be linked structurally to a penitential and pastoral itinerary, in order to work through the bereavement after the death and the pardon of the sin. A logic of the "original" must be accompanied or substituted by a "logic of the before and after" that accepts historical time as a criterion of judgment.
3. The *"experience of crisis and of death"* that the partners live in their separation and divorce must be interpreted not only with the aid of the "penitential categories", but also with the aid of the "categories of infirmity, of fragility, and of death". In its pastoral work, the Church knows "two paths" of healing: that of the crises due to guilt (penance) and that of the crises "without guilt" (the anointing of the sick). Recovering a *therapeutic approach to broken marriages* means not only "opening up penitential itineraries" that recognize all the defects and the guilt that caused the death of the bond. It also means integrating the "broken" couples into "the ecclesial refugee camp". From this point of view too, the eastern tradition has known a praxis of "anointing" sick couples. Direct imitations of this would perhaps be inappropriate, but it could provide inspirations and an exact synthesis between tact on the part of the Church and the couple's own delight in the relationship.
4. When the "death of a marriage" is registered, this declaration would not prevent the subject from remaining faithful to his or her partner in the marriage that has been declared extinct, on the analogy of widowhood. This idea would, however, make it impossible to regard the "second marriage" as "continued adultery" (according to an abstract and unjust logic).
5. It is obvious that this hypothesis would not block any of the prerogatives that belong to the institution of the recognition of the nullity of a marriage. On the contrary, these would remain unchanged, and would be better guaranteed. They would doubtless also be slimmed down and restored to their most authentic meaning. This means that the *praesumptio iuris* would be much further removed from the *fictio iuris.* And this institution would be brought back within the "original river banks" from which it overflowed at least fifty years ago.
6. An *obvious discrepancy between civil divorce and the death of an ecclesias-*

> *tical matrimony* would nevertheless be confirmed. This would objectively remain an insuperable difference. It would guarantee the necessary space for the Church's prophecy in response to the logic of the world, which always risks "putting at people's own disposition" that which every man and every woman can recognize, in their depths, as something they have received primarily as a gift, even when they did not know how to accept it, to value it, and to comprehend it – or were not able to do so – and even when they were not capable of living this gift.

Let me conclude with a very precious admonition that comes from Bishop Ambrose. The bishops at the Synod should not only meditate on the questions that are raised there. They must also remember always these words of their great predecessor in Milan: *Ubi gratia largienda est, Christus adest; ubi exercenda severitas, soli adsunt ministri, deest Jesus.*[24]

[24] AMBROSE: *De Abraham,* I, 6, 50.

The Indissolubility of Marriage and the Civil Second Marriages of Baptized Persons

Eberhard Schockenhoff

The church's magisterium, down to the present day, has repeatedly defended the praxis of excluding Christians who live in a civil second marriage from full participation in ecclesial life, and from the reception of the sacraments. This usually relies on two arguments. First of all, the relevant documents of the church's magisterium refer to Jesus' logion about divorce (see Mk 10,8–9 and parallels), which re-establishes God's original will in the creation with regard to marriage. This is regarded as the most important biblical testimony to the doctrine of the indissolubility of marriage. On the basis of the impossibility of dissolving a marriage between baptized persons that has been contracted in the presence of God, the second argument draws an inference about the existential situation of those whose first marriage has broken down and who then enter a civil second marriage. In the experience of those concerned, they live in this second marriage many of the moral values that, according to the church's understanding of marriage, go to make up a marriage: fidelity, reliability, and the willingness to take responsibility for each other in joy and in sadness, in happiness and in unhappiness, as well as responsibility for the children either from their marriage or from the first marriage of one of the partners. Although the second partnership has stood the test as a lived reality and has proved – unlike the first marriage – to be a reliable basis for a stable shared life of the new partners, the church refuses to give it moral recognition and qualifies it as an "irregular situation," as "continued adultery," or as an "obstinate persisting in a publicly grave sin"[1] that excludes these persons from the reception of the sacraments.

In the most recent discussion, the advocates of the present pastoral praxis of the church introduce a further argument that elevates the question of the right way to deal with persons who live in a civil second marriage to the rank of a fundamental theological question. They argue that by maintaining the exclusion of divorced and remarried persons from the sacraments, the church is defending her faith in

1 See CIC 1983, can. 915.

the indissolubility and the sacramental dignity of marriage. At a period when the convictions of the faithful with regard to the church's teaching are undergoing a process of erosion, and – according to the verdict of the former Pope Benedict XVI – unbelief is penetrating the innermost ranks of the church, a more flexible pastoral praxis in dealing with baptized persons who have married again after the breakdown of their first marriage would be seen as a departure on the part of the church from her previous teaching about the indissolubility of marriage.[2] According to this logic, the sanction of a lifelong exclusion from the sacraments is absolutely necessary, if central affirmations of the church's faith are to be protected. If one accepts the diagnosis of a progressive disintegration of faith even inside the church, the exclusion of divorced and remarried persons from the sacraments seems the perfect shibboleth of orthodoxy, a yardstick of reliable fidelity to the church's faith, an *articulus stantis et cadentis ecclesiae.*

This stylization of the conflict to a kind of cultural war inside the church, in which nothing less is at stake than the defense of the substance of the Gospel against a creeping surrender to the zeitgeist of modern pluralistic society, must be countered by an insistence on an exact description of the question that Pope Francis wanted the Synod of Bishops to take up. It is not a question of a "yes" or a "no" to the indissolubility of marriage. It is not a question of fidelity to the convictions of the church's faith or of falling away from these convictions. It is a question of an appropriate pastoral way of communicating God's offer of reconciliation to Christians who live in a second marriage and of letting them experience his mercy, without linking this to conditions that they cannot meet.

In support of such a de-dramatization of the conflict, we may mention the fact that important representatives of the line of argumentation that I have just presented, such as Pope Emeritus Benedict XVI and the present Prefect of the Congregation for the Doctrine of the Faith, Cardinal Gerhard Ludwig Müller, have themselves presented in the past proposals for an admission of divorced and remarried persons to the sacraments. Indeed, they reckoned on the possibility of a low-threshold official admission by the local parish priest, or of an approving reaction on the part of the ecclesial community of faith to the decision taken in conscience by the individual believers who live in a second civil marriage.[3] It is true that after these authors were appointed to the office of bishop, they withdrew

2 See J. RATZINGER: "Zur Frage nach der Unauflöslichkeit der Ehe", in: ID.: *Gesammelte Schriften*, vol. 4, Freiburg: Herder, 2014, 600–621, esp. 616.

3 See J. RATZINGER: "Zur Frage nach der Unauflöslichkeit der Ehe", in: F. HENRICH/V. EID (eds.): *Ehe und Ehescheidung: Diskussion unter Christen,* Munich: Kösel, 1972, 35–56, esp. 54; and G.L. MÜLLER: "Glaubensvollzug und Sakramentalität der Ehe", in: T. SCHNEIDER (ed.): *Geschieden – wiederverheiratet – abgewiesen? Antworten der Theologie,* Freiburg: Herder, 1995, 202–212, esp. 211.

from their earlier theological positions. Nevertheless, they bear witness that one can present these proposals with good arguments and without casting even the slightest doubt on the doctrine of the indissolubility of marriage. There is no author in the contemporary debate who seriously calls into doubt this conviction of the church's faith. One who alleges that this is the case is making a contribution to the conscious dramatization of the conflict, which dislocates the real point of dispute. The assertion that what is at stake, in the debate about the admission to the sacraments of divorced and remarried persons, is faith in the indissolubility of marriage is, in fact, a knockout argument that is meant to discredit new proposals.

This is why we must emphatically insist that the theological debate that Pope Francis wished to see prior to the Synod of Bishops must be an objective debate. It is not a question of the fundamental principles of the theology of marriage – the unity, indissolubility, and exclusiveness of marriage, or the requirement of marital fidelity and of a reliable decision for each other. Instead, it concerns the correct understanding of the indissolubility of marriage, that is to say, the question of when and how God irrevocably unites two human beings. These questions put into words important and open problems that have certainly not been clarified once and for all in the ecclesial tradition. And on closer inspection, these problems are more complicated and broader than is supposed by those who want to defend the current church praxis as the only possibility that is in accordance with the Gospel.

1 How Does Marriage Become Indissoluble?

According to the usual understanding in scholastic theology, the indissolubility of marriage has a double reason, namely, the bond of marriage that is constituted between the two partners through the marriage promises, and the character of marriage as a sacramental sign that makes it an image of God's fidelity to his people, or of Christ's love for his church. The relationship between these two factors has always been a matter of dispute. It is very helpful for the correct understanding of the indissolubility of marriage when Andrea Grillo, with Jean-Paul Vesco, reminds us that an inherent element of married love as such is its reaching out towards its own permanence and its unlimited ability to grow.[4] The indissolubility of marriage is not a normative expectation that is imposed upon marriage from the outside by means of a law or a sacramental symbolism. On the contrary, it is a requirement that every genuine and authentic love makes of itself. It is based on what love truly wants and on that which is love's goal for a whole lifetime, if it wishes to remain faithful to its own self.

[4] See J.-P. VESCO: *Tout amour véritable est indissoluble: Plaidoyer pour les divorcés remariés*, Paris: Cerf, 2015.

The first and real reason why marriage is a long-term fellowship [*Gemeinschaft*] that is of its very nature indissoluble, and thus demands an irrevocable decision taken by the partners in favor of each other, can be seen clearly. Marriage is the expression of the personal truth of two human beings who wish to respect and acknowledge each other in their existence as persons. Grillo rightly quotes the reflections of Thomas Aquinas in the *Summa contra gentiles* III, 123, where he derives the indissolubility of marriage from the essence of marital love as the highest possible friendship between two human beings. Thomas declares explicitly that this common bond of the married couple, which spans all the dimensions of life – the private-intimate dimension, that of living together in a home, and that of the public life of citizens – is enough to make marriage *omnino indissolubile*. The salvation-historical symbolism, whereby a marriage between baptized persons points to the fidelity of God and to the love of Christ, adds a further objective reason to this indissolubility that is inherent in marital love as such; but this symbolism is not constitutive of the indissolubility.[5]

Along the lines of this solution by Thomas, the Roman school theology of the nineteenth century drew a distinction between an *internal* indissolubility, based on the nature of the marriage contract, and an *external* indissolubility that is added to this through the symbolism of Christ and the church. For example, we read in Giovanni Perrone that the character as a symbol of the union between Christ and his church is not "the real reason for the indissolubility of marriage, but rather an additional sign".[6] If one takes seriously this logic of a possible referential character of the sacrament, it means that Christian marriage is not indissoluble because it is a symbol of the unity between Christ and the church. On the contrary: because marriage, as a human reality, is indissoluble on the basis of the claim it makes, it can become a symbol of the love of God for human beings that has been actualized once and for all in the incarnation of God.

However, this symbolic function applies in the full sense only to a marriage that is successful in human terms. A broken marriage remains an indicator of the fellowship between God and the human person, or between Christ and the church, only in virtue of the fact that when they got married, the partners had the intention to live in an indissoluble bond for life, a bond that would be an image of God's irrevocable fidelity and of the unconditional decision that he has taken in favor of

---

5 *Summa contra gentiles*, III, 123, 7: "Lex autem divina supernaturalem quandam rationem apponit ex significatione inseparabilis coniunctionis Christi et Ecclesiae, quae est una unius." In another passage, Thomas explains: " ... quod unio Christi ad Ecclesiam non est res contenta in hoc sacramento, sed res significata non contenta: et talem rem nullum sacramentum efficit" (*Summa theologiae*, III, suppl. 42, 1 *ad* 4).

6 See G. PERRONE: *De matrimonio Christiano,* vol. 3, Rome: Congregatio de Propaganda Fide, 1858, 145f.: "Et significatio coniunctionis Christi cum Ecclesia non sit *proprie indissolubilitatis causa,* sed potius *signum posteriori*."

the human person.[7] If one takes seriously this irreversible orientation of the possibility for marriage to be a sacramental sign, it has far-reaching consequences that have scarcely begun to be considered. In that case, even a civil second marriage must be thought of theologically as an indissoluble union between the two partners; it certainly must not be called a *matrimonium nullum,* still less, an irregular concubinate – as the conventional language of canon law dictates. It is a matter of fact that the couple often experience in their second civil marriage the human and moral values – faithfulness, exclusiveness, marital love and friendship, reliable mutual support, and so on – that they were not able to realize with the partner in their first, sacramentally valid marriage.

This means that a civil second marriage must be regarded as a reality that deserves moral respect because of the anthropological values that are lived in it. It deserves to be respected and recognized by the church. If the married couple find in their faith the motivation for the way they lead the life they share, their civil marriage also possesses a spiritual dimension for them. This entitles them in this attitude to ask the church for God's blessing, which ought not to be refused them. Since, however, a civil second marriage has its origin in the breach of a sacramental marriage, it cannot count as a sacramental sign of God's unbreakable fidelity – since that would empty out the symbolic function of the sacramental sign.

We must, however, also pay heed to the logic of the sacramental pointer to the unity between Christ and the church when we look in the other direction, to the first marriage. This is because the sacramental symbolism of marriage proves to be even more controversial when we ask to what extent the broken first marriage can count as an image of God's fidelity. In its human reality – that is to say, in its breakdown, the marriage, which is valid in terms of canon law and is regarded by the church as sacramental, does *not* represent what it claims to represent, namely, God's unconditional fidelity and the decision he has taken in favor of the human person. While it is true that this decisiveness on God's part continues to exist even after the breach of the first marriage, it can no longer become effective in this marriage. A broken sacramental marriage is like a spiritual torso. The claim it makes survives only as an admonition that God's grace cannot attain its goal without the free collaboration of the human persons whom this grace empowers to engage in their individual activity.

This contradiction between the bitter experience of a broken marriage and the claim that it possesses a sacramental symbolic function makes the predominant understanding of the indissolubility of marriage remote from reality and real life

---

7 On this, see G. TENHOLT: *Die Unauflöslichkeit der Ehe und der kirchliche Umgang mit wiederverheirateten Geschiedenen,* Münster: LIT, 2001, 178 and 227.

in the eyes of those affected. A more realistic interpretation of the collaboration between divine grace and human freedom ought to restrict itself to a more modest affirmation, namely: The marriage that both partners want to live as an indissoluble life together, thanks to their marriage promises, can become the sacramental sign of God's irrevocable fidelity to the human being, provided that they allow this grace of God to become effective in the life they share. This means that it is only on the basis of the successful realization of this intention – not already at the precisely datable beginning of the marriage, when they exchange their consent – that we can say that this marriage, in all its heights and its depths, but above all in the continuous struggle by both partners to understand each other better, to forgive each other, and to make progress on the path of love, is a sign and image of God's fidelity to the human person and of Christ's love for his church. At the time of the wedding, however, the marriage is a sacramental sign of God's fidelity only in an initial, proleptic sense. Its success, which still lies in the future, is anticipated in the liturgical celebration of the sacrament. The couple is assured of this success, as a promise by God that they must then realize in their shared life.

In view of the precarious sociological framework conditions and the high psychological expectations, however, the success of a marital bond for life can no longer be presupposed as something taken for granted. The external and internal dangers to which this bond for life is exposed are not removed by the grace of the sacrament of marriage. The grace of Christ that is received in baptism does not preserve the married couple against the risks and threats to their marriage, against their temptations and afflictions by what is evil, against getting injured to the humdrum of every day, or against the dangers to which their historical existence exposes them. The grace that is linked to the sacrament of marriage is not a miraculous power that guarantees on its own the success of a marriage. Rather, it is the grace that was given to these Christians in baptism and is meant to strengthen them on their shared path through life, so that they fill out their marriage promises with life day by day, through deeds and signs of love, through little gestures of attentiveness, through endurance and patience, but also through great steps of reconciliation and the request for forgiveness.[8] When their marriage is

8 This interpretation of the working of grace through the sacrament of marriage corresponds to the answer that Thomas Aquinas gives to question that was discussed in the controversies of the high Middle Ages: *Utrum matrimonium conferat gratiam?* He distinguishes between three possibilities; he regards the first two as inappropriate, because they fail to recognize the newness of the church's sacraments in comparison to the signs of salvation in the Old Testament. The first position, maintained by Peter Lombard, assumes that marriage is only a sign of the grace of God – not in any way its cause. According to a second explanation, which goes back to Albert the Great, the grace of the sacrament of marriage brings it about that marriage is consummated without sin. According to Thomas' own solution, in which he follows Bonaventure, the grace of Christ supports the married couple in a *positive* manner, so that they perform all the acts

lived in communicative days, gestures, and signs, it will be successful, and the couple will see this success as a happiness that has been bestowed on them, as a great gift that surpasses their own efforts and that, in this sense, is grace. In that case, their marriage will correspond to the divine promise of being a sign of the dawning of the kingdom of God and of the unity between Christ and the church.

Since the sacramental fellowship of life between husband and wife remains exposed to temptations to dishonesty, infidelity, and deception, it can also break down – either temporarily, so that it remains possible to rekindle it to life; or definitively, so that it is no longer possible to heal it. In the latter case, it is meaningless to speak of a sacramental bond that continues to exist. When the marital bond of life is extinguished, the sacramental sign likewise disappears. To put it in the categories of the classical sacramental theology: when the communicative acts in which the marriage exists concretely as a fellowship of life between husband and wife are no longer performed, the "matter" that can serve God's grace as a "clue" in human experience, and that can point beyond itself, no longer exists.

2 The Anthropological Basis of the Church's Teaching

The classical definition of the relationship between the indissolubility of marriage, as an anthropological given, and its sacramental function of pointing to the grace of God, is called into question by many today. They argue that the knowledge of the definitiveness and indissolubility of marriage no longer exists in the present-day consciousness of most of our contemporaries. This also applies to the so-called "baptized pagans" in the church. The question whether the church can, as a matter of fact, assume that her faithful, when they ask to receive the sacrament of marriage, do so with the will to accept the definitiveness and the unconditional decision taken for each other, is decisively important. For when this will to "go all the way" and bind oneself permanently is lacking, there is no marriage (as Jesus and the church understand it). This is why some proposals about how best to tackle the contemporary crisis of marriage no longer wish to understand its indissolubility on the basis of the natural longing of every genuine love for definitiveness, but exclusively or primarily on the basis of the sacramentality of marriage. Marriage is under attack by the zeitgeist, and it is only in trust in God's offer to the human person of a covenant that is represented sacramentally in the marriage between

---

that are necessary for the success of the marriage: " … quod matrimonium, inquantum in fide Christi contrahitur, habet ut conferat gratiam adiuvantem ad illa operanda quae in matrimonio requiruntur" (*In IV Sententiarum*, 26, 2, 3). In view of this spectrum of opinions in mediaeval theology, one can scarcely speak of a uniform tradition with regard to the sacramentality of marriage.

two baptized persons that it is still possible to think of marriage as indissoluble, and to live it as such.[9]

We must, however, ask whether a primarily salvation-historical and symbolic foundation of the indissolubility of marriage could really strengthen the recognition of this indissolubility in the awareness of the faithful. When the anthropological basis of the affirmations of the church's faith begins to crumble, one must attempt to salvage this basis, or to make it more comprehensible. If one chooses instead to rely on a genuinely salvation-historical argumentation that no longer has any need of support from the theology of creation, one would convince – even within the church – only small groups with a particular spiritual orientation. A reasoning of this kind would be supported by the spiritual authority of faith, and it could only favor the regrettable tendencies to withdraw from the modern world. It would scarcely be able to help us bear witness more convincingly to the disputed church teaching about the indissolubility of marriage.

3 The Processual Character of Marriage and the Theory of the Marriage Bond

The indissolubility of marriage is usually understood as a quality that is inherent in the first marriage and that continues to exist even after this marriage breaks down. In the history of theology, this supposition goes back to Augustine's understanding of the marriage bond, which left its mark on the praxis of canon law in the Western Latin church. This theory of the marriage bond must, however, not be equated directly with the Gospel or with the authority of the Word of God in the church, since it interprets the Gospel on the basis of one particular form of theological thinking, which is certainly not the only possible form. Augustine reads the logion at Mark 10,8–9 on the basis of the metaphysical presuppositions of Platonic ontology. This gives the biblical words – "And the two shall become one flesh. So they are no longer two but one flesh. What therefore God has joined together, let not man put asunder" – a new meaning, so that the biblical text is interpreted in a different direction. Augustine understands the *quod ergo Deus coniunxit, homo non separet* of the Latin Bible not as: "What God has joined together, the human being *must* not separate", or as: "The human being *ought* not to separate what God has joined together", but in the sense of a metaphysical essential affirmation *à la* "the human being *cannot* separate". He thus gives the biblical words a new meaning that is foreign to their original affirmation.

---

9 This approach is represented in the current debate above all by T. RUSTER/H. RUSTER: *Bis dass der Tod euch scheidet? Die Unauflöslichkeit der Ehe und die wiederverheirateten Geschiedenen: Ein Lösungsvorschlag,* Munich: Kösel, 2013.

This is only a slight shift, which Augustine himself may not even have noticed, since the background presuppositions of his Platonic worldview form the framework of understanding when he reads the biblical text. In its practical consequences, however, Augustine's shift in meaning has considerable effects. Jesus' logion no longer speaks of God's promise, which gives the human person the strength to keep the commandment of marital fidelity and to fulfill reliably the declaration in the marriage promise that he or she will make the total gift of self. In the Augustinian interpretation, Jesus' logion speaks of a metaphysical impossibility. The consequence is that the married couple no longer have any possibility whatever of dissolving their marriage, even if they can no longer realize its moral claims in their concrete life. In this way, an absolute moral claim *and* the promise that one can meet this claim if one trusts in God's fidelity are transformed into a metaphysical reality that is detached from concrete life, that swings over the heads of the married couple and can be dissolved only by the death of one of the two partners.

Andrea Grillo's proposal rightly takes its place in the attempts of the contemporary theology of marriage to think of marriage as a process over the course of a lifetime. This binds together the biography of two persons to form a shared development (psychoanalytic couple therapy speaks of a "coevolution"). The "marriage bond" is no longer thought of in static-ontological terms, but in historical-processual terms. This change of perspective also leads to a new understanding of divine grace and of how it becomes effective in married life. The grace of the sacrament of matrimony is no longer understood as an act that happens at one specific point in time, an act tied to the moment when the couple exchange the consent that is constitutive of the marriage bond. On the contrary, the assurance of divine assistance must be thought of as a processual event that encompasses the entire shared path that the partners take through life. If one interprets the grace that is brought about by the sacrament of marriage in this way – no longer on the basis of the metaphysical presuppositions of an ahistorical ontology, but in view of the processual character of a shared life history – it becomes easier to understand in theological terms why even the marriages of baptized persons can break down. As Grillo convincingly argues, they can "become sick". They can be threatened by breakdown and human failure, until finally, they are no longer alive, but are "dead", and there is no longer any possibility of resuscitating them and renewing them.

This historical-processual conception sees in the indissolubility of marriage a divine promise and a moral demand addressed to the will of the two marriage partners. It does not see indissolubility as a metaphysical reality detached from concrete life. It is not only closer to life than the Augustinian theory of the marriage bond; it also corresponds better to the biblical idea that the married couple "become one flesh" (see Mark 10,8). The biblical anthropology that is presupposed in this metaphor sees in the *sarx* the place of the concrete, bodily lived existence of the human person – not a transhistorical reality that would be utterly unaffected by the joys and exertions, the struggles and defeats of this life. "Being one flesh" refers not only to the act of sexual union, although many exegetes hold that this is the immediate background against which the biblical symbolism is to be understood.[10] In the entire wealth of its meaning, "being one flesh" denotes the fact that the married partners have become a common "we". They no longer lead their own individual existence as persons only alongside one another or against one another. They lead their individual existence *with* one another. They belong totally to one another. The Second Vatican Council expresses this through the idea of a total communion of life and of the unreserved gift of self.[11]

4 The Freedom of Baptized Persons to Get Married

The approach that understands the situation of divorced and remarried persons in the church with its starting point in the conciliar Declaration on Freedom of Religion, *Dignitatis humanae,* can in fact indicate the path to a better solution. This, however, presupposes that one understands religious freedom, which has its foundations in the dignity of the person, more comprehensively than in the old theological doctrine of the freedom of the act of faith. In keeping with the Augustinian axiom *Non potest credere nisi volens* ("It is only of one's free will that one can believe"), this theology saw only the unique act of accepting faith as free. Once one's assent had been given to the truth, this entailed abiding permanently in the truth and accepting the religious, moral, and legal obligations connected to it, in keeping with church order. An integral theology of freedom would need to take much more seriously the fact that faith must be completely free not only in its origin, but in the totality of its exercise in life.[12] Unlike the situation in secular civil society, the freedom of the individual in the church cannot mean freedom *from* faith or the freedom to deny the faith. But the baptized have their own right to interpret and to shape the specific situation of their lives in responsibility before God. Freedom in the church thus means the freedom to give expression to one's own faith in one's own life, and to realize this faith in accordance with one's own conscience.

[10] See R. PESCH: *Das Markusevangelium*, vol. 2: Kommentar zu Kap. 8,27 – 16,20, Freiburg: Herder, 1977 (Herders Theologischer Kommentar zum Neuen Testament; 2/2), 124.

[11] See *Gaudium et spes,* 48–50.

[12] See the address in the Council aula by Cardinal Henriquez of Santiago in Chile: "Activitas … fidei est omnino libera, non solum in sua origine, sed in tota sua vitalitate" (*Acta Synodalia Sacrosancti Concilii Oecumenici, Vaticani Secundi*, vol. IV/1, Rome: Typis polyglottis Vaticanis, 1977, 228).

The freedom to articulate one's faith in the church and to realize it in an authentic personal form of life also includes the right to speak of one's personal experiences in one's own marriage, even when these are linked to a painful breakdown that was ultimately unavoidable. Social-scientific diagnoses of the postmodern era, and reflective modern persons, see this era as characterized by an expansion of options with regard to fundamental forms of life, by a greater risk in the personal conduct of life, and thus also by an increasingly fragmentary quality of responsibly lived biographies. Christians do not remain untouched by these basic characteristics of the modern world in which they live, when they attempt to shape the life they share in their marriage in mutual responsibility. Despite their initial decision to live an indissoluble sacramental marriage, it can happen that they finally are faced by the broken fragments of their marriage. If it is no longer possible for them to put the fragments of their happiness together again to form a coherent life, separation can be the only reasonable option for them – and thus, even a desirable option.

What right does the church have to refuse them the freedom to enter a civil second marriage, if they already live the moral values of marriage *de facto* in a second partnership? Immediately after the Council, the church acknowledged the freedom of her faithful to enter a "mixed marriage" – today, we speak of a "marriage that binds the churches together". In the same way, a deeper reflection on the consequences of religious freedom in the church could show her that the right of the faithful to lead their lives responsibility under the claim that the Gospel makes on them also includes the right to enter a civil second marriage, provided that certain conditions are met. These conditions will certainly include a declaration that the first marriage has broken down irreversibly, and is in this sense "dead", so that, as far as we can judge, it is impossible to return to the first partner. Further conditions could be inferred from a reflection in no. 84, section 4 of the Apostolic Exhortation *Familaris consortio,* which requires careful distinctions to be drawn with regard to the individual situations and living conditions of baptized Catholics after the definitive breakdown of their first marriage. It also demands a differentiated judgment with regard to possible personal guilt or to a moral responsibility that has been taken on after this breakdown. But although no. 84 of *Familiaris consortio* speaks of the necessity of an examination of individual cases, it does not infer from this that the church has more than one possibility of reacting to divorced and remarried persons. This break in the argumentation is regrettable. On the one hand, we are told to examine carefully and to do justice to the specific situation of the individuals concerned; but this obligation to draw distinctions has no consequences that would justify a differing treatment of those concerned.

If the church were to acknowledge the right of believers to contract a civil second marriage on certain conditions – or, at least, to tolerate such a civil second marriage – that would not in the least amount to a total breach with the previous doctrinal tradition of the church. One can adduce parallels from the testimony of the ecclesial tradition in past centuries that are certainly comparable, although the details are, of course, the object of controversial debates among the historians of theology.[13] When the relevant patristic texts are interpreted, however, one should follow the hermeneutical rule that the intention in what they state should be identified against the background of their historical period. One should resist the temptation to neutralize awkward texts from an earlier stage of the tradition by "flattening them out" in the light of the later formation of tradition. The path to a toleration of civil second marriages that I have indicated would not only be able to appeal to models in the history of theology. It would also remove a problematic weakness in the exposition of no. 84 of *Familiaris consortio,* which demands a differentiated evaluation of individual situations. By indicating different ways in which the church could react to this evaluation, we would remove the breach in the argumentation that deprives of inherent stringency the church's doctrine of the indissolubility of marriage and the pastoral consequences that are inferred from this doctrine.

The possibility that the church could tolerate civil second marriages would not in the least amount to a "whitewashing" that would justify *a posteriori* every intentional breakdown of one's marriage. The individual examination that is necessary can doubtless lead to the conclusion that the presuppositions for a process of penance and repentance do not exist, because the person concerned lacks all insight into his or her own blame for the breakdown of the marriage, or is completely unwilling to accept this portion of blame. Besides this, a very serious guilt may have arisen only in the course of the conflict around the separation, a guilt that excludes one from participation in the eucharist and in the full life of the church. For example, this could be the ruthless brutality with which one's own interests were asserted, at the expense of one's partner or of the children of the first marriage. Another example would be the refusal to meet the continuing obligations to material solidarity vis-à-vis one's own family. This human wrongdoing can be a grave scandal. Or it can do such damage to the credibility of the church that the conditions under which a civil second marriage can be tolerated as a responsible decision in conscience by the individuals involved do not exist.

We must not, however, assume that a negative judgment of this kind is the rule. On the contrary, we must assume that the persons involved make a judgment, in the personal responsibility of their own consciences before God, about their own share of blame for the breakdown of the first marriage and about their willingness

---

13 See E. SCHOCKENHOFF: *Chancen zur Versöhnung: Die Kirche und die wiederverheirateten Geschiedenen,* Freiburg: Herder, 2011, 49–70.

to make amends in honest penance and repentance. And the church can recognize this as a binding and legitimate self-assessment. This does not in any way call into question the ecclesial doctrine of the indissolubility of marriage. What it does is to indicate a path on which the church can make it possible for the divorced and remarried persons in her midst to be reconciled to their own life stories and to be reconciled to God.

5 The Indissolubility of Marriage and Divorced and Remarried Persons

It is only in very recent times that we have heard the argument that maintaining the conviction of faith in the sacramental dignity of marriage, which is the reason for its absolute indissolubility, forbids any attempt to find more flexible pastoral paths. This argument has been an inappropriate dramatization of a present-day theological conflict in the lead-up to the Synod of Bishops in Rome. Besides this, the sanction of a lifelong exclusion from the sacraments contradicts the spiritual orientation of the penalties that are envisaged by canon law. These are oriented to the penance and repentance of those on whom they are imposed. The idea that one should threaten to inflict the sanctions of penal law in order to protect the general norm derives from civil penal law. More precisely, the threat of sanctions causes a general deterrence that is meant to keep others from committing the same crime. It is in this sense that it is intended to protect one particular normative prohibition, and a deterrence of this kind certainly exists in many areas covered by civil penal law. But it is highly doubtful whether anyone refuses to end his or her irreparably broken marriage, or refrains from contracting a second marriage, in order to avoid the sanction of a lifelong exclusion from the sacraments. More importantly, such a sanction contradicts the true meaning of the penalties of canon law, which are meant to show the individual the situation before God and before the church into which he or she has landed by committing some specific deed.

In their genuine meaning, the penalties of canon law aim at the repentance of the person concerned and at his or her reconciliation to the church. They are meant to initiate a process of spiritual maturity and to make possible an inner turning away from the wrong that has been done. But the sanction of a lifelong exclusion from the sacraments cannot make possible a repentance of this kind, which leads to reconciliation to God and to the church. On the contrary, this sanction leads those who live in a civil second marriage into a blind alley in their life story, from which there is no realistic possibility of escape. This is why the idea that the church must fence off the sacraments against divorced and remarried persons, in order to protect her own faith in the indissolubility of marriage, contradicts the spiritual aim of the penalties of canon law. These always aim at the repentance and the reconciliation of the individual. It is incompatible with the dignity of baptized persons to regard their individual life situation as a hinge on which one can hang protective measures that are thought to be necessary from the perspective of something that is allegedly higher (the church's conviction of faith, the tradition, the *bonum ecclesiae,* and so on). This instrumentalization of individuals for the protection of a general norm contradicts the dignity of the baptized – who do not lose this dignity when their first marriage breaks down and they then marry again. This is why the sanction of an exclusion from the sacraments that lasts until the death of the first partner does not prevent any public scandal in the church. No: it is this exclusion itself that constitutes a continuous scandal.

On the Specific Theological Character of the Sacrament of Matrimony

Peter Hünermann

The specific character of the sacrament of marriage, which is very closely connected to the "dying" of the marriage bond of which Andrea Grillo has spoken, has scarcely been the object of theological reflection, and is almost unknown in the consciousness of the bishops. In the Apostolic Exhortation *Familiaris consortio,* John Paul II explicitly emphasizes the "*living tradition* of the ecclesial community throughout history".[1] But although he speaks of the continuous renewal of this message, he does not define the differences of the innovation over against earlier positions. *Familiaris consortio* does not cite *Casti connubii,* but defends *Humanae vitae.* The teaching of Pius XI constitutes the dogmatic foundation in *Humanae vitae*, supplying the justification for the condemnation of the contemporary changes in marriage in the social sphere and for the moral questions that are connected with these changes.

How then are we to interpret *Familiaris consortio*? Does it bid farewell to *Casti connubii* on certain points, or not?

It is clear from the declarations of the Congregation for the Doctrine of the Faith that *Casti connubii* continues to supply the dogmatic foundation. Here, there is a direct trajectory from the pontificate of Paul VI onwards.

Furthermore dogmatic clarification is important here, precisely in view of statements like the ones found in *Remaining in the Truth of Christ*[2] or in the volume *Eleven Cardinals Speak on Marriage and the Family*[3], and in view of corresponding submissions to the Synod of Bishops by episcopal conferences. It is impossible that what have hitherto been alleged to be doctrines of the faith with regard to the sacrament of matrimony should be changed thanks to the pressure of public opinion, in an adaptation to the *Zeitgeist*.

---

1 *Familiaris consortio*, 29.

2 R. DODARO (ed.): *Remaining in the Truth of Christ: Marriage and Communion in the Catholic Church*, San Francisco: Ignatius Press, 2014.

3 W. AYMANS (ed.): *Eleven Cardinals Speak on Marriage and the Family: Essays from a Pastoral Viewpoint*, San Francisco: Ignatius Press, 2015.

In order to reach such a clarification, my argumentation begins from *Casti connubii*. I compare the definition of the sacrament of matrimony in this encyclical with the theological tradition. In the third section, I outline the specific dogmatic characteristics of the sacrament of matrimony, which emerge from a critical comparison of *Casti connubii* with the Catholic tradition.

1 The Sacrament of Matrimony According to *Casti connubii*

Casti connubii, written in 1930 by Franziskus Hürth S.J. during the pontificate of Pius XI, is the first document of the papal magisterium that claims to present "Christian marriage, taking into account the present-day conditions and necessities, errors and crimes". The encyclical is not about some questions connected with marriage; on the contrary, it is marriage as such that occupies center stage. Contemporary conditions and necessities, errors and crimes are to be taken into account and judged on the basis of this central point.

Casti connubii was written during the European and American discussions and developments after the First World War. These included battles of words in the Berlin Reichstag and social debates in the Anglo-Saxon and French-speaking countries about civil marriage, the emancipation of women, the right to divorce and remarry, the limitation of the number of children, and the meaning and essence of marriage and the family in modern society.[4]

4 See M. LAROS: "Revolutionierung de Ehe", in: *Hochland* 27/3 (1930), 193–207. Laros (1882–1965) was ordained to the priesthood in 1907. He was for many years the general secretary of the Görres Society and translated works by Blaise Pascal and John Henry Newman. Bishop Korum of Trier blocked his appointment as professor in Strasbourg. Laros did meritorious work later on in the Una Sancta Movement, as the follower of M.J. Metzger, who had been executed by the Nazis. See V. COMENIUS: *Propheten und Vorläufer: Wegbereiter des neuzeitlichen Katholizismus,* Einsiedeln: Benziger, 1972, 193–205, and K. UNTERBURGER: "Phänomenologie der ehelichen Liebe gegen neuscholastisches Naturrecht? Die Kontroverse um Laros' Aufsatz "Die Revolution der Ehe" vor dem Hintergrund der Enzyklika 'Casti connubii' und der Entwicklung der katholischen Ehe- und Sexualmoral", in: J. SEILER (ed.): *Matthias Laros (1882–1965): Kirchenreform aus dem Geiste Newmans*, Regensburg: Friedrich Pustet, 2009 (Quellen und Studien zur neueren Theologiegeschichte; 8), 131–187. The representative dialogue partner for Laros in this article is Marianne Weber, a Lutheran Christian, the wife of Max Weber. She had published *Ehefrau und Mutter in der Rechtsentwicklung* in 1907. She had been the president of the Association for Women's Education and Studies in Heidelberg since 1897, and was a member of the governing body, and later national president, of the Association of German Women's Societies. See M. RAINER LEPSIUS: "Weber, Marianne", in: *Religion in Geschichte und Gegenwart,* 4th ed., vol. 8, Tübingen: Mohr Siebeck, 2005, 1320f. – There has been an intensive study in recent decades of the public and the church discussion in the various European states and in Northern America of questions concerning the understanding of marriage and the family, as well as of connected questions such as birth control. See, inter alia, J.T. NOONAN: *Contraception: A History of its Treatment by Catholic Theologians and Canonists,* Cambridge,

What theological definition does *Casti connubii* give of marriage itself? The introduction is followed by a definition in the form of three statements:

1. "Matrimony was not instituted or restored by man but by God; not by man were the laws made to strengthen and confirm and elevate it but by God, the Author of nature, and by Christ Our Lord by Whom nature was restored, and hence these laws cannot be subject to any human decrees or to any contrary pact even of the spouses themselves. This is the doctrine of Holy Scripture; [*Gen.*, I, 27–28; II, 22–23; Matth., XIX, 3 sqq.; *Eph.*, V, 23 sqq.] this is the constant tradition of the Universal Church; this the solemn definition of the sacred Council of Trent ... [Conc. Trid., Sess. XXIV)".[5]
2. Although it is instituted by God, "the human will, too, enters into it ... for each individual marriage ... arises only from the free consent of each of the spouses ... by which each party hands over and accepts those rights proper to the state of marriage ... but the nature of marriage is entirely independent of the free will of man."[6] "By matrimony, therefore, the souls of the contracting parties are joined and knit together more directly and intimately than are their bodies, and that not by any passing affection or sense of spirit, but by a deliberate and firm act of the will; and from this union of souls by God's decree, a sacred and inviolable bond arises."[7]
3. "Hence the nature of this contract, which is proper and peculiar to it alone, makes it entirely different both from the union of animals entered into by the blind instinct of nature alone in which neither reason nor free will plays a part, and also from the haphazard unions of men, which are far removed from all true and honorable unions of will and enjoy none of the rights of family life."[8] "From this it is clear that legitimately constituted authority has the right and therefore the duty, to force (*coercere*), to prevent, and to punish those base unions which are opposed to reason and to nature."[9]

The decisive affirmation is found at once, in the first core proposition: marriage

MA: Belknap Press, 1966; M. SEVEGRAND: *Les enfants du bon Dieu: Les catholiques français et la procréation au XX siècle,* Paris: Albin Michel, 1995; A. GEMELLI: "L'eugenetica fascista e l'enciclica Casti connubii", in: *Annali di storia dell'educazione e delle istituzioni scolastiche* 19 (2012), 161–174.

5 PIUS XI: *Casti connubii*, 5, http://w2.vatican.va/content/pius-xi/en/encyclicals/documents/hf_p-xi_enc_19301231_casti-connubii.html; retrieved 15.11.2015.

6 Ibid. 6.

7 Ibid. 7.

8 Ibid.

9 Ibid. 8. For the Latin text, see LEO XIII/PIUS XI: *De matrimonio christiano: "Arcanum divinae sapientiae" 10 febr. 1880, "Casti connubii" 31 dec. 1930,* ed. F. HÜRTH, Rome: Pontificia Universitas Gregoriana, 1942 (Textus et documenta in usum exercitationum et praelectionum academicarum: Series theologica; 25: Litterae encyclicae; 1), 34–36 passim.

is instituted by God himself, and is also strengthened, confirmed, and elevated by Christ, the "restorer of nature". This means that marriage is not in any way subject to the free will of the human person. Marriage comes about formally by means of a contract, the free consent of the spouses, through which the indissoluble *vinculum,* which has the character of a gift of grace, arises. The ensuing words of *Casti connubii* about the "goods of marriage" – their presentation follows Augustine –, the "errors and depraved morals", and the "remedies of marriage" confirm in detail the fundamentalist conception of revelation, and the corresponding biblical hermeneutic, that underlies this concept of "sacrament". Given the nature of marriage as something wholly elevated above time, the consideration of societal conditions, necessities, errors, and crimes that the encyclical proposes to set out can be displayed only with regard to the errors and crimes. And the basic remedy can lie only in "God's idea and norm" for marriage.

It is striking that the author of *Casti connubii,* far from taking up the ample discussion[10] among canon lawyers of the *ius divinum* and the *lex naturalis,* makes no mention of this discussion at all. The same applies to the classical conceptual instruments that mediaeval scholasticism had developed in order to identify and classify sacraments. These instruments remained in use, via Baroque scholasticism, down to Neo-Scholasticism.[11]

2 Observations on the Theological Development of the Concept of the Sacrament of Matrimony

The historical development of a concept of the sacrament of matrimony encompasses the entire history of Christianity from the very beginnings. The first centuries form, as it were, a period of incubation. For many of the church fathers, God is (so to speak) the "bride-conductor" who brings the bride to the husband

---

[10] See J.I. ARRIETA (ed.): *Ius divinum*, Venezia: Marcianum, 2010.

[11] The encyclical does not speak of the matter and form of the sacrament, the minister of the sacrament, or of its mode of operation. With regard to the *bonum sacramenti,* we find only these brief remarks: "But this accumulation of benefits is completed and, as it were, crowned by that blessing of Christian marriage which in the words of St. Augustine we have called the sacrament, by which is denoted both the indissolubility of the bond and the raising and hallowing of the contract by Christ Himself, whereby He made it an efficacious sign of grace" (*Casti connubii*, 31). With regard to the indissolubility of the *vinculum,* the author writes: "If we wish with all reverence to inquire into the intimate reason of this divine decree, Venerable Brethren, we shall easily see it in the mystical signification of Christian marriage which is fully and perfectly verified in consummated marriage between Christians. For, as the Apostle says in his Epistle to the Ephesians, the marriage of Christians recalls that most perfect union which exists between Christ and the Church: Sacramentum hoc magnum est, ego autem dico, in Christo et in ecclesia; which union, as long as Christ shall live and the Church through him, can never be dissolved by any separation" (ibid. 45, quoting Eph 5,32).

and sets his seal on their union; the consequence is the unity and indissolubility of the bond. The church fathers presuppose here the *pactio coniugalis* in Roman law, that is to say, the consent of the two persons who enter the marriage.[12] The early church already inferred the consequence of monogamy as the form of life. *Univira* is an honorific title of widows, although a subsequent second marriage is certainly possible, and various regulations are tolerated for a variety of boundary situations. These begin with the so-called *privilegium Paulinum* (1 Cor 7,10–16).[13] Approaches to legal regulations concerning the assent by the bishop to marriages, impediments to marriage, and marriages with heretics, Jews, and pagans led to a differentiating praxis in the various regions in East and West.

It is only from the Second Lateran Council in 1139 onwards that marriage is mentioned in the same breath as the sacrament of the Body and Blood of the Lord, infant baptism, and priestly ordination. Groups who deny this view "with the appearance of piety" are condemned as heretics.[14] This is the period in which Gratian presents a general canonistic definition of the sacrament of matrimony. In the same period, Hugh of Saint Victor presented an extensive discussion of the sacrament of marriage;[15] unlike Peter Lombard, Hugh demarcated the sacraments much more following Augustine.[16] Peter Lombard restricted the number of the sacraments to seven.

In the Augustinian tradition, Hugh portrays this sacrament as an act of tolerance by God with regard to marital sexual intercourse: God tolerates a *malum*. In this sense, the sacrament of marriage is not a mediation of grace.

Abelard, a contemporary of Hugh, teaches explicitly that although marriage is a sacrament, it does not mediate any grace. It is an aid for a *malum*: "It is given to rein in the incontinence" of human beings.[17]

Peter Lombard's characterization of the sacraments differs from that by Hugh of Saint Victor, since he recognizes only seven sacraments. In the case of marriage, however, he brackets off his own emphasis on the fact that the sacraments bring

---

12 See the excellent overview by H. CROUZEL: "Ehe/Eherecht/Ehescheidung V. Alte Kirche", in: *Theologische Realenzyklopädie*, vol. 9, Berlin-New York: De Gruyter, 1982, 325–330, with an ample bibliography.

13 A large number of exegetes reject the term "Pauline privilege", because it is not an "exceptional regulation" that is a *burden* on the married person, but precisely a presentation of the *freedom* of the Christian: "The secular status cannot exercise any coercion on the Christian; it is secular, not negative-sacred." On the interpretation, see inter alia H. CONZELMANN: *Der erste Brief an die Korinther,* Göttingen: Vandenhoeck & Ruprecht, 1969, 146. With regard to the present-day situation, see P. KNAUER: "Gibt es wirklich ein 'privilegium' Paulinum?", in: *Herder Korrespondenz* 69 (2015), 267–269.

14 H. DENZINGER: *Enchiridion*, 718.

15 HUGH OF SAINT VICTOR: *De sacramentis christianae fidei,* PL 176, 310–318.

16 Ibid. 317–327.

17 ABELARD: *Epitome theologiae christianae,* PL 178, 1745–1748.

about grace. Peter sees marriage as an *indulgentia,* an act of tolerance, after the fall; it has the character of a permission.[18] Peter Lombard understands a *permissio* to apply to smaller goods and lesser evils, and one such lesser evil is the *coitus, qui fit causa incontinentiae.* This teaching persisted throughout the entire Middle Ages in some theologians, such as Durandus.

In this early period of the elaboration of a theological concept, it is Thomas Aquinas who presents a highly reflected theology of marriage in his Commentary on the *Sentences,* and develops this further in the *Summa contra gentiles.*[19]

What differentiations and clarifications does Thomas undertake in the state of the theological discussion in his period?

First, Thomas distances himself from the positions of Hugh of Saint Victor or Peter Lombard that although matrimony is a sacrament, thanks to Christ, it does not mediate any grace;[20] there is merely the toleration of a particular *malum.* On the basis of his Aristotelian anthropology, Thomas has another access to the bodiliness and sensuousness of the human being. Sensuous desire has a different value for Thomas than for Augustine. At the same time, Thomas specifies more precisely how he understands the favor and grace of God. Through baptism, the *sacramentum fidei,* the human being is justified, and sanctifying grace – which is won (*opere operato*) by the salvific Christ-event – is betokened and communicated. What is betokened and communicated by marriage as a sacrament? In agreement with Bonaventure, Thomas teaches that marriage, "provided that it is entered into in the faith of Christ", bestows "helping grace (*gratiam adiuvantem*) in order to accomplish what is required in marriage". "Accordingly, through marriage, thanks to divine institution, the human being is given the ability to make use of his wife for the procreation of children; and he is given the grace without which he cannot do this in the appropriate manner."[21] The aid of God, who is the friend of the human being, corresponds thus to the mutual aid that the marriage partners offer each other, when this aid is enacted in faith.[22] The aid of this "friend"

---

18 Peter Lombard draws a distinction between permission, something that is granted, and a remission of guilt (*Sent.* IV, *Dist.* XXVI C.L 3).

19 The remarks about the sacrament of marriage in the *Summa theologica* are found in the Supplement, which was added by a pupil of Thomas on the basis of the positions he takes in his Commentary on the *Sentences.*

20 See *Summa theologiae*, III, Suppl., q. 42, a. 3.

21 Ibid.

22 In the overall conception of Thomas' teaching about grace, the gifts of grace that people receive for one another from God are treated in his teaching about the charisms. But since grace can be granted only by God himself, all that human beings can ever mediate to each other is the disposition to receive this grace. Thomas repeatedly refers here to the principle: *facienti quod est in se Deus non denegat gratiam* ("God does not deny grace to the one who does what he is able to do").

accompanies the human being from the creation onwards.[23]

Secondly, this theological clarification of the mediation of grace results in a sharper definition of the specific sacramental sign of marriage. Thomas underlines explicitly that the relationship of Jesus Christ to the church, which is mentioned in Ephesians 5,12, is not contained as a sign in marriage itself. Thomas teaches that this relationship of Christ to the church and the indissolubility of this relationship are not contained (*non contentum*) in the sacrament itself.[24]

This relationship between Christ and the church is something that goes beyond the significance of marriage itself, something that is seen only where marriage is lived in faith. This, however, means that the *sacramentum matrimonii* differs very fundamentally from the sacraments of baptism and the eucharist. Both baptism and the eucharist are signs that point directly to Christ and his redeeming work, signs that mediate this grace. It is only in the sphere of faith that one can speak of marriage as a *sacramentum Christi.* In this sense, marriage is a sacrament of the second rank, which can be founded only on baptism and the eucharist, as the fundamental sacraments. Let me point out here that this opens the door to ecumenical conversations, above all with the Churches of the Reformation and numerous Free Churches.

Thirdly, Thomas makes a specification with regard to the "establishing" or "instituting" of marriage by God. Like the theological tradition and reflection before him, and like the Jewish teaching about marriage, Thomas speaks of marriage as an *officium naturae,* a *lex naturalis,* that has its origin in God. But how is this *lex naturalis* of the Creator, the creational mandate, to be defined more precisely? Thomas notes on a very fundamental level that the nature of the human person inclines (*inclinat*) towards something.[25] But this *inclinatio,* in which God's will is expressed, is not something unambiguous and unilinear. Rather, the *inclinatio naturalis* must always be accompanied by the free will.[26] Let me merely note in passing that this contradicts the teaching of *Casti connubii* that the perfect legal regulation of marriage is not in any way subordinate to the will of the human being. At the same time, Thomas, who did not think in the same historical fashion as

---

23 See *Summa theologiae*, I-II, q. 110, a. 1.

24 See *Summa theologiae*, III, Suppl., q. 42, a. 1 ad 2.

25 See *Summa theologiae*, III, Suppl., q. 41, a. 3c.

26 Thomas explicitly draws a distinction between that "which is caused as a necessity by the principles of nature, such as the upward movement that belongs to fire, and so on; thus, marriage is not natural, nor is it something else that must be accomplished through the free decision of the will" (*Summa theologiae*, Suppl., q. 41, a. 1). In the following article, Thomas points out that all the fundamental inclinations that human nature, as a social nature, implies necessarily include the free choice of willing and the option for this or that, in accordance with the individuality of human beings, and so on.

modern people, opens the door to an appreciation of the history of the institutions that have elaborated marriage and its various culturally influenced forms.

Fourthly, Thomas makes an explicit distinction between the marital *consensus* and a *contractus* (a contract). He defines the marital consent in the words of Hugh of Saint Victor: "Those who enter marriage must give their consent in such a way that they receive one another spontaneously (freely); this is expressed when they do not contradict one another in the celebration of matrimony." According to Thomas, the *consensus matrimonialis* and the marital union are declared *ad modum*, "in the manner of" the obligation in material contracts.

On points of detail, Thomas demarcates the marital consent that is enacted in the reciprocal *receiving of each other* and handing oneself over to the other, over against the forms taken by contracts.[27] The reciprocal receiving of each other can be carried out only in the present. Unlike contracts, this bond for life has no conditions and reservations; it is indissoluble. Although this consent begins in time and has a beginning, it cannot be made only for a certain space of time. It is (as we might say) a reciprocal, unconditional "yes" in freedom. Contracts are very different from this consent, which has a "holistic character" that needs to be "made true", and to prove itself, in each present moment.

This, however, means that this consent and its specific indissolubility are at the same time highly precarious, since they are endangered by all kinds of situations and events, and by differences of opinions and decisions by the marriage partners. Indeed, this consent can be killed off. Thomas does not actually engage in these reflections, but they are a consequence of the specific character of the sacrament of marriage. The consent given by the couple might be "mixed" or "impure": the consent intending matrimony is in itself an honest aim. "But all what is in itself an aim can imply in itself secondary aims and an infinite number of aims 'per accidens'."[28]

Fifthly, in the *Summa contra gentiles,* the teaching about the pluri-dimensionality of marriage[29] corresponds to the specific character and the essential elements of the sacrament of marriage, as Thomas describes them. Thomas speaks explicitly in the *Summa contra gentiles* of the various goals that are aimed at in and through the specific "nature" of marriage. He presents three dimensions in marriage:

"Since (marriage) is thus oriented to the *bonum naturae,* that is, the preservation of the species, it is led to this goal by the inclination (*inclinatio*) of nature; this is why it is called *officium naturae,* a natural obligation. Since it is oriented to the political good, it is subordinate to the ordering of civil law. Since it is ori-

[27] See *Summa theologiae* III, Suppl., q. 45–47.

[28] See *Summa theologiae*, III, Suppl., q. 48, a. 2 ad 1.

[29] See *Summa contra gentiles*, IV, capit. 78.

ented to the ecclesial good, it is subordinate to ecclesiastical regulation."[30] But precisely this threefold dimension is the reason why God's helping grace, which is bestowed on human beings, is "highly necessary" for them, in order that "they may turn to the things of the flesh and of the world in such a way that they do not separate themselves from Christ and the Church."[31]

Thomas did not regard his understanding of marriage as complete once and for all, nor as "*the* church teaching on marriage". He is aware that he is on the path of history with his teaching about marriage, and thus he explicitly calls the distance he takes from the theology of Peter Lombard and Hugh of Saint Victor the "more probable" solution.[32]

In order to sketch the further development of the struggle to achieve the appropriate concept of the sacrament of matrimony, I have decided to have recourse to the dogmatics of Giovanni Perrone S.J. This Jesuit was one of the most important dogmatic theologians after the Jesuits were allowed to establish themselves in Rome once more. He was a collaborator of several Roman Congregations and played an important role in the renewal of the school theology in its Neo-Scholastic form in Rome.[33] He had an extensive theological education, and was a specialist in the theology of the Early Modern and Counter-Reformation period down to the First Vatican Council. I want to show that Neo-Scholasticism cannot be reduced to the simplistic kind of theology of marriage that Pius XI and Franziskus Hürth presented in *Casti connubii.* I want to show that the essential paths laid down by Thomas for the conceptual comprehension of the sacrament of marriage remained present as guidelines throughout the history of theology.

My basic text here is the *Praelectiones theologicae* of Perrone, a book that went through many editions.[34] One notes at once the reception of Thomas in the conceptual definition of marriage in the first sentence in ch. 1: "De matrimonio in se spectato". "One can look at marriage as such either as an *officium naturae* or as a sacrament, or, more clearly, as the *officium* that is sanctified by Christ, who has raised it to the dignity of a sacrament and has added the sacramental grace to it."[35]

Perrone goes on to state more precisely: "Nature, even the nature that is held fast in sin, makes the human being *inclined* to the procreation of children." It is in this sense that he also interprets the statements of Trent. This rejects the fundamentalist conception of revelation in *Casti connubii.*

30 Ibid.

31 Ibid.

32 See *Summa theologiae*, III, q. 42, a. 3.

33 Giovanni Perrone was born in Chieri in Piedmont in 1794, and died on August 28, 1876 in Rome.

34 The following quotations or notes refer to J. PERRONE: *Praelectiones theologicae,* vol. 7, Regensburg: Manz, 1855.

35 Ibid. 201.

With regard to the difference between *consensus* and *contractus,* Perrone underlines[36] that he follows the language of Trent on this point, although he is obliged to recognize "that marriage is completely different from every other contract". Here too, Perrone adduces a whole sequence of theologians who object to the use of the word "contract". Perrone presents a long list of well-known theologians such as Cajetan, Vasquez, and Estius, who explicitly argue against the idea that one could prove from Ephesians 5,2 that marriage is a sacrament. Perrone uses the language of Trent, which said that Paul had only "hinted at" this truth here. This nullifies the identification – found in *Casti connubii* – of the "indissoluble *vinculum*" with a "contract".

Perrone dialogues very intensively with theologians who maintain that although marriage is a sacrament, it does not mediate any grace. Here, he relies explicitly on Erasmus, who had demonstrated how the church fathers had disputed with Gnostics, Manicheans, and so on, and had condemned them as heretics. He thereby corrects the Augustinian tradition in keeping with Thomas.

In addition to this group of material points on which Perrone certainly identifies with the definitions by Thomas, there are a number of other questions that Thomas had not confronted so explicitly. One such question was raised by Cano: ought not the priest to be the minister of marriage, if it is a sacrament? And what considerations speak against the mutual administering of the sacrament by the spouses?

When one reads through Perrone's reflections, one sees that there were many open questions about the theology of marriage. There is no trace in *Casti connubii* of the significance and importance of these questions.

In the next section, on the basis of Thomas' clarifications and guidelines, I shall set out consequences and inferences for the conception of the sacrament of matrimony in the context of our present-day experience. Accordingly, although these consequences do not accord with the conception of *Casti connubii,* we are certainly moving on the great theological trajectory from the beginning of the real study of the concept of "sacrament" in the twelfth and thirteenth centuries down to the nineteenth century.[37] We do not in any way break with this tradition.

---

36 See ibid. 204.

37 I have not presented any specific interpretation of the theological doctrines and condemnations of the Council of Trent, since the "*doctrina*" of the Council represents the mainstream of the Catholic theology of marriage. In its anathemas, it defends the customary ecclesial praxis against Reformation propositions, without making any direct contribution to the further formation of dogmatic concepts. I have already referred above to the distance taken by numerous theologians, and by Perrone himself, to the statements in the *Catechismus ad parochos*, p. II, c. VIII, XVI.

3 Consequences for a Contemporary View of the Sacrament of Matrimony in its Specific Character

The third section brings us to the task of elaborating the specific dogmatic characteristics of the sacrament of matrimony that emerge in today's situation from the critical comparison of *Casti connubii* and the Catholic theological tradition, especially the theology of Saint Thomas. We proceed in two steps. First, I shall present the specific characteristics of the sacrament of marriage, which I have noted in the second section of this paper. At the same time, I shall offer a new interpretation of them. The modern situation is not something external, but a co-constitutive element of marriage. In the second step, I shall elaborate some reflections on the modern form of the sacrament of marriage.

3.1 The Modern Properties of the Sacrament of Marriage

Our starting point are the affirmations by Thomas Aquinas or by the theological tradition about the "establishing" or "instituting" of marriage by God. We take up the *third* clarification in the second section. This runs through the theological tradition from Thomas to Perrone. How did God establish or institute marriage?

The theological tradition has given us the answer that God instituted marriage as an *officium naturae, a lex naturalis,* that has its origin in God. But how can this creational mandate be defined more closely? Nature brings it about that the human being *inclines* towards something. But this *inclinatio,* in which God's creative will finds expression, is not unambiguous and unilinear. The *free will must accompany* the *inclinatio naturalis.*[38] This means, therefore, that the concept of the sacrament of matrimony inherently means that the absolute presupposition of this sacrament is the historical development of marriage, which is generated from the inclination of the nature of the human person and by the shape given to human life in its various cultural forms. If we translate this into our contemporary horizon, this means that marriage and family unfold from the biophysical and biopsychic givennesses of the species *homo,* with its two sexes, with the lengthy immaturity of the child, and the fact that the human being comes late to sexual maturity or to adulthood. This includes the cultural deployment of marriage and parenthood to a "cultural *universale*".[39] Kaufmann insists, that given the inclination of nature to marry and given the disposition to accept children and bring them up, this natural predisposition or inclination must necessarily take a societal and cultural form and be stabilized. Parenthood – as marriage – must be cultivated in societal forms, if it is

[38] See the third point in section 2 above.

[39] Thus the very felicitous expression of Franz Xaver Kaufmann (F.X. KAUFMANN: "Ehe und Familie, II", in: *Staatslexikon: Recht, Wirtschaft, Gesellschaft,* 7th ed., vol. 2, Freiburg: Herder, 1985, 99f.)

to be realized at all. Precisely in view of the worldwide forms of the abandonment of children, the direct murder of children, and so on, there exists everywhere "the institution of parenthood, that is to say, the attribution of births to specific persons – usually the biological parents – and it is expected, as a norm, that they will take on a defined responsibility as mothers or fathers".[40] The formation of relatedness, societal position, and so on, is linked to this. The lengthy process by which children become adults means that they are dependent on stable personal relationships, which of course bear the marks of the most fundamental human needs of a socio-economic kind and of the need for recognition. Without such an original institutionalization of marriage and parenthood, it is impossible for demographic groups to survive in the long term.

All these fundamental elements of the historical genesis of marriage and the family lead to a plurality of historical forms of marriage and family "systems". Present-day research holds that there are no unambiguous patterns of evolutionary development in this process. It is obvious that forms of polyandry, polygyny, group marriage, and so on co-existed, as well as a strong development of monogamous forms. The form taken by marriage is consistently linked to the specific societal and economic position of the parents and of their children. With regard to the human race as a whole, contemporary research indicates monogamy as the most customary arrangement.

The forms of marriage and family that are mentioned in the Old Testament take their place in this long sequence of historical forms, as does the monogamous form of marriage that we find in the Christian communities in the early age of the church. But the bourgeois marriage of the eighteenth and nineteenth centuries belongs here too, as does the modern marriage based on partnership.

The consequence for the sacrament of marriage is that it is a reality that must be updated, because the forms of its constitutive presupposition change in the course of history. It is important to be aware of this. The sacrament of marriage is not simply the "system of marriage" instituted once and for all by God; it is a sacrament that must be understood and lived ever anew. This is rather different from what Father Hürth envisaged in *Casti connubii.* Marriage as sacrament must take into itself contemporary elements – in a constitutive, that is to say, an essential manner.

The *second point* of our confrontation with the doctrine of marriage in *Casti connubii* had brought out the fact that Thomas explicitly emphasizes that the relationship of Jesus Christ to the church, as this is set out in Ephesians 5,1, is not contained as a sign in marriage itself.

In this definition, Thomas and the theology that came after him are concerned

[40] Ibid. 99.

about the precise characterization of the sacramental sign of marriage. The relationship of Jesus Christ to the church (and the church's relationship to him) is a *significance* that goes beyond the significance of marriage itself. Marriage, as such, does not point from itself out to Jesus Christ and his relationship to the church. It is only on the basis of the Christian faith that this relationship can be discovered and understood – and affirmed. It is only in the total view of things that is determined by faith in Jesus Christ that one can speak of marriage as a *sacramentum Christi.* To speak of the sacrament of marriage thus presupposes faith in Jesus Christ. And the grace that, according to this faith, is mediated in marriage helps to accomplish what is required in *marriage.*

It is vital to know this, because it opens the door to the correct understanding of the biblical texts and of the New Testament writings. Both the Bible and the New Testament testimony proclaim the faith in God, and faith helps to accomplish what is required *in marriage.* Alfons Auer observes: "The creation narratives do not talk explicitly about marriage and the family. Rather, they presuppose a family group and want to justify the necessity of its coming into existence by presenting the values that give meaning to human sexuality. The older Yahwistic narrative speaks of the meaningful values of reciprocal complementarity (Gen 2:18), union in 'becoming one flesh' (Gen 2:24), and knowledge through the reciprocal uncovering of the physical and mental sphere of intimacy (Gen 4:1.17, and elsewhere). The more recent Priestly narrative adds fruitfulness (Gen 1:28). These immanent values are accompanied by a transcendental value that gives meaning: being the image of God (Gen 1:27). Since the fellowship of sexual love leads to becoming the image of God, the woman is given the same dignity as the man. The placing of the more recent narrative before the older account is surely meant to protect the latter against misunderstanding. The creation of the woman from a rib of the man (Gen 2:22) is not meant to be understood in the sense of an undervaluing of the woman."[41]

The same applies to the understanding of Jesus' logia about marriage and the family. Here too, marriage is placed in a new overall framework that has consequences for marriage. Jesus links to the preaching of the dawning kingdom of God the sharp rejection of adultery and of the legitimated praxis of divorce for any reason, or for one of a more narrowly limited number of reasons. This divorce contradicts the original will of God. Here too, there is no "foundation of marriage and family" or of a system of marriage and family; this is neither presented nor envisaged. In the kingdom of God, in faith, there is no legitimation for adultery. A marriage that is entered into in faith in the kingdom of God gives no one the

---

41 A. AUER: "Ehe und Familie, I. Theologisch", in: *Staatslexikon: Recht, Wirtschaft, Gesellschaft,* 7th ed., vol. 2, Freiburg: Herder, 1985, 90.

right and the authority to exalt himself to be a judge over this union between husband and wife, and to declare it null and void for this or that reason. In faith, no husband can dismiss his wife from the marriage because she frequently burns the soup – in other words, for some arbitrary reason. Nor is there a narrowly limited group of reasons that would justify such a "dismissal" of husband and wife. Does this mean that the words of Jesus can be the basis of a perfect legal system that applies to every possible case and solve the most various cases? No – one cannot say this, precisely when one looks at the different answers that have been given to this problem in the history of the church in East and West.[42]

An important clarification comes from the positions set out in the fourth point of the second section, above, on the definition of the sacrament of marriage.

Thomas draws an explicit distinction between the marital consent and a "contract". He writes that the marital consent is given merely *ad modum,* "in the manner of" contracts, from which it fundamentally differs. The reason for this lies in the more precise description of the marital consent that Thomas takes over from Hugh of Saint Victor: "Those who enter marriage must give their consent in such a way that they receive (*recipiant*) one another spontaneously (freely); this is expressed when they do not contradict one another in the celebration of matrimony."[43] This is fundamentally different from *Casti connubii,* where the marital consent is explicitly described, in formal terms, as a contract, whereas Thomas (and the tradition with him) draws an essential distinction precisely on this point. The reciprocal "receiving" implies the persons as a whole. Marriage is not a matter of a contractually regulated reciprocal supply of sexual services. It is highly significant that Trent took over this tradition. The Catechism of Trent speaks of this consent as an *abalienatio,* an "expropriation" or "alienation" whereby the husband gives the wife authority over his body, and the wife gives the husband authority over her body. The handing over of the *ius corporis* is understood in keeping with the idea that an essential characteristic of the human being is self-determination with regard to his body, being master of one's own self.[44] In marriage, however, there is a handing over of oneself to the other, and a receiving in a reciprocal lov-

---

42 See the analysis by J.D. FARIS: "Marriage in Eastern and Western Churches", in: *Canon Law Society of America: Proceedings of the Seventy-Sixth Annual Convention (2014),* Washington, DC: Canon Law Society of America, 2015, 42–72. (A somewhat different version in U. RUH/M. WIJLENS (eds): *Zerreißprobe Ehe: Das Ringen der katholischen Kirche um die Familie,* Freiburg: Herder, 2015, 157–185.) Faris brings together, from the ecclesial tradition in East and West, an impressive plurality of forms of dealing with adultery and the "divorce" of husband and wife. At the same time, we see the substantial limits on the ability of these legal forms to give a juridical interpretation of the words of Jesus, which are on the level of principles.

43 See Section 2, fourth point, above.

44 Compare the Habeas Corpus Acts of 1697 as the precursor of the modern history of human rights.

ing reception. It is a "yes" to the other, a promise to hold fast to him or her no matter what may happen.

This means that the marital consent is seen on a pre-legal level, and that it fundamentally differs in its form from formal contracts between persons. Logically, it is on this level that indissolubility comes into play. Thomas identifies this consent and its characteristic indissolubility – which consists precisely in the fact that it must continuously be perceived and realized – as that which makes it a sacrament in the eyes of faith, because it is elevated to a sign and a promise of the aid of God, who helps to realize this consent and make it true.

It is obvious that this consent, in the bodily sphere in which it must be realized, is at great risk, because it can never be accomplished and made true otherwise than in particular gestures, modes of conduct, words, expressions of relationship, and so on. This means that it is exposed to misunderstandings and errors, but also to abuses of every kind; it can become deeper or more shallow. It is equally obvious that the grace of God does not transform the human being once and for all, without any possibility of backsliding and falling away – in short, without the possibility of sin. And this means that this consent can be killed off.

However, it is true that even where the believer is unfaithful to God, God's fidelity does not cease. His aid and his mercy are not exhausted. This confidence of faith is expressed in many Psalms, and it likewise leaves its mark on the New Testament.[45] This has led the early church to develop the sacrament of penance. Correspondingly, it is true that thanks to the Christian marital consent, it is possible to hold fast – with the help of God – to the consent of the other marriage partner even in the face of denial and breach. Repentance and reconciliation are possible. There are, however, also forms of acknowledgment of a partner, even the admission of one's own guilt or of a reciprocal entanglement, that are not linked to a renewed acknowledgment of the consent, because it is no longer possible to realize the consent in its bodily concretion. There are developments and histories between human beings that make marriage as a *cohabitatio* impossible.

Casti connubii affirms that the consent is a contract, something involving the couple's souls, a firm decision of the will. But this is not correct. The consent is merely *expressed* or *attested* in the form of a contract. This means that the marital consent can cease to exist. What remains is a dead consent, a failed consent, which in such cases can no longer be perceived, realized, and "made true".

To speak of the continuing existence of the consent in the form of a contract, when a marriage has definitively broken down, is to proclaim a "wooden iron", so to speak. It is a theological absurdity. This must be rejected by the church's magisterium. This is not to deny the indissolubility of the consent. But it does mean

45 See 1 Jn 1,8–12.

rejecting one type of indissolubility that is the product of an error of the imagination. In the course of its history, the magisterium of the Catholic Church has often undertaken differentiating rejections of assertions that were defined inexactly, and has made the necessary corrections.

This means that it is possible, in a new freedom and openness on the part of the responses made by canon law, to discuss various possibilities of penitential regulations that are appropriate with regard to broken marriages.

Let us finally turn to the fifth point that I mentioned in the second section, above; this forms the introduction to the second step in our final reflections. Thomas speaks of the pluri-dimensionality of marriage and of the various goals at which it aims, thanks to the specific nature of marriage. He calls marriage a *bonum naturae,* he calls marriage an institution that is oriented to the political good, and finally, a good of the church that is subordinate to ecclesiastical regulations. Theologians from Thomas to Perrone continually point to this pluri-dimensionality, which raises the question how new perspectives might arise in the modern age. This is because the realities of "species", the "nature of the human being", the good of the state, and the relationship of marriage and family to this good, as well as the type of marriage and its interconnection with other social realities change. When changes occur here, they have an effect on the sacrament of marriage.

3.2 Remarks on the Modern Form and Corresponding Shaping of the Sacrament of Marriage

If we see a variety of ways in which constitutive interconnections to the various historical situations occur, we finally face the question of the present-day form of the sacrament of marriage. In other words, how does a partnership-based Christian marriage look?

When the modern type of marriage is called a marriage based on partnership, this means first of all that the "decisive basis of stability" is the relationship between the couple themselves. In earlier historical types of marriage and family, the basis of stability was much more strongly guaranteed by the established societal circumstances, that is to say, the economic and cultural situation.

A high vulnerability of modern marriage is the consequence. Moreover modern marriage is functionally interwoven with different social conditions as economy, modern professional live, dependence from institutions as kindergarten, school, public health, associations etc. The functional competence of these institutional structures reduces marriage and family to a specific section of live with less public weight than other dimensions of society with their specific dynamics and power. Kaufmann notes: Matrimony and family represent a societal conjunction centered on the theme of all-day-life, affectivity, solidarity, holistic recognition of the person, the "humanity" of which is in sharp contrast to the growing anonymity of social life. What are the conclusions to be drawn for the concept of the Sacrament of marriage in continuity with the marked points?

It is obvious that if a relationship between a couple, that is essentially stabilized by the partners themselves, is to last for a lifetime, and faces decisive phases such as the family phase with children and then a phase as a group consisting of two persons, it needs a lengthy period of testing and preparation, with the relevant goals in view. From the beginnings of the church, the catechumenate belonged to the celebration of the sacrament of baptism. What does this "catechumenate" for the sacrament of matrimony look like? This sacrament ought to be celebrated and experienced as the grace that God bestows in order that the couple respond to the requirements of marriage. The dispositions that the married couple ought to bring to each other should – and must – be known, understood, and (at least incipiently) practiced. Bishops and pastors of souls have a completely different point of access here than in the general pastoral praxis and preaching that have been customary up to now, as well as in the conflictual discussions with young people, young men and women, in the context of the Questionnaire prior to the Synod of Bishops in 2014. The pre-marital period of young Christians needs a new consideration, a new evaluation and an acknowledgement in the dogmatic doctrine of marriage. The sociological investigations of the vulnerability and risks of marriages today offer an indispensable basis for the elaboration of the cardinal points of a catechumenate of this kind.

It is also important that this catechumenate should communicate a balanced view of the many relationships between couples that today's society often sees as equal in rank and importance to marriage; such relationships enjoy public recognition. It is no miracle, if in an epoch, in which marriage assumes the form of partnership and stabilization must be guaranteed by the couple itself, arises the necessity to have stabilized partnerships for people, who are not gifted by nature with hetero-sexual inclination. To see here an explosion of sin is as unreasonable as the negation of every difference between marriage and homosexual partnership. The church's magisterium is urgently asked to revise the traditional attitude.

The liturgical celebration of the sacrament of marriage documents only to an extremely limited extent the specific character of the marital consent, which needs particular attention in a marriage, that is based on partnership. There is scarcely any indication that this is a consent that must be renewed every day, in the very sober mysticism of a shared life. The renewal of marriage and of its consent has no definite place in the liturgy. The feast of the Holy Family, in its present form, is not capable of performing this service. Nor is it performed by a somewhat more intensive pastoral contact in the context of the children's first communion or confirmation.

It is not by chance that many divorces occur when the married partners are making the transition in the phase of older age. They part company when the family phase is running out. This transition poses a huge challenge to many people, because their lifestyle and the way they live with each other must change. How is the sacramental sign of faith attested here? How is its efficacy sensed?

These few indications must suffice here to indicate the way in which the sacrament of marriage must be opened up anew in the church, and what our orientation should be in this regard.

Part IV

THE SENSE OF THE FAITHFUL

Church Teaching on Marriage and Family: A Matter of *sensus fidelium*?

Thomas Knieps-Port le Roi

The synodal process initiated in 2013 by Pope Francis to discuss the church's vision on marriage and family life has been remarkable in at least two respects. First, the Pope's decision to put marriage and family (again) on the church's agenda carried the implicit admission that there is a problem with the current teaching on these issues. Thirty years ago, also at the beginning of his pontificate, Pope John Paul II had already called a synod of bishops on that same topic and afterwards spelled out a firm magisterial position in his post-synodal exhortation. Since then many had regarded *Familiaris consortio* as the *magna carta* of the church's teaching in this field. But why then revisit that teaching today – unless it is found misconstrued or neglected and therefore in need of clarification and inculcation, or otherwise regarded as deficient or outdated in the present situation? Perhaps even more notable, secondly, has been Pope Francis' choice to hold broad consultation processes among the faithful in the local churches to feed into both the extraordinary and ordinary assemblies of the synod. Apparently, the pope was of the opinion that the aforementioned problems with the church's conjugal and family morality cannot properly be redeemed either by a new, single-handed pronouncement of the magisterium or by intensified scholarly theological reflection alone or by a joint endeavor of the magisterium and the theological academia. It is here that the theological concepts of the *sensus fidei* and *sensus fidelium* enter the current scene.[1]

[1] Pope Francis himself referred to the *sensus fidei* in his address at the closing of the 2015 Extraordinary Assembly of the Bishops' Synod: "And when the Church, in the variety of her charisms, expresses herself in communion, she cannot err: it is the beauty and the strength of the *sensus fidei*, of that supernatural sense of the faith which is bestowed by the Holy Spirit so that, together, we can all enter into the heart of the Gospel and learn to follow Jesus in our life. And this should never be seen as a source of confusion and discord"; http://en.radiovaticana.va/news/2014/10/18/pope_francis_speech_at_the_conclusion_of_the_synod/1108944; retrieved 14.10.2015. According to the Secretary General of the International Theological Commission, S.-T. Bonino, *sensus fidei* is a key concept in the theology of Pope Francis; see his lecture "Pour lire le doc-

In this paper I will ask whether, and in what way, the theological concepts of the *sensus fidei* and *sensus fidelium* can contribute to elucidating the current reflection and discussion about marriage and family issues in the context of the 2014 and 2015 synods of bishops, and, vice-versa, whether these debates may advance our understanding of the *sensus fidei et fidelium*. This question is based on the two-fold assumption that the synodal process has on the one hand been without parallel in more recent church history and that on the other hand the notion of *sensus fidei* is still searching for its *Sitz im Leben* in the life of the church. I will first briefly recall and summarize what I think is the well founded and widely agreed upon understanding of the *sensus fidei/fidelium* in theology and ecclesiology after Vatican II. In a second step I will explore the significance of the *sensus fidei/fidelium* in "matters of morality" as they have been discussed during the 2014 and 2015 bishops' synods. Inspired by this current debate about marriage and family, I will conclude by setting out some points of reference for further orientation and study.

1 Theological Foundations of the *sensus fidei et fidelium*

The *sensus fidei* is a complex theological concept which finds its expression in a variety of terms that have been used throughout the history of church and theology to cover a wide range of meanings.[2] Three notions recur in contemporary theology that indicate the main fields of theological investigation in which the "sense of the faith" has played a role.

The basic notion is indeed (1) *sensus fidei* and refers to the individual believer's subjective capacity to receive and respond to God's call in personal faith. Medieval scholastic theology in particular was interested in understanding the act of faith as a specific kind of knowledge which was effected by the working of the Holy Spirit and provided the believing person with an unfailing sense of the truth of the Gospel. Thomas Aquinas referred to a "sympathy or connaturality for Divine things" which the virtue of faith establishes between the believing subject

ument: 'Le sensus fidei dans la vie de l'Eglise'", http://www.vatican.va/roman_curia/congregations/cfaith/cti_documents/rc_cti_20140610_cerf-sensus-fidei_fr.html; retrieved 14-10-2015.

2 For an overview on the history of the term and its meanings, see W. BEINERT: "Bedeutung und Begründung des Glaubenssinnes (*sensus fidei*) als eines dogmatischen Erkenntniskriteriums", in: *Catholica* 25/4 (1971), 271–303; ID.: "Der Glaubenssinn der Gläubigen in Theologie- und Dogmengeschichte: Ein Überblick", in: D. WIEDERKEHR (ed.): *Der Glaubenssinn des Gottesvolkes – Konkurrent oder Partner des Lehramts?*, Freiburg: Herder, 1994 (Quaestiones disputatae; 151), 66–131; D. VITALI: *"Sensus fidelium": Una funzione ecclesiale di intelligenza della fede*, Brescia: Morcelliana, 1993; D.J. FINUCANE: *Sensus Fidelium: The Use of a Concept in the Post-Vatican II Era*, San Francisco: International Scholars Publications, 1996.

and the object of faith, the truth revealed in Scriptures.[3] Unlike an act of rational discernment and discursive reasoning, faith is in the first place a Spirit-given instinct, a spontaneous knowledge of the heart which enables the believing person to empathically discern whether or not a teaching or practice is coherent with truth and likewise to put into practice one's witness to that truth. In so far as this connotation of the *sensus fidei* focuses on the individual person's faith, one can speak here more precisely of the *sensus fidei fidelis*.[4]

A second notion is that of the (2) *sensus fidelium*. As the sense of faith of the individual believer cannot be conceived independently of the community of believers, i.e. the church, it always originates from and flows into the *sensus fidei fidelium* which is nothing else than what the entire church or all faithful believe. This sense of the faith given to the church as a whole provides a more objective criterion of truth than individual faith. Even though also the individual Christian senses the divine truth, the faith of the church is a manifestation of the fullness of Christian doctrine, practice and life and therefore more easily accessible and verifiable than the subjective faith of the individual believer. This also qualifies the *sensus fidelium* as a proper source of theological knowledge alongside Scripture, tradition, the magisterium and scholarly theology. Theological epistemology became indeed the field within which theologians from the times of Counter-Reformation up to the 19th century got interested in the *sensus fidei*.

Finally, the interplay between the individual's and the entire church's sense of faith evokes a third connotation of the *sensus fidei* which is commonly referred to as (3) *consensus fidelium*. Whenever the church as a whole and all individual believers express their agreement on a specific aspect of the faith, they provide the most tangible and most compelling proof of Christ's assurance that they are held in the truth. The church's infallibility has its basis and strongest evidence in such a consent of all. It was the church in the patristic era in particular which was convinced that the consent of the whole community, "from the Bishops down to the last of the lay faithful"[5], was a necessary and sure criterion for the authenticity and truth of an article of faith.

For a further, although brief systematic unfolding of the *sensus fidei*,[6] I start

---

3 Cf. THOMAS AQUINAS: *Summa theologiae*, IIa-IIae, q. 45, a. 2.

4 Cf. INTERNATIONAL THEOLOGICAL COMMISSION: Sensus fidei *in the Life of the Church*, 2014, ch. 2, http://www.vatican.va/roman_curia/congregations/cfaith/cti_documents/rc_cti_20140610_sensus-fidei_en.html; retrieved 14.10.2015; see also O. RUSH: "*Sensus Fidei*: Faith 'Making Sense' of Revelation", in: *Theological Studies* 62 (2001), 231–261.

5 The formulation by Augustine (*De praedest. sanctorum*, 14, 27) is taken up in *Lumen gentium*, 12.

6 A review of post-Vatican II theological scholarship on the *sensus fidei* is provided by J.J. BURKHARD: "*Sensus Fidei* since Vatican II: I 1965–1984", in: *Heythrop Journal* 34 (1993), 41–59; "*Sensus Fidei* since Vatican II: II 1985–1989", in: *Heythrop Journal* 34 (1993), 123–

from the second notion, the sense of faith given to the church as a whole. This is also where the Second Vatican Council locates the *sensus fidei* in *Lumen gentium* 12 when pointing out that (1) the "prophetic" or teaching office is not a prerogative of a specific elite or expert group within the church but a common responsibility of the people of God in its entirety and that (2) "the entire body of the faithful" (*universitas fidelium*) has been given by the Holy Spirit that unfailing instinct for the truth of the Gospel which prevents it from erring in matters of faith.[7] Such "infallibility" *in credendo*, as the Latin formulation puts it, has of course to be distinguished from the indefectibility *in docendo* attributed to the magisterium, but the council text makes it clear that all teaching authority in the church cannot be separated, but must be derived from the sense of the faith of all faithful. Receiving and witnessing to the Word of God, which is what the *sensus fidei* enables the collective of the faithful to do, is indeed the basic activity from which all truth-finding and truth-attesting in the church comes forth. The council describes it in terms of an unwavering adherence to the true Word of God which is deeply penetrated with right judgment and applied ever more fully in daily life. Although the text notes that the people of God is guided in this by the magisterium of the pope and the bishops which it faithfully obeys, it does not treat the believers as passive recipients of a message that is proclaimed by the magisterium nor does it reduce the *sensus fidelium* to merely echoing what the hierarchy teaches. The council definitely dismisses the distinction between a teaching church (*Ecclesia docens*) and a listening or learning church (*Ecclesia discens*). All faithful, including the bishops, are infallibly guided and sustained in their faith by the Spirit, just

---

136; "*Sensus Fidei*: Recent Theological Reflection (1990–2001). Part I", in: *Heythrop Journal* 46 (2005), 450–475; "*Sensus Fidei*: Recent Theological Reflection (1990–2001). Part II", in: *Heythrop Journal* 47 (2006), 38–54. The most comprehensive systematic treatise on the *sensus fidei* has recently been provided by O. RUSH: *The Eyes of the Faith: The Sense of the Faithful and the Church's Reception of Revelation*, Washington, DC: The Catholic University of America Press, 2009.

7 *Lumen gentium*, 12, reads as follows: "The holy people of God shares also in Christ's prophetic office; it spreads abroad a living witness to Him, especially by means of a life of faith and charity and by offering to God a sacrifice of praise, the tribute of lips which give praise to His name (cf. Heb 13:15). The entire body of the faithful, anointed as they are by the Holy One (cf. Jn 2:20,27) cannot err in matters of belief. They manifest this special property by means of the whole peoples' supernatural discernment in matters of faith [*sensus fidei*] when 'from the Bishops down to the last of the lay faithful' (Augustine, *De Praed. Sanct.* 14,27) they show universal agreement in matters of faith and morals. That discernment in matters of faith is aroused and sustained by the Spirit of truth. It is exercised under the guidance of the sacred teaching authority, in faithful and respectful obedience to which the people of God accepts that which is not just the word of men but truly the word of God (cf. 1 Thess 2:13). Through it, the people of God adheres unwaveringly to the faith given once and for all to the saints (cf. Jud 3), penetrates it more deeply with right thinking, and applies it more fully in its life."

as the entire church is faithfully proclaiming God's Word, including all those who do not fulfil any magisterial function.

If the church as a whole is held in the truth, then also the individual believer must be given that spiritual instinct which makes him/her adhere to the truth. The *sensus fidelium* implies, and in turn builds upon, the *sensus fidei* of the individual believer. A reciprocal relation is included here: the individual believer has that spontaneous knowledge of the truth because the church as a whole, from which s/he has received the faith, has been "anointed by the Spirit of truth" (cf. 1 Jn 2,20.27); this is also true the other way around: the entire church can only stand firm in the truth to the extent to which also every single believer has that interior disposition to adhere to what God has revealed. One has to recall here a fundamental ecclesiological principle which says that the community of the believers is neither a collective in which the individual's identity is being absorbed within the mass nor a conglomerate of self-sufficient individuals without any shared identity. This organic structure of the church community is also reflected in the way it finds and attests to the faith and its truth. There is no subsistent truth in the church unless it is received and held by concrete persons in specific contexts. As such the faith of the church bears the index of historicity which explains why its discernment of truth can grow and also change over time.[8] It also implies that any authoritarianism in the church has to be avoided. The French moral theologian Paul Valadier has drafted a sort of "code of conduct" for everyone who teaches in the church. According to him, the *sensus fidelium* urges that the

> one who speaks or teaches will seek to grasp the reaction of the one whom he is addressing, to find out about his agreements or his reservations, to discover whether his own remarks have been well received, and whether they seem capable of summoning people to a life that is truly in accord with the gospel. This means that one emerges *ipso facto* from the solitude that surrounds everyone in authority; one looks for some kind of test of the validity and pertinence of one's remarks; one guards against the dangers of an authoritarianism that it utterly contrary to an ecclesial life formed by the precepts and practices

---

8 Vatican II's Dogmatic Constitution on Divine Revelation, *Dei verbum*, explicitly links the *sensus fidei*, along with the specific tasks of theologians and of the magisterium, with a development in the understanding of the tradition: "This tradition which comes from the Apostles develops in the Church with the help of the Holy Spirit ... For there is a growth in the understanding of the realities and the words which have been handed down. This happens through the contemplation and study made by believers, who treasure these things in their hearts (cf. Lk 2:19,51) [= theology, TK], through a penetrating understanding of the spiritual realities which they experience (*tum ex intima spiritualium rerum quam experiuntur intelligentia* [= *sensus fidei*, TK], and through the preaching of those who have received through Episcopal succession the sure gift of truth [= magisterium, TK]." (*Dei verbum*, 8) It has to be noted that the conciliar concept of *sensus fidei* rests upon both the ecclesiological redefinition of the church as "people of God" and the revision of the instruction-theory which had reduced divine Revelation to a set of propositional statements.

of the Sermon on the Mount; and one gives oneself the chance to discern the relevance of the teaching one has imparted.[9]

From the above it is clear that the interplay between personal and ecclesial aspects in the *sensus fidei* works best when it is based upon, and finds its expression in, the *consensus fidelium*. Consent within the entire church and among all believers is a sure criterion for a particular teaching or practice to be in accord with the truth revealed by God. Inasmuch as the church relies on the apostolic tradition, of which the Scriptures are the authoritative written witness, it expresses consent retrospectively, with regard to the past. But the people of God is also oriented towards the future and on its pilgrim way it regularly needs to maintain and express such consent, and thus to recover and restore it when it has been wanting. It may take a long time before processes of discernment come to a conclusion, the *sensus fidei* is clarified among all its bearers, and a true *consensus fidelium* is achieved. In these mutual interactions the magisterium exercises a specific ministry of oversight for which it has been given "the sure gift of truth"[10]. It is thus expressed that the judgment concerning the authenticity of the *sensus fidelium* does ultimately not belong to the faithful themselves. The First Vatican Council even stipulates that decisions of the highest teaching authority do not require the consent, whether antecedent or consequent, of the whole church.[11] But while such factual consent is perhaps not an absolute prerequisite, one can hardly assert that it is accidental, certainly not on the basis of Vatican II's understanding of the *sensus fidei*. It is characteristic of the *sensus fidei* in the broad sense as we have summarized it here, that it allows the faithful to receive and recognize in the teaching that is proposed to them God's true Word – and to make it their own. Moreover, when the magisterium's infallibility is referred to in this context, this is not to exalt in any way the church's competence but rather to stress God's fidelity to his work of salvation. As L. Örsy has put it: "When Catholics speak about infallibility of the Church, of the bishops' college, or of the pope, they really want to state their belief in the fidelity of God: in matters of salvation he will not let his people fall victim to falsehoods and become captive to fallacies. If that could happen, so Catholics believe, the saving word of God would be dead."[12]

9 P. VALADIER: "Has the Concept of *Sensus Fidelium* Fallen into Desuetude?", in: J. KEENAN (ed.): *Catholic Theological Ethics in the World Church*, New York: Continuum, 2007, 187–192, at 189f.

10 *Dei verbum*, 8.

11 See DH, 3075.

12 L. ÖRSY: "On Interpretation, on Infallibility: A Response to Fr. Sullivan", in: K.W. WILDES/A.C. MITCHELL (eds.): *Choosing Life: A Dialogue on Evangelium vitae*, Washington, DC: Georgetown University Press, 1997, 98–102, at 100.

2 The *sensus fidei fidelium* in "Matters of Morality"

Vatican II affirms that the *sensus fidei* pertains to both "matters of faith and morals" (*de rebus fidei et morum*)[13] but it seems that substantial theological reflection on the *moral* sense of the faithful is largely missing.[14] James F. Keenan has recently pointed out that one of the reasons why the *sensus fidei et fidelium* has received so little attention is that "many theologians who write about *sensus fidelium* are systematic theologians, who tend to think that the *sensus* is solely about matters of faith and therefore do not think of these as matters of conscience".[15] As a matter of fact, both systematic and moral theologians have extensively dealt with the unfailing sense of the faith in the aftermath of the promulgation of *Humanae vitae* in 1968, but what was mainly at stake in these debates was, next to the issue of birth regulation raised in the encyclical, the magisterium's infallibility in matters of moral teaching. The discussions focused almost exclusively on the status and obligatory force of such teaching, the kind of response it calls for from the side of the faithful, and the possibility, conditions and consequences of legitimate dissent, especially the legitimacy of following one's own judgment if it differs from that of the magisterium.[16] Since then, if moral theologians refer to the *sensus fidei* at all, they seem to locate it in the narrowly demarcated space between ecclesiastical authority and personal conscience which opens up when the individual believer finds himself or herself in dissent with a moral teaching of the church.[17] The discussions around the 2014 and 2015 synods of bishops suggest, however,

---

13 See *Lumen gentium*, 12.

14 The issue has recently been addressed by A. AUTIERO: "The *Sensus Fidelium* and the Magisterium from the Council to the Present Day: Moral-Theological Reflections", in: *Asian Horizons* 9 (2015), 57–75. See also B. SESBOÜÉ: "Le 'sensus fidelium' en morale à la lumière de Vatican II", in: *Le Supplément* 181 (1992), 153–166.

15 J.F. KEENAN: "Redeeming Conscience", in: *Theological Studies* 76 (2015), 129–147, at 131.

16 For an overview on these discussions see D.J. FINUCANE: *Sensus Fidelium*, 388–401; J. MAHONEY: *The Making of Moral Theology: A Study of the Roman Catholic Tradition*, Oxford: Clarendon Press, 1987, 259–301; J.-F. CHIRON: *L'infaillibilité et son objet: L'autorité du magistère infaillible de l'Eglise s'étend-elle aux vérités non révélées?*, Paris: Cerf, 1999, 321–394. For a more general overview on dissent from church teaching, cf. C.E. CURRAN/R.A. MCCORMICK (eds.): *Dissent*, New York-Mahwah, NJ: Paulist Press, 1988 (Readings in Moral Theology; 8).

17 F.A. Sullivan describes the room current teaching and theology allocate to the moral sense of the faithful in reference to Vatican II's statement in its Declaration on Religious Freedom which says that "[i]n the formation of their consciences, the Christian faithful ought carefully to attend to the sacred and certain doctrine of the Church" (*Dignitatis humanae*, 14). Sullivan concludes: "It seems to me that this way of expressing the obligation of the faithful in the face of the moral teaching of the magisterium leaves a certain amount of room for them to exercise their personal judgment in the formation of their consciences. This, I take it, is an expression of respect for the moral sense of the faithful" (F.A. SULLIVAN: *Magisterium: Teaching Authority in the Catholic Church*, Dublin: Gill and Macmillan, 1983, 170).

that the time is ripe to enlarge the perspective – and possibly to start by reverting it. The question is then not so much in what way the church – be it in a more strict sense through its official teaching, be it in a broader sense as a narrative community – contributes to the formation of the believers' moral discernment, but also how the moral sense of the faithful in their daily decision-making and practice can feed into the moral insight of the church.[18] This reversal of perspective is not only legitimate but even imperative – if what we said above about the reciprocal interaction between the individual believer and the church community is true, and if the moral practice of Christians is not accidental to their faith but an integral part of it as one may assume. We will therefore briefly show that the realm of morality is an inherent extension of Christian doctrine and religious practice in the more restricted sense.[19]

The sense of the faith enables and urges individual believers and the whole people of God to proclaim the truth of the faith but also to put this faith into a lived practice. Prayer life, devotion and worship, sacramental and liturgical life are all concrete and immediate expressions of that faith by which the faithful respond to the Word of God which has been addressed to them. It would be a grave misunderstanding to restrict the unfailing sense of the faith to such moments in which the whole church arrives at, and agrees upon, doctrinal formulations. Dogmatic formulas are essential as they are attempts of the believing community to recall God's revelation as faithfully as possible, to preserve it, to keep it alive and pass it on to future generations, but they are just one way in which the faith finds its expression. We get the full picture only if we realize that "the Church, in her *teaching, life and worship*, perpetuates and hands on to all generations *all that she herself is, all that she believes*".[20] It is in view of all these dimensions of an

---

[18] For a similar approach in the field of marriage and family ethics cf. P. BORDEYNE: *Ethique du mariage: La vocation sociale de l'amour*, Paris: Cerf, 2010, esp. 191–225.

[19] It has to be noted here that the formula *fides et mores* which indicates the realm to which the Church's infallible sense of the truth pertains, has undergone significant semantic transformations throughout history. P. FRANSEN has outlined the history of the formula in his article "A Short History of the Meaning of the Formula 'fides et mores'", in: ID.: *Hermeneutics of the Councils and Other Studies*, Leuven: Leuven University Press-Peeters, 1985 (BETL; 69), 267–318. While roughly from its first emergence in Augustine up to the Council of Trent the formula referred to the Christian doctrine along with the manifold (especially sacramental and liturgical) forms of Christian life as rooted in the living tradition of the church, a more narrow meaning became established with Vatican I. *Fides* is conceived of here as the propositional content of faith connected with divine revelation and authentically interpreted by the Magisterium, while *mores* now cover the ethical principles and moral obligations ensuing from a correct interpretation of the revealed truth. Interpreting morals as part of the broader spectrum of Christian practice, as we suggest in this paper, can possibly reconnect with the earlier and broader understanding of faith life which Vatican II has recalled and encouraged.

[20] *Dei verbum*, 8; my emphasis.

integral faith life that the *sensus fidei* has to be understood.

Although Vatican II explicitly distinguishes between matters of doctrine and morality when dealing with the *sensus fidei*, it goes without saying that moral practice is another realm in which faith necessarily takes shape. Christian witness is always "a transmission of the faith in words and deeds".[21] The Gospel is even more explicit in this regard: "If anyone says, 'I love God,' and hates his brother, he is a liar; for he who does not love his brother whom he has seen cannot love God whom he has not seen" (1 Jn 4,20). If then the entire body of the faithful cannot err in matters of doctrine and religious practice, that same steadiness in the faith also pertains to the field of behavior and conduct. A common, but ultimately narrow, understanding often restricts the church's inerrancy in matters of morality to its explicit moral teaching, in particular its reference to ethical principles derived from a natural law that, although not directly revealed by God, can be deduced from Revelation and observation of nature by means of human reasoning. But here again, it has to be recalled that the sense of the faithful covers more than that and ultimately also something different from it. In fact, it is implied here that the community of the faithful, seen in its entirety, preserves a sense of morality which does not fail. And just like in matters of Christian doctrine, the moral sense of the faithful is not so much a cognitive capacity but a practical sense which intuitively realizes what is good or bad moral practice. Explicit moral norms and rules have certainly a role to play in nurturing that capacity but it basically remains a non-discursive intuition which has as its goal not so much the intellectual assent to a moral prescription but good moral practice itself. What this moral sense of the faith, for instance, urges Christian spouses to do, is to live a faithful relationship day by day rather than to believe in or contemplate the "indissolubility" of marriage. It is again in this broad way that the entire body of the faithful has been given an unfailing moral sense.

It is obvious that this moral sense of the faithful directly refers to the classic Christian concept of moral conscience. It is striking, however, as we have already mentioned, how little attention has been given in theological and magisterial discourses to clarifying the relation between these two concepts. Pope Francis has recently recalled that within the Christian tradition conscience is understood as "the interior space in which we can listen to and hear the truth, the good, the voice of God. It is the inner place of our relationship with Him, who speaks to our heart and helps us to discern, to understand the path we ought to take, and once the decision is made, to move forward, to remain faithful."[22] This description comes close

21 *Catechism of the Catholic Church*, 2472.

22 FRANCIS: "Angelus", 30.06.1013, https://w2.vatican.va/content/francesco/en/angelus/2013/documents/papa-francesco_angelus_20130630.html; retrieved 14.10.2015). See also the Pastoral Constitution on the Church in the Modern World, *Gaudium et spes*, 16.

to that of the *sensus fidei* which, as we have seen above, is essentially a *sentire*, a comprehensive perception of the truth of the Gospel inspired by God's Spirit. While conscience has been understood in the Catholic moral tradition predominantly as that act of intellectual discernment and judgment by which objective moral principles and truths are applied to a concrete situation by way of a rational deduction,[23] the *sensus fidei* refers to that aspect of conscience that has been described in the tradition as *synderesis*, i.e. as that innate inclination by which the human person is drawn to act in the way God wants him or her to act. We intuitively desire and commit to live this truth and make it our own, even before we understand it intellectually and understand what precise conduct it demands. But just as this sense of the faith is not only given to the believer individually, there is also something like a "collective conscience" of the entire church which makes the entire body of the faithful inclined to, and hold fast to, good moral practice even before its concrete actions are to be validated against its explicit moral teaching. It seems useful in the present context to remind the hierarchy that they do not have to regard themselves as the sole defenders of Christian moral values.

If there is indeed something like a "magisterium of the faithful" also *in rebus morum*, it seems anyway to be more vulnerable and frail than in matters of Christian doctrine and religious practice. More than doctrinal propositions of the faith which find their expression in and shape existing thinking patterns (*Denkformen*) that are usually long-living, morality has to do with concrete life and thus with infinitely variable types of action and circumstances and is therefore more easily affected by rapid social and cultural transformations that make less unequivocal the markers of what can be regarded as consistent Christian moral practice. In addition, the moral practice of Christians is by definition situated at the intersection of church and secular world, much more so than for example liturgical and devotional practice. How are we to avoid then that especially in today's cultural mentality secular ideologies and public opinion infiltrate and distort Christian morals?[24] Moreover, diachronic consent, i.e. a shared belief over a long time, which is a proven criterion for the sense of the faithful in doctrinal and devotional matters, can hardly be invoked in the field of morality where constantly new questions and dilemmas emerge for which there is no precedent in earlier periods. All these are grave and serious concerns which have to be dealt with carefully, but they do not relieve us of the task to further elaborate a viable understanding of the *moral*

23 See C.E. CURRAN: "Conscience in the Light of the Catholic Moral Tradition", in: ID. (ed.): *Conscience*, New York-Mahwah, NJ: Paulist Press, 2004 (Readings in Moral Theology; 14), 3–24.

24 See G. ANGELINI: "The *Sensus fidelium* and Moral Discernment", in: J.F. KEENAN (ed.): *Catholic Theological Ethics in the World Church*, 202–207; also J.F. KEENAN: "Redeeming Conscience".

sense of the faithful and to give it a place in the church's life. The current discussions of marriage and family issues in the context of the bishops' synods present a promising test-case for further elaborating the moral sense of the faithful and for integrating it more solidly in the life of the church and of all faithful. By way of conclusion I will offer four observations and reflections in this regard.

3 Marriage and Family Morality – a Test Case for the *sensus fidei fidelium*

With his epoch-making initiative to consult the faithful in the course of the synodal process on marriage and family issues, Pope Francis has not only reminded the post-conciliar church of a much neglected concept and principle of its life but has also indicated how the sense of the faithful can be called upon and collected. As we have shown above, the authentic faith of the church does not only, and even not primarily, find its expression in the official pronouncements of the magisterium but is manifested in the manifold forms of life of the church, in "all that she herself is, all that she believes". The Preparatory Document for the extraordinary assembly of the bishops' synod in 2014 and the *Lineamenta* for the 2015 ordinary synod both contained a series of questions which were meant to map what the church as a whole – all faithful "from the Bishops down to the last of the lay faithful" and "all components of the particular churches and academic institutions, organizations, lay movements and other ecclesial associations"[25] – believes, celebrates and practices in the field of marriage and family life. Even though the planning, realization and mode of evaluation of the consultation process as such may be in need of improvement, the operation shows that there is a practical way of drawing out and collecting the sense of the faithful in a particular matter.

Secondly, there can be hardly any doubt that the consultation provides a fuller picture of the church's belief in this field than a study of the *Enchiridion on the Family* would do.[26] The question is however, whether it also yields a more adequate and, what is more, a true and legitimate picture of that belief. In other words, where precisely is the *sensus fidelium* to be located? A conservative position would argue that any opinion that is in disagreement with the church's official

[25] SYNOD OF BISHOPS: XIV ORDINARY GENERAL ASSEMBLY: *The Vocation and Mission of the Family in the Church and Contemporary World: Lineamenta*, 2014, Preface; http://www.vatican.va/roman_curia/synod/documents/rc_synod_doc_20141209_lineamenta-xiv-assembly_en.html; retrieved 14.10.2015.

[26] The *Enrichidion on the Family* is a compilation of recent church teaching on marriage and the family; see PONTIFICAL COUNCIL FOR THE FAMILY: *Enchiridion on the Family: A Compendium of Church Teaching on Family and Life Issue from Vatican II to the Present*, Boston: Pauline Books & Media, 2000.

teaching cannot by definition be the expression of a genuine *sensus fidelium*. Referring to the manifest opposition to the teaching of *Humanae vitae* by a great portion of the faithful, Kathleen Kirk has recently expressed that "there does not at present exist among the faithful as a whole a *sensus fidelium* of a truly Christian depth as far as marriage and sexuality are concerned; that is to say, I find lacking in this area the qualities of a genuine *sensus fidelium*".[27] Kirk was writing before the synodal consultation was held, but its result would probably have corroborated her view. If one looks indeed more closely at the responses given to the Vatican questionnaires, there is overwhelming evidence that a large proportion of the faithful (at least in western societies) disagrees on some specific aspects of the church teaching on marriage, in particular with regard to contraception, divorce and remarriage, homosexual relationships and unmarried cohabitation.[28] Does dissent in these matters automatically disqualify these voices placing them outside of the *sensus fidelium*? Kirk's argument, however, is a circular one which undermines and finally neutralizes the *sensus fidelium* in an inacceptable way. If a genuine expression of the *sensus fidelium* can only be what is in full congruence

[27] K. KIRK: *The Sensus fidelium, with Special Reference to the Thought of Blessed John Henry Newman*, Leominster: Gracewing, 2010, 2.

[28] I refer here in particular to the more extensive summaries of the responses to the questionnaires which were made public e.g. by the German and Swiss Bishops' Conferences; see DEUTSCHE BISCHOFSKONFERENZ: *Pastoral Challenges to the Family in the Context of Evangelisation: Summary of the Responses from the German Dioceses and Archdioceses to the Questions Contained in the Preparatory Document for the III Extraordinary General Assembly of the Synod of Bishops 2014*, 2014, http://www.dbk.de/fileadmin/redaktion/diverse_downloads/presse_2014/2014-012b-ENG-Fragebogen-Die-patoralen-Herausforderungen-der-Familie.pdf; DEUTSCHE BISCHOFSKONFERENZ: *The Vocation and Mission of the Family in the Church and Contemporary World: Response by the German Bishops' Conference to the Questions Aimed at a Response to and an In-Depth Examination of the Relatio synodi in the Preparatory Document for the XIV Ordinary General Assembly of the Synod of Bishops of 2015*, 2015, http://www.dbk.de/fileadmin/redaktion/diverse_downloads/dossiers_2015/2015-Synode -Lineamenta2015-Antworten-engl.pdf; SCHWEIZER BISCHOFSKONFERENZ: *"Die Pastorale Herausforderung der Familie im Kontext der Evangelisierung": Synthesebericht der Schweizer Bischofskonferenz über die Umfrage der Diözesen unter Seelsorgenden und Experten in der Schweiz*, 2014, http://www.kath.ch/skz/upload/20140211135608.pdf; SCHWEIZER BISCHOFSKONFERENZ: *Bericht aus der katholischen Kirche in der Schweiz zu den Fragen der Lineamenta in der Vorbereitung auf die Bischofssynode in Rom 2015*, 2015, http://www.bischoefe.ch/dokumente/communiques/synodengespraeche-in-der-schweiz. Likewise, I refer to the outcome of two quantitative surveys which were carried out for the 2014 synod, cf. SCHWEIZERISCHES PASTORALSOZIOLOGISCHES INSTITUT (SPI): *Umfrage zu Partnerschafts-, Ehe- und Familienpastoral der katholischen Kirche*, 2014, http://www.pastoralplanungskommission.ch/documents/umfragepef/pef_umfrage-ergebnisse_2014-02-04.pdf; all documents retrieved 14.10.2015. See also A. DILLEN/T. KNIEPS-PORT LE ROI/K. KRYSINSKA: "A Growing Gap? Catholic Pastoral Workers and Volunteers' Perceptions of Family Life and Church Teaching in Flanders", in: E. OSEWSKA/J. STALA (eds.): *Modern Family: Local and European Perspectives*, Krakow: The Pontifical University of John Paul II in Krakow Press, 2015, 159–177.

with the magisterial teaching, then the sense of the faithful is being downgraded to a merely passive reception of the church's instruction and eliminated as a proper source of theological knowledge and the sharp distinction between a teaching and a listening church is being perpetuated – a position that is, as we have shown, incompatible with the teaching of Vatican II. Paul Valadier rightly reminds us

> that "dissent" is not necessarily the fruit of disobedience on the part of believers or theologians. In many cases, it is the byproduct of an authoritarianism that is incapable of offering a theological justification of its positions. This dissent ought to alert the hierarchy to its own inability to make itself heard, and thus to the crisis of authority that the hierarchy itself engenders by its own praxis; nor should it forget that it is both incorrect and disrespectful to apply the term "dissidence" ... to every formulation of criticism or questioning of the positions taken by the ecclesiastical magisterium. This ill-will and injustice are further evidence of a deafness that cuts off those in authority from the ecclesial community and locks them into their own inability to communicate – and hence to hand on the Word.[29]

A majority of Catholics who have actively participated in the presynodal consultation processes concur with Valadier's analysis. The German Bishops start out their 2014 summary report by stating that "[a]s a matter of principle, [Church] statements made at universal level are regarded as not being suited in terms of their linguistic style and their authoritative approach to be understood and accepted among the baptized".[30] The Swiss synthesis report seconds this and points out that church documents are "for many people hardly acceptable" because of their language, style and attitude which all contribute to widening even more the existing gap between the Gospel and contemporary culture.[31] Many respondents find it simply contrary to the Gospel that the church's teaching frightens off especially those who are in need of its understanding and care. When the respondents complain about a morality that is characterized by highly idealistic expectations on the one side and rigorist claims on the other, their criticism and rejection is directed in the first place against the manner in which the church pronounces its teaching.[32] It would be a grave error if the magisterium would ignore or even condemn these critical voices as going against or even undermining the Catholic faith. Pope Francis at least seems to have understood that the church's moral teaching has a serious deficit here when he writes: "Before all else, the Gospel invites us to

---

29 P. VALADIER: "Has the Concept of *Sensus Fidelium* Fallen into Desuetude?", 190.

30 DEUTSCHE BISCHOFSKONFERENZ: *Summary of the Responses from the German Dioceses and Archdioceses*, 2.

31 See SCHWEIZER BISCHOFSKONFERENZ: *Synthesebericht*, 3.

32 For a further analysis of the responses see T. KNIEPS-PORT LE ROI: "Bischofssynode 2014/2015 zur kirchlichen Ehe- und Familienlehre: Ergebnisse, Einblicke und Erwartungen", in: *Familien-Prisma* 7 (2015), 4–10.

respond to the God of love who saves us, to see God in others and to go forth from ourselves to seek the good of others. Under no circumstance can this invitation be obscured! All of the virtues are at the service of this response of love. If this invitation does not radiate forcefully and attractively, the edifice of the Church's moral teaching risks becoming a house of cards, and this is our greatest risk."[33]

Thirdly, the question what portion of the faithful represents the *sensus fidelium* and should therefore be consulted to establish it, has not only been limited to the aspect of strict adherence to the church's teaching but extended to further requirements. Canonically the faithful are being defined as those who have been incorporated into Christ through baptism and have thus received a particular vocation and mission in the church.[34] This definition assumes that every baptized person practices the faith and leads a life according to it which is, however, no longer the case today. Some have therefore suggested to use devotion and faith practice as a criterion for *sensus fidelium* and to include only "those who accept the whole Gospel, who are willing to carry the cross every day, who lead a serious prayer life, who accept the teaching magisterium commissioned by the Church".[35] Others push even further by arguing: "It is those whose Christian discipleship is costing, yet who stick to what they believe through thick and thin, who should be most listened to by the theologian concerned to hear the authentic accents of the Tradition."[36] Why then not assume that the *sensus fidelium* is to be found in those "heroic sufferers in the cause of chase wedlock" who unfalteringly defend the position of *Humanae vitae* against today's contraceptive mentality?[37] On the other side of the spectrum are those who point to the indispensable role of critical, dissident and prophetic voices that help the church to remain faithful to the Gospel.[38] Again others emphasize that the *sensus fidei* "pertains to all the faithful, and that we can learn from the ordinary, distracted, confused, ill-informed, sinful, and ecclesially marginalized members, e.g., the divorced and remarried,

---

[33] *Evangelii gaudium*, 39.

[34] According to the CIC of 1983, can. 204, §1, "[t]he Christian faithful are those who, inasmuch as they have been incorporated in Christ through baptism, have been constituted as the people of God. For this reason, made sharers in their own way in Christ's priestly, prophetic, and royal function, they are called to exercise the mission which God has entrusted to the Church to fulfill in the world, in accord with the condition proper to each."

[35] T. DUBAY: "The State of Moral Theology: A Critical Appraisal", in: C.E. CURRAN/R.A. MCCORMICK (eds.): *The Magisterium and Morality*, New York-Ramsey: Paulist Press, 1982 (Readings in Moral Theology; 3), 332–363, at 352.

[36] A. NICHOLS: *The Shape of Catholic Theology*, Edinburg: T&T Clark, 1991, 229f.

[37] Cf. K. KIRK: *The Sensus Fidelium*, 126f.

[38] See e.g. B. HÄRING: *Theologie im Protest – Die Kirche im Konflikt*, Salzburg: Otto Müller, 1971, 36ff.; G. O'COLLINS: "Note a proposito della consultazione dei fedeli", in: *La Civiltà Cattolica* 138/4 (1988), 40–45.

homosexual persons, alienated women, etc."[39] And the question has also been raised whether baptized Christians from other churches should not be included in a Catholic determination of the *sensus fidelium*.[40]

One can hardly deny that the faith life of committed and practicing Christians is of particular value and reflects to a great extent what the church as a whole believes and stands for. If, for instance, one wants to know what the belief of Catholics today is with regard to marriage, one cannot afford to pass over the various ecclesial groups and movements that are dedicated to promoting and living a marital spirituality. In some of the surveys organized in preparation of the 2014 bishops' synod, the initiators attached quite some importance to the fact that a majority of the respondents had turned out to be strongly practicing and church-related Catholics.[41] This gave them the opportunity to point out that not only marginal or nominal Christians had difficulties in accepting the church's moral teaching and that the hierarchy should feel alarmed about the growing distance among its core members.[42] If, however, we take seriously the concept of the *sensus fidelium* as we have unfolded it above, we have to conclude that there is no criterion at hand to decide who the faithful are whose voices must be heard. Since it is ultimately God's sovereign decision to bring to the faith whom He wills, no one in the church can place himself above the work of the Holy Spirit. Even the magisterium – or should we say: the magisterium in particular – is not in a position to determine whom it finds worthy to feed into the *sensus fidelium*. It may rightly have the function and authority to assess the authenticity of a particular belief in last resort, but it cannot preselect to whom it is willing to listen and whom it is going to ignore or exclude in establishing its teaching. Would it do so, it would again disregard the *sensus fidelium* as a *locus theologicus* and proper source of theological knowledge which for that reason does not have to rely on a magisterial accreditation. Baptism and faith commitment may then be the most evident criteria for the sense of faith, they are not certain ones either. How would the church otherwise make sure that she is cognizant of Jesus' praise to this Fa-

---

39 J. J. BURKHARD: "*Sensus Fidei*: Recent Theological Reflection (1990–2001). Part I", 452.

40 See P.J. HARTIN: "*Sensus Fidelium*: A Roman Catholic Reflection on Its Significance for Ecumenical Thought", in: *Journal of Ecumenical Studies* 28 (1991), 74–87.

41 See e.g. A. DILLEN ET AL.: "A Growing Gap"; SCHWEIZERISCHES PASTORALSOZIOLOGISCHES INSTITUT: *Umfrage zu Partnerschafts-, Ehe- und Familienpastoral der katholischen Kirche*.

42 Interpreting the responses to the questionnaire in Switserland, Arnd Bünker concludes that "die ... sichtbar werdenden Differenzen zur kirchlichen Lehre keineswegs nur an den Rändern der Kirche spürbar werden, sondern längst in der Mitte der Kirche angekommen sind." A. BÜNKER: "Kirche in der Schweiz auf dem Weg zur Familiensynode", in: *INTAMS Review* 20/1 (2014), 61–68, 64.

ther for having "hidden these things from the wise and the intelligent and revealed them to infants" (Mt 11,25)?

Fourthly, we have argued above that many Catholics' disagreement with the church's moral teaching is partly due to a misplaced style and attitude adopted by the magisterium. Furthermore, the responses to the questionnaires have also revealed that this disagreement must be qualified as a "differentiated dissent" inasmuch as a majority of the faithful appreciates and welcomes the church's commitment to marriage and family and still holds fast to the most essential marital and family values as pronounced by the church.[43] Still, it can hardly be denied that there is also real dissent on some particular contents of the church teaching. Many Catholics can be suspected of having adopted a "heterodox morality" which means that they do not only disagree with and act contrary to the church's regulations but regard their dissenting lived convictions as morally acceptable and at times even desirable.[44] How the church should respond to it, is a matter of ongoing debate. Some see in this refusal of an official church teaching a blunt act of disobedience which cannot be tolerated. More moderate voices argue that the teaching has not adequately been communicated or lacks argumentative consistency – both shortcomings which could and should be redeemed. At the opposite end of the spectrum are those who are convinced that the incriminated aspects of the teaching are incoherent, outdated or false and should therefore be revoked. These two latter positions are at least in accord that when a moral teaching is met with persistent reservation and criticism, and the faithful refuse to accept it over a long period, this is a clear indication that something is wrong with that teaching. But does this insight necessarily leave one with the binary conclusion that this teaching is either beyond reproach (and its non-reception simply an *accident de parcours* which can be repaired) or completely wrong?

A different approach would suggest that a teaching is not necessarily false when it is consistently ignored or refused; it may even contain some truth. Its non-reception on the other hand cannot readily be taken as a sign of disobedience on the part of the faithful; it may again be a reaction to a magisterium that does not care about the effective reception of its message. In both regards, the fact that the teaching is not received calls for an act of discernment by the church's magisterium. We quote again P. Valadier who has convincingly explained what this might include:

This necessary discernment entails investigating the reluctance of the people of God (or

[43] See T. KNIEPS-PORT LE ROI: "Bischofssynode 2014/2015 zur kirchlichen Ehe- und Familienlehre".

[44] See R. BURGGRAEVE: "Historical Building Blocks for a Consistent Relational and Sexual Ethics", in: J.F. KEENAN (ed.): *Catholic Theological Ethics: Past, Present, and Future: The Trento Conference*, Maryknoll, NY: Orbis Books, 2011, 86–95.

of large portions of it), and reexamining the reasons that underlie the message of the magisterium. In many spheres, the persistent refusal to listen seriously to the reactions of the people is not a sign that all the truth is on the side of the magisterium, and that the faithful are merely being disobedient; an elementary discernment may lead one to the conclusion that the people of God, in whom the Spirit dwells, does not recognize its own life in a particular teaching (in whole or in part), and that this is why it cannot receive the teaching. A persistent refusal to listen helps devalue the teaching that is set forth. When there is no genuine adherence to the teaching, the faithful are left to their own devices. Lacking orientation, they conform to the environment in which they live. And this means that the magisterium has failed to perform its essential role.[45]

Who has carefully listened to the testimonies of so many faithful in the pre-synodal consultation rounds, will not have missed the explicit and implicit longing for moral orientation and guidance in the fields of sexual and relational life which secular worldviews fail to provide and which the church is obviously no longer able to provide for a majority of Catholics. This should be reason enough for the teaching office of the church to submit to a careful and critical scrutiny both the lines of argument that underlie its moral discourse on marriage and family and the reluctance with which that teaching is met by large portions of the faithful. It is time for the magisterium to recognize the *sensus fidelium* as a proper source of moral knowledge and to accept it as a critical interlocutor that does not undermine its competence and authority in the field of sexual and conjugal morality but will ultimately help to restore it.

[45] P. VALADIER: “Has the Concept of *Sensus Fidelium* Fallen into Desuetude?”, 192.

Sensus fidelium and the Ecclesial Dynamics

Serena Noceti

Introduction: A Question that Is Debated, a Possible Perspective

In *Evangelii gaudium,* the programmatic document of his pontificate, Pope Francis refers to the *sensus fidei et fidelium,* recalling the fact that all Christians are subjects who speak a necessary and authoritative word in the proclamation of the faith and the interpretation of the Gospel: "In all the baptized, from first to last, the sanctifying power of the Spirit is at work, impelling us to evangelization. The people of God is holy thanks to this anointing, which makes it infallible *in credendo* ... God furnishes the totality of the faithful with an *instinct of faith – sensus fidei* – which helps them to discern what is truly of God."[1] The explicit reference here is to the conciliar text *Lumen gentium* 12, which he cites a second time further on, in number 130 of the Exhortation, where the Pope presents the value of the charisms for the growth and the life of the church.[2] This is indubitably one of the keystones of the ecclesiological thinking of Pope Francis, which opens up significant perspectives for a profound rethinking of the ecclesial dynamic, of theological elaboration, and of the interpretation of the faith and of the form of the Christian life. The organization, the method of working, and the form of celebration of the two Synods of Bishops in 2014 and 2015 seem to express this ecclesiological conviction and to wish to activate it.

The words of Pope Francis help to bring back to the center of discussion a theme that is undoubtedly prominent in the corpus of the documents of Vatican II, but which seems to have been undervalued and basically marginalized in the post-conciliar hermeneutic of the papal magisterium. Explicit quotations are rare, and tend to define the limits and the scope of ecclesial speaking – especially of theological speaking – over against the exercise of the episcopal (and *in primis,*

---

1 *Evangelii gaudium,* 119.

2 See D. VITALI: "Una chiesa di popolo: Il *sensus fidei* come principio dell'evangelizzazione", in: H.M. YÁÑEZ (ed.): *Evangelii gaudium: Il testo ci interroga,* Rome: Gregorian & Biblical Press, 2014, 53–66.

papal) magisterium.[3] There has seldom been any attempt, on the level of the praxis and the reform of the church, to look for ways and forms to give concrete reality to what *Lumen gentium* 12 affirms about the prophetical *munus* of the people of God.[4] Fifty years after the close of the Council, in the present stage that looks like a prelude to significant ecclesial reforms, it seems important to return to reflect on the *sensus fidei et fidelium,* in the attempt to identify its unexplored potentialities and its undefined implications.

I should like, therefore, to enter into dialogue with Thomas Knieps-Port le Roi's proposal. I begin with the questions that he has raised (subjects; the determination of a moral *sensus fidei*; the authoritative discernment of the *sensus fidelium*), and I declare my substantial agreement with the complex picture that has been presented by him. Within this picture, I wish to offer some further suggestions in an ecclesiological perspective. I shall concentrate on the communicative and participatory dynamics that are implied, and on what this means for the life of the ecclesial Body. I believe that my suggestions can help to define more closely the "interplay between personal and ecclesial aspects in the *sensus fidei*" that Knieps-Port le Roi postulates as the keystone of his interpretation of the *sensus fidelium* and the point where our perspective changes, allowing us to identify the consequences for moral theology.

I shall develop my reflection in four moves. After an examination of the ecclesial dynamics of the development and discernment of the *sensus fidelium,* and a reflection on the subjects who are involved, I shall present some elements of the ecclesial figure that is implied in the programmatic recovering of the *sensus fidelium,* in order to demonstrate the open challenges with regard to a comprehensive reform of ecclesial praxis. In all three sections, my starting point will be, not the faithful situation of the individual Christians (*sensus fidei fidelis*), but the collective subject that is the "church" (*sensus fidei ecclesiae*), in order to look at the interaction between individual believers and the ecclesial "we".[5] A more

---

3 See PONTIFICAL COUNCIL FOR SOCIAL COMMUNICATIONS: *Communio et progressio*, 1971, 25, 32, 116, 117 (on public opinion); CONGREGATION FOR THE DOCTRINE OF THE FAITH: *Mysterium ecclesiae*, 1973, 2; CONGREGATION FOR THE DOCTRINE OF THE FAITH: *Libertà Cristiana e liberazione*, 1986, 98; CONGREGATION FOR THE DOCTRINE OF THE FAITH: *Donum veritatis*, 1990, 35 ("the opinions of the faithful cannot be purely and simply identified with the 'sensus fidei'"); *Catechism of the Catholic Church*, 91–93, 785, 889. See also INTERNATIONAL THEOLOGICAL COMMISSION: *Sensus fidei in the Life of the Church*, 2014.

4 There are no references to the *sensus fidei* in the Code of Canon Law; cf. the allusion in can. 750 §1.

5 See especially D. VITALI: *Sensus fidelium: Una funzione ecclesiale di intelligenza della fede,* Brescia: Morcelliana, 1993; D.J. FINUCANE: *Sensus fidelium: The Use of a Concept in the Post-Vatican Era,* San Francisco: International Scholars Publications, 1996; O. RUSH: *The Eyes of Faith: The Sense of the Faithful and the Church's Reception of Revelation,* Washington: Catholic University of America Press, 2009; J. BURKHARD: "*Sensus fidei*: Meaning, Role and Future of

consciously critical rediscovery of the dynamic of the *sensus fidelium/consensus fidelium* will allow us to identify some open perspectives that were undervalued in the post-conciliar phase, but that are necessary if we are to understand the theme of the Synod.

1 Thinking or Rethinking the *Sensus fidelium* in an Ecclesiological Perspective

Even a rapid examination of the theological literature on this topic shows very clearly the risk of conceptual overlappings and slippages on the interpretative levels of the concepts of *sensus fidei* and *sensus fidelium.* Knieps-Port le Roi reacts to this risk, firstly, by showing us the polysemy of the lemma *sensus,* which goes from "meaning" to an immediate intuition, to feeling or senses, and unites a passive, receptive aspect to a dimension of the activity of revealing.[6] Secondly, he presents the three fields in which this concept has been elaborated in the course of the history of theology, and in which the debate is located even today. He then chooses the *sensus fidelium* as the starting point for his argumentation, in order to recover the *consensus fidelium,* which he calls a "necessary and sure criterion for the authenticity and truth of an article of faith".

I too wish to focus on the identity of the subjects who are involved, and on the dynamics that are in action in the *sensus fidelium.* But I shall take the collective subject that is the "church" as my starting point and as the perspective of my argumentation here. I believe that it is helpful here to draw a distinction on the conceptual level between the *sensus fidei fidelium* (that which is proper to the totality of individual Christians, on the level of the *universa ecclesia* or of the local church) and the *sensus fidei ecclesiae,* where *ecclesia* refers to the constituted or institutional ecclesial "we". This "we" is more than the sum of the faithful, because it implies relationships between the believers and the institutionalized forms of such relationships. This perspective allows us to grasp the *consensus fidelium* as a dynamic of ecclesial life that characterizes the empirically discernable form taken by ecclesial life. I wish to grasp the centrality of the *sensus fidelium* for

a Teaching of Vatican II", in: *Louvain Studies* 18 (1992), 18–34; J. BURKHARD: "*Sensus fidei*: Recent Theological Reflection (1990–2001)", in: *Heythrop Journal* 47 (2006), 38–54.

6 It is useful to recall terms similar to *sensus fidei* or *sensus fidelium* that appear in the conciliar documents: *sensus fidei* (LG 12; PO 9); *sensus christianus fidelium* (GS 52); *sensus christianus* (GS 62); *sensus religiosus* (NA 2; DH 4; GS 59), *sensus Dei* (DV 15; GS 7); *sensus Christi et ecclesiae* (AG 19). See O. RUSH: "*Sensus Fidei*: Faith 'Making Sense' of Revelation", in: *Theological Studies* 62 (2001), 231–261; C. OHLY: *Sensus fidei fidelium: Zur Einordnung des Glaubenssinnes aller Gläubigen in die Communio-Struktur der Kirche im geschichtlichen Spiegel dogmatisch-kanonistischer Erkenntnisse und der Aussagen des II. Vatikanum*, St. Ottilien: EOS Verlag, 1999, 273–282.

the form – in a permanent state of coming into being – of a church that is born of the proclamation of the Gospel and that lives thanks to a permanent dynamic of the communication *of* the faith and *in* the faith of believers. The fundamental text to which I shall refer is *Lumen gentium* 12, correlated to what is stated in *Dei verbum* 8 on the *Traditio ecclesiae.* These two texts must be read in relation to *Lumen gentium* 25 and 35, which speak (respectively) of the prophetical *munus* of the bishops and of the laity.[7]

1.1 A Collective Subject, the Baptismal Root

As is well known, number 12 of the Dogmatic Constitution on the Church as we have it today is a part of the second chapter, *De populo Dei,* but it largely repeats what had been stated in the Philips schema and then in the *textus prior* about the prophetical *munus* of the laity (*De ecclesia,* 24).[8] Its present location (before the

---

[7] In discussing my proposal, I shall not cite explicitly the ample secondary literature to which Knieps-Port le Roi has drawn attention. I shall suggest only a few studies that contextualize and motivate my interpretative proposal, especially those in Italian: Z. ALSZEGHY: "Il senso della fede e lo sviluppo dogmatico", in: R. LATOURELLE (ed.): *Il Vaticano II: Bilancio e prospettive venticinque anni dopo,* Assisi: Cittadella, 1987, vol. 1, 36–151; R. BROSSE: "Consensus fidelium: un dialogue? Réflexions herméneutiques sur la théologie fondamentale et l'ecclésiologie", in: *Revue théologique de Louvain* 29 (1998), 331–344; L. SARTORI: "Il 'sensus fidelium' del popolo di Dio e il concorso dei laici nelle determinazioni dottrinali", in: *Studi ecumenici* 6 (1988), 33–57; C. DUQUOC: "Il popolo di Dio, soggetto attivo della fede nella chiesa", in: *Concilium* 21 (1985), 574–585; H. WAGNER: "Glaubenssinn, Glaubenszustimmung, Glaubenskonsensus", in: *Theologie und Glaube* 69 (1979), 263–271; J. KERKHOFS: "Le peuple de Dieu est-il infaillible? L'importance du 'sensus fidelium' dans l'église post-conciliaire", in: *Freiburger Zeitschrift* 35 (1988), 3–19.

[8] It is helpful to recall the history of the redaction of LG 12 and the interaction between this paragraph and the entire literary-doctrinal corpus of the documents. This approach allows us to identify the theoretical links at play, as these progressively emerged, and to demonstrate the novelty of the conciliar perspective. Although the expression was known to theologians from the sixteenth century onwards, the interpretative perspective adopted by Vatican II was original. When the debates in the aula and the *animadversiones scriptae* presented after the second session are compared with what is stated in the *Relatio* (*Acta Synodalia* II/III, 504–505), they allow us to reaffirm the choice made by the Council to change the interpretative paradigm. The Council abandons the idea of a passive *indefectibilitas* for the faithful (which had been reaffirmed in the Council itself by Cardinal Ruffini); it decisively abandons the model of "*ecclesia docens – ecclesia discens*" (with its location of the *sensus fidei* in this second pole); and it is not limited to the laity alone. The expression, and an initial elaboration, were present from the preparatory phase onwards, and in the document presented to the Council fathers in 1962, as well as in the first Philips schema (they occur respectively in the chapter about authority and obedience, and in the chapter about the laity), taking up anew the post-Tridentine theology of the "*indefectibilitas in credendo*". But the final redaction of the text permits us to grasp a new vision of this topic, thanks to its location in the text and to the subjects and dynamics that are indicated therein. On the history of the redaction of LG 12, with a precise comment on this topic, see the essay by D. VITALI in S. NOCETI/R. REPOLE (eds.): *Commentario ai documenti*

two chapters on the hierarchy and the laity) indubitably shows the *intentio* of the Council fathers: the *sensus fidei* defines the people of God and describes its messianic mission. It does not refer exclusively to the experience and the expression of the faith of the lay faithful. In order to understand the significance of this expression, we must locate it in the foundational horizon, which precedes it in the text – namely, that which is "*held in common*" because it belongs to every one of the ecclesial components (since it is rooted in the baptismal subjecthood), and is "*held in common*" because it is made real and possible for the collective subject only by the coexistence and cooperation of all the ecclesial subjects. The prophetical *munus* of Christ, his mission as prophet of the kingdom, is shared by every baptized person and by the entire church, which in its entirety is a "prophetical community".[9]

This text defines the identity of the church and of all the *christifideles* (both the ordained ministers and the laity) by means of three vectors that "converge" upon each other and are "correlated" to each other – each of them defines the existence of the others and is characterized by this fact. First, there is the *reference to the root* (*faith*, as an interior adherence to the Gospel of salvation, a living obedience to the Word that one has heard). Secondly, there is the *specific form* (the text insists on the plurality of *charisms* that is the distinguishing mark of the people of God, in a variety and complementarity of experiences of speaking and living the faith that determines the face of the church). Thirdly, there is the *dynamic of a church* that is oriented towards a *consensus* – in the faith and of the faith. Everyone is summoned to offer a necessary contribution to this living consensus of a charismatic, cultural, ministerial, and constitutive plurality. All share in a collective dynamism that is a dynamism of communion, in the sense that it is oriented towards a *union* that is to be attained thanks to the contribution by every believing subject who is a subject who shares in constituting the church.[10]

1.2 On the Basis of the Sensus fidei ecclesiae

In order to grasp the *sensus fidelium* in its activity of generating or regenerating the ecclesial subject, and in order to define its specific nature in the circumincession

---

del Vaticano II, II. *Lumen gentium*, Bologna: EDB, 2015, 176–185.

9 J. SANCHO BIELSA: *Infalibilidad del Pueblo de Dios: Sensus fidei y infalibilidad orgánica de la Iglesia en la Lumen gentium*, Pamplona: Universidad de Navarra, 1979; B. VAN LEEUWEN: "La partecipazione comune del popolo di Dio all'ufficio profetico di Cristo", in: G. BARAÚNA (ed.): *La Chiesa del Vaticano II: Studi e commenti intorno alla Costituzione dogmatica "Lumen gentium*, Florence: Vallecchi, 1965, 465–490; D. VITALI: "'Universitas fidelium in credendo falli equità' (LG 12): Il sensus fidelium al concilio Vaticano II", in: *Gregorianum* 86 (2005), 607–628.

10 See S. NOCETI: "Laici e *sensus fidei* (LG 12)", in: C. MILITELLO (ed.): *I laici dopo il Concilio: quale autonomia*, Bologna: EDB, 2012, 87–101.

between the individual believing subjects and the collective subject that is the "church", I believe it is useful to take our starting point not so much in the *sensus fidei fidelis,* but in the *sensus fidei ecclesiae,* which enjoys a priority that is both logical and chronological. There is no absolute and univocal equivalence between the *sensus fidelium* and the *sensus fidei ecclesiae.*

The people of God, the church as a collective subject, is characterized by the *faith* that is a fundamental element shared by all. This faith makes possible at one and the same time the subjecthood of the individual believers and the communion among the many. The people of God is marked by a *sensus fidei,* as the collective form and content of its awareness. This is bestowed by the ability to "understand the implications, as yet not elucidated, of a reality that is already possessed" (Congar) and by the capacity to grasp and understand the object of faith. These abilities belong to every member of the church, but it is always through the collective subject that is the "church" that they are "activated" and come into operation. Only a stable collective subject can be the adequate subject that preserves the *memoria Christi apostolica* that is at the heart of the proclamation that makes believers and that makes the church. This is because the *sensus fidei* presupposes the *fides qua* of the individual subject, who defines himself as a "Christian" and is recognized as such because he has received the proclamation of the Word from other believers, and because he has been baptized or initiated into the faith of the church – a faith that is ecclesial in its content and in its form.

Each one's profession of faith – and antecedently to this, the *sensus fidei fidelis* – thus combines an objective content (the story of Jesus) and a subjective and personal dimension.[11] The identities of Christians have characteristics that are absolutely unique and irreplaceable, in their sharing together in one single faith. Every Christian is a Christian in virtue of the faith that is received in the ecclesial *mediation,* but his or her specific identity takes shape and is determined between personal appropriation and personal re-expression of the story of Jesus and of the Christian event.[12] The individual *Christian* believes only "in" the church and "as" church, but each one receives from the Holy Spirit the capacity or faculty that permits the interpretation – the comprehension – and the personal actualization of the Word that is revealed and heard (these are the verbs used in *Lumen gentium,*

[11] See S. DIANICH: *Ecclesiologia: Questioni di metodo e una proposta,* Cinisello Balsamo: Paoline, 1993, 143–150; IDEM: "Teorie della comunicazione ed ecclesiologia", in: D. VALENTINI (ed.): *L'ecclesiologia contemporanea,* Padua: Messaggero, 1994, 134–178; J. CAILLOT: *L'évangile de la communication,* Paris: Cerf, 1985; H.J. HÖHN: *Kirche und kommunikatives Handeln: Studien zur Theologie und Praxis der Kirche in der Auseinandersetzung mit den Sozialtheorien Niklas Luhmanns und Jürgen Habermas,* Frankfurt a.M.: Knecht, 1985.

[12] See S. NOCETI: "La fede della comunità", in: SEGRETARIATO ATTIVITÀ ECUMENICHE: *Se aveste fede quanto un granello di senape: Atti della XLII sessione di formazione ecumenical,* Milan: Ancora, 2006, 80–95, 269–271.

12). The *sensus fidei ecclesiae* basically represents a "symbolic universe" that is the matrix of all the meanings that are objectified societally and are subjectively valid.[13]

The church becomes present and works in history as an institutionalized "collective subject" that manifests and realizes the communion of the believers with God and among themselves in a communication *of* the faith and *in* the faith of all the baptized. In their uniqueness and in the variety of the charisms that they bear, they jointly constitute this faith. On this basis, it is possible to recognize that Christian subjecthood is a "subjecthood of word". On this basis, a doctrinal authority of *all* in the church is sanctioned, under the unique Word of God, despite the difference of ministries. On this basis, we can understand that the *sensus fidei* is always an active capacity or faculty – not receptive or passive, as it was presented in the pre-conciliar texts. This perspective allows us to grasp that the *sensus fidei ecclesiae* has a historical character that comes from the individual subjects, from the ecclesial "we" that unfolds across the generations, and from the object of faith; and we see that the *sensus fidei ecclesiae* always entails the confrontation with an irreducible pluralism.

Every new believing subject, in the uniqueness of his identity (history, culture, gender, age ...), makes his own profession of faith with a *receptio* of the words that have been transmitted to him. He bears witness to this profession in a unique form, in accordance with an original re-expression. Every transmission of the constitutive meanings of the church is their reaffirmation, transformed in the course of the unique and personal life stories of the individual subjects. Those who believe in Christ, on the basis of the apostolic faith in which they share, thus continually "re/generate" this shared reality – the form of the church as a subject bearing witness to the common faith – by means of their actions and of their communicative interactions (verbal, symbolic-liturgical, pragmatic).[14]

1.3 The Consensus fidelium: Universitas fidelium and the Role of the Magisterium

The ecclesial dynamic towards the *consensus,* and the process that leads to the recognition of the existence of a *consensus fidelium,* are central to the church's life, because it is the *consensus* that brings to light, transmits, and expresses the *sensus fidei ecclesiae* on the public and empirically discernable level. The *consensus* needs to see protagonists – hence the plurality of the ecclesial subjects – and it entails a differentiated plurality of witnessing and interpretative functions. The

[13] According to DV 8, in the *sensus fidei ecclesiae* is incomplete in some aspects, thanks to its specific eschatological openness.

[14] See P.L. BERGER/T. LUCKMANN: *The Social Construction of Reality,* New York: Anchor, 1967.

consensus does not come about through a homogeneity of thinking and of verbal forms that is spread among everyone or imposed upon everyone. It is actualized around the Word of God that is heard by everyone in keeping with a historical-eschatological understanding of the truth.[15] The process can admit various levels of achieved consensus (it is useful to think of this in relation to the idea of the hierarchy of truths,[16] or to the forms of differentiated consensus that we find in the ecumenical sphere).[17] The thesis of Vincent of Lérins that "that which is believed by all, always, and everywhere" is true,[18] remains a fundamental point of reference, but this truth must be recognized by means of a dynamic of *conspiratio* (which involves both the individuals and the local churches) and with an intelligent look at how the *traditio ecclesiae* came into being. This involves the ability to discern and to interpret the discontinuities and the emergence of new forms in the continuity of identity. To speak of the *consensus fidelium,* in the diachronic and synchronous senses, means recognizing oneself as a necessary part of the ecclesial subject – as one who shares in a unique manner in constituting the ecclesial subject. But it also means recognizing my indebtedness to the faith that binds me to the others, and grasping the "relativity" of every personal understanding of the *traditio.* We can say that the *consensus fidelium* is a genuine and proper *locus theologicus.*

The specific identity, function, and ministry of the ordained ministers and of the laity emerge clearly when this ecclesial dynamic "towards the consensus" takes place. *Lumen gentium* presents the bishops (and the other ministers) as custodians and guarantors of the apostolicity of the faith and as servants of the unity of the people of God. It assigns the lay faithful the task of serving the outward spread of the church in the world, and of understanding and proclaiming the Gospel in human society. This means that the process towards the *consensus fidelium* cannot exclude the involvement of the laity, for otherwise we risk forgetting the languages of the time in which we live, and undervaluing the signs of the times as signs of the coming of the kingdom of God in history.[19] At the same

---

15 See H. VORGRIMLER: "Dal 'sensus fidei' al 'consensus fidelium'", in: *Concilium* 21 (1985), 489–500; P. SCHARR: *Consensus fidelium: Unfehlbarkeit der Kirche aus der Perspektive einer Konsensustheorie der Wahrheit,* Würzburg: Echter, 1992.

16 UR 11. See also Pope FRANCIS: *Evangelii gaudium,* 34–36; G. THILS: "Hierarchia veritatum", in: *Revue théologique de Louvain* 10 (1979), 209–215; S. NOCETI: "Gerarchia delle verità: Interrogativi e suggestioni dal dialogo ecumenico", in: *Vivens Homo* 26 (2015), 69–86.

17 See A. BIRMELÉ: "Un choix fundamental dans le dialogue oecuménique moderne: La différence comme partie intégrante du consensus", in: *Nouvelle revue théologique* 124 (2000), 3–29; ID.: *La communion ecclésiale: Progrès oecuménique et enjeux méthodologiques,* Paris: Cerf – Geneva: Labor et Fides, 2000.

18 VINCENT OF LÉRINS: *Commonitorium* 2, PL 50, 640.

19 See D. BIANCHI/S. NOCETI: *Trattato sulla chiesa,* Brescia: Queriniana, 2002, 390–428.

time, the *consensus* is the arrival point of a process in which the bishops have a specific role to play. Precisely because it is the church as a whole that mediates and transmits the revelation, the *sensus fidei ecclesiae* does not come into being autonomously through the exercise of the magisterium of the ordained ministers – but it does demand this exercise. The people of God is indefectible and infallible in believing *and in teaching* (and it contains the ordained ministers *within itself*); in the first aspect, "in believing", this is thanks to the contribution of everyone (the *sensus fidei fidelium*, with laity and ministers jointly involved in the search for the truth and in bearing witness to the faith); in the second aspect, "in teaching", this is thanks to the ministry of some, in relation to the life of the ecclesial "we" – and this ministry is guided by the Spirit. But the ministerial subject on whom magisterial competence is bestowed is inside the responsible communion of all the believers, and his task is to serve this communion. All are under the same Word of God (*Dei verbum*, 10), and the magisterium must "hear, nourish, and receive" the *sensus fidei fidelium.* This reminds us that the magisterium is primarily exercised *a posteriori*, as an act of discernment about the extent to which a consensus exists. The magisterium and the *sensus fidei* of the other Christians have a normative function that is reciprocal, critical, and complementary, with regard to the recognition of the content of the faith. This overcomes the exclusive (and sometimes excluding) centrality of the magisterium.[20] Besides this, the magisterium must be the promotor and guarantor of the process towards consensus, and the guarantor of the consensus itself. This is the basis on which it serves the correlation between the *sensus fidelium* and the *sensus fidei ecclesiae,* and it helps to maintain the distinction between these two. As Walter Kasper affirms, the ecclesiastical magisterium is the service of the event of communication of the ecclesial community, in safeguarding the apostolicity of the proclamation. It must therefore guarantee "the institutional space in which an open and public dialogue is possible", because "the normal and ordinary datum in the church must be the collective and dialogical discovery of the truth".[21]

2 The Dynamics of Communication and the Experience of Faith

If it is true, as Paulinus of Nola wrote, that "*de omnium ore pendeamus, quia in omnem fidelem Spiritus spirat*", I would be inclined to think that all the baptized

[20] D. WIEDERKEHR (ed.): *Der Glaubenssinn des Gottesvolkes – Konkurrent oder Partner des Lehramts?,* Freiburg i.Br.: Herder, 1994; see also B. SESBOÜÉ: *Le magistère à l'épreuve: Autorité, vérité et liberté dans l'Église,* Paris: Desclée de Brouwer, 2001.

[21] W. KASPER: *Die Lehre von der Tradition in der Römischen Schule*, Freiburg: Herder, 2011 (Gesammelte Schriften; 1) [first published 1962]; translated here from H. FRIES: "C'è un magistero dei fedeli", in: *Concilium* 17 (1985), 598 (Italian edition).

are subjects in the full sense of the term. We must, however, bear in mind an important distinction: between (interior) faith and the profession of the faith (which is empirically discernable and can therefore be judged). The latter is the true criterion of belonging to the church. The church, and every believer, lives from an interior faith that must necessarily be symbolized, communicated, and professed in order to make history and to keep alive the memory of Jesus. We must submit to the labor of interpretation and of the confrontation or conflict between various interpretations. The communicative acts of the faith – which have their foundation (in terms of their content and of their effect) on the level of *mystery* of a *credo in Deum* and of a *credo ecclesiam* – are empirical. Faith is the "co-generator" of the church only if it is symbolized and communicated, both verbally and symbolically. The criterion of belonging to the church – if we take our stance on the empirical level – is not faith, which remains interior and is known only to God, but the profession of the faith, celebrated in baptism and expressed anew in the symbolical-liturgical or interpretative-witnessing actions of believers. The ecclesial "we" exists and develops in a dialectical process, in a triple dynamism that is proper to its own members: the dynamisms of exteriorization, of objectification, and of interiorization. In their communicative interactions, these dynamisms have created, and create, societal reality. They make their own the objective reality of society, and they bear witness to it as something that is subjectively relevant.[22] The ecclesial tradition has never forgotten the importance of listening to the prophetical voices that speak out both inside and outside the church.

The dynamic of "reception" and "decoding", and the dynamic of "appropriation" and personal re-expression form the context in which we should think of the *sensus fidei* in relation to the word-pair *fides* and *mores*.[23] The symbolized and verbal profession of the church's faith (which is necessary for the *consensus fidelium*) brings into play experience, praxis, and attestations, both on the symbolic level and on the level of structures. This is recalled by *Dei verbum* 5, when it outlines the dynamic of faith as handing oneself over to God, the assent given by a heart moved by the Spirit, an intelligence that grows, the praxis of testimony with the totality of one's life, and so on. The *sensus fidei* (*fidelis*) thus has both a cognitive and a soteriological dimension, since it is a personal interpretative experience of the salvation that has been revealed. These two dimensions are distinct, and

---

22 See P.L. BERGER/T. LUCKMANN: *The Social Construction of Reality,* 132–147 and 179–183 of the Italian translation (*La realtà come costruzione soziale,* Bologna: Il Mulino, 1969).

23 The expression "*fides et mores*" occurs five times in LG 25. It cannot be limited only to doctrinal questions; the entire existence of the believer stands under the light of revelation. The formula "*de fide et moribus*" seems, in reality, to be influenced by an intellectualist conception of the "*fides*" – it is as if the "*mores*" were not included in it. This formula comes from the Council of Trent, and it reached the Council via *Divino afflante Spiritu* of Pius XII.

each develops according to its own specific characteristics (circumstances, life, age, culture, gender, formation of the conscience, and so on) in an existential re-expression. The living contexts make it possible to comprehend (and not merely to understand with the mind) the content of the faith and its implications, in experiencing the power of salvation. (This dynamic becomes evident in the mystagogy of the sacraments.)

3 *Sensus fidelium* and the Form of the Church: Thinking and Rethinking the Ecclesial Dynamics

The *sensus fidelium* touches deeply the nature and the mission of the church, the fundamental form of the church and the configurations that have been assumed in the course of history. The way in which the *sensus fidelium* has been thought of, and the manner of its interpretation, reveal how the identity of the ecclesial subject is understood, and how the internal relationships in the church are promoted, because the *sensus fidelium* is at the heart of the constitutive and transformative dynamics of the ecclesial subject. The recognition of its value allows us to grasp three features of the face of the church in relation *to that which is foundational, to the permanent ecclesial dynamic* that guarantees development, and *to the* necessary *empirical configuration* – the church in *traditio,* the church as a hermeneutical community, and the synodal church.

As we have seen, the teaching of *Lumen gentium* 12 on the *sensus fidei* or *fidelium* tells us that *the societal construction of the ecclesial "we"* takes place in the communicative and interpretative *medium.* This is true both with regard to the individual believer, who is generated as a Christian subject and as a "co-constitutive subject of the ecclesial subject", and with regard to the form of the church, which is generated and regenerated by every new member. The network of ecclesial relationships is sustained and animated by a network of significant constructs that are reinterpreted and communicated, constructs that are shared and acknowledged by the members. As a reality that is societally constructed, the "church" is continually "given a new shape" by its members, by means of interactions that are symbolically mediated and communicated, on the basis of an original meaning that is attainable only in terms of *tradition.* The apostolic church exists in *tradition.*[24]

The church draws its life from a fundamental *hermeneutical process.* Ecclesial communion remains alive and authentic if it knows how to develop in accordance

[24] See J.G. BOEGLIN: *La question de la Tradition dans la théologie catholique contemporaine,* Paris: Cerf, 1998; D. WIEDERKEHR (ed.): *Wie geschieht die Tradition? Überlieferung im Lebensprozess der Kirche,* Freiburg-Basel-Wien: Herder, 1991; S. NOCETI: "Che cos'è la Tradizione? Una lettura ecclesiologica", in: *Vita Monastica* 67 (2013), 139–154.

with a permanent dynamism of communication among believers. The object of this dynamism is the ever-new understanding of the Gospel in the "today" of history and of cultures (see *Gaudium et spes*, 44: we must know and understand the languages of our age, in order to be able to proclaim and understand the Gospel better).[25] The church exists in the "form of a hermeneutical community" that lives from the reinterpretation of the foundational experience on the basis of the *norma normans* of scripture, in the stream of the *paradosis,* incarnated in different cultures, in a human history that Christians believe is marked by the manifestation of the sovereignty of God through the work of the Spirit.

Finally, to think and rethink ecclesiology with the *sensus fidelium* or *ecclesiae* as the keystone means rethinking the *model of communication* that has been adopted. Behind every form of the church lies a model of the communication of the faith. The Tridentine model insisted on a communication that was prevalently one-directional – from one who knows to one who does not know; from one who is a clergyman to the laity; from the men to the women. Chapter II of *Lumen gentium* begins to propose an ecclesiology that lives from the communicative dynamics of multidirectional networks where each point in the network is both a receiver and a transmitter, though within the asymmetry of the functions (thanks to the specific role that is taken by the ordained ministry). A synodal church.

4 The *Sensus fidelium* and the Synod "in Two Acts" in 2014 and 2015: On the Open Building-site of the Reception of Vatican II

The theme of the *sensus fidelium* is a nodal point of the ecclesiological vision of the Second Vatican Council, because it touches the question of subjecthood, of the constitutive dynamics, of the form of the church. We find in *Lumen gentium* 12 a "lofty declaration of principles", but this has been received only to a limited extent in the praxis and the self-awareness of the post-conciliar church. The lack of a reception – or the merely partial reception – of the Council's intuitions on this point has had profound repercussions on the hoped-for ecclesial reform and

25 The understanding of the traditional topic of the *sensus fidei* or *fidelium* that Vatican II develops is new in so many ways. It is broadened in the post-conciliar theological debate, and it finds expression in the reception of new languages and new experiences of human life in society: the spread of a democratic-participatory *mens* (the perception of the right to speak and to be present, in the West and in many parts of the world, overcoming and denouncing every reductionist condition of inferiority and every inequality based on sex, race, wealth, or other factors of identity); the development of a civilization of communication and the accelerated spread of instruments of information that make possible a multidirectional communication, constant access to an enormous amount of information, the extremely rapid diffusion of news and documents in every part of the world, with profound and very rapid modifications both on the anthropological level and in terms of societal belonging.

on the process of reception of Vatican II,[26] which necessarily included the recognition of the *sensus fidelium* and the development of a synodal church. Although the synodality of the church[27] and the necessity of founding anew a "collective rationale" with regard to communicative negotiations have been sensed, there has been a complete lack of institutions in the church that would guarantee the state of reform, welcoming the synodal awareness and the vision of a synodal form of the church, in which the subjects who are a part of the church would have their differing responsibilities and contributions. There has been no structural reform that would correspond to the synodal awareness and form of the conciliar church. Such a reform would make the synodal awareness and form concrete – teaching it, mediating it, and transmitting it. That would make it possible to listen continuously to the local churches in a church that had become a worldwide church. Fifty years after the close of Vatican II, we must ask how we can strengthen the awareness of the Christian laity that they are subjects with full responsibility in a church that is a hermeneutical and synodal community. How can we make real and efficacious the exercise of the *sensus fidelium*? And how can we work to attain a genuine *consensus fidelium*?

Thinking more specifically of these two Synods (or better, of this "Synod in two acts") centered on the vocation and the mission of the family in society and in the church, I believe that there are three questions that "invoke" the realization of the perspective of the *sensus fidei fidelium* and the *consensus fidelium*: the question of gender, the recognition of the ecclesial ministeriality of the one who "marries in the Lord", and the relationship between the synodality of the church and the synod of bishops.

In the church, the authoritative guardianship of the apostolicity of the faith and of doctrine is entrusted exclusively to men. Up to the present, no female voice is heard in this authoritative guarantee of the faith we share. It is only in a genuine and concrete confrontation with the *sensus fidelium* that we can receive *the word of women,* their unique and singular experience of life as a couple, the value of a bodiliness that has a female gender, the meaning of maternity (physical and internal), and the perception of the relationship with one's partner. Secondly, if we attach value to pluri-directional communicative dynamics, it will be possible to arrive at a real *recognition of the ecclesial ministeriality that the couple* takes on

26 I have in mind "reception" in the perspective of Y.M. CONGAR: "La réception comme réalité ecclésiologique", in: *Revue des sciences philosophiques et théologiques* 56 (1972), 369–403, and G. ROUTHIER: *Il Concilio Vaticano II: Recezione ed ermeneutica,* Milan: Vita e Pensiero, 2006.

27 See H. LEGRAND: "La sinodalità, dimensione inerente alla vita ecclesiale: Fondamenti e attualità", in: *Vivens Homo* 16 (2005), 7–42.

with the celebration of the sacrament of matrimony.[28] The "singular-plural We" of the couple who have married in the Lord brings a unique word, both on the level of the verbal proclamation and on the level of the testimony of life and of praxis. They bear witness to the essence of the kingdom of God – unity in difference, made fertile in love. In view of the theme of the Synod, it is essential to receive and to study in breadth and in depth the experience of the "ecclesial *locus*" that is the life of the couple and of the family. Finally, there is *the relationship between the synodal church and the synod of bishops.*[29] In particular, to precede the celebration of the Synod by a phase of consultation of the churches means, not only consulting the laity, but also listening to the contribution to the *sensus fidei fidelium* from the priests, the deacons, and the bishops who are not delegates, and thus are not present at the Synod. It means being able to listen to the voice of the local churches in the legitimate plurality with which the Gospel is welcomed in the various cultures and peoples. The *consensus* demands recognition and discernment with regard to the processes of communication of the faith and in the faith – and these processes are always inculturated. I conclude with a suggestion. Why should we not celebrate brief synodal events in the local churches before every Synod of Bishops, in which we can listen to the *sensus fidei fidelium* and receive it? Such events would allow every local church, gathered around its bishop, to make a genuine contribution of its own towards the *consensus fidei,* giving due value to the plural riches that the Gospel generates when it is proclaimed in the various human places and contexts. In this way, there would be a real recognition of the contributions and the ministries of so many persons – women and married couples – who are heard only rarely in the church. An "unheard-of" word that is necessary for the renewal of the church.

---

[28] M. ALIOTTA: *Il matrimonio,* Brescia: Queriniana, 2002; K. RAHNER: "Il matrimonio come sacramento", in: IDEM: *Nuovi Saggi,* Rome: Paoline, 1968, III, 575–602.

[29] See R. BATTOCCHIO/S. NOCETI (eds.): *Chiesa e synodalità: Coscienza, forme, processi,* Milan: Glossa, 2007.

Authors

Emmanuel Agius is the Dean of the Faculty of Theology at the University of Malta. He is the Head of the Department of Moral Theology at the Faculty of Theology, a member of the European Group of Ethics in Science and New Technologies (EGE), a member of Malta's National Bioethics Committee and a member of the Scientific Committee of the Centro di Ateneo di Bioetica at the Catholic University of the Sacred Heart, Milan, Italy. He is the author of three books and co-editor of five publications about future generations. His articles on bioethical issues have appeared in a number of international academic journals.

Aldegonde Brenninkmeijer-Werhahn is the founder and Director of the International Academy for Marital Spirituality (INTAMS) in Brussels. Since 1995, Senior Adviser in Marriage and Family Spirituality and in vocations to ordained and lay ministries. She is the co-editor of the following books: *Christian Marriage Today* (with K. Demmer), Washington, DC: Catholic University of America, 1997; *Das Herz spricht zum Herzen: Reflexionen über die Ehe* (with K. Demmer), Freiburg: Herder, 2012; *Close to Our Hearts: Personal Reflections on Marriage*, Berlin: LIT, 2013; *A cuore aperto: riflessioni sul significato del matrimonio*, Rome: Città Nuova, 2014.

Roger Burggraeve, SDB, is professor emeritus of Theological Ethics at the Faculty of Theology and Religious Studies, Catholic University of Leuven, Belgium, where he taught, inter alia, the course *An Ethics of Growth for Difficult Pastoral and Educational Situations*. He has recently published *Meaningful Living and Loving: A Christian Ethics of Growth for People on Their Way*, Leuven: Peeters, 2016. For 37 years he was also part-time collaborator and team member of the Salesian youth pastoral Centre *Eigentijdse Jeugd* (Youth Today) in Dilbeek, Brussels.

Andrea Grillo teaches Theology of the Sacraments and Philosophy of Religion at the Pontifical Athenaeum of St. Anselm in Rome and Liturgy at the Institute of Pastoral Liturgy of the Abbey of Santa Giustina in Padua. Among his many publications are *Rite che educano*, Assisi: Cittadella, 2011; *I sacramenti spiegati ai bambini*, Assisi: Cittadella, 2012; *Genealogia della libertà*,

Cinisello Balsamo: San Paolo, 2012; *Indissolubile? Contributo al dibattito sui divorziati risposati*, Assisi: Cittadella, 2014.

Peter Hünermann was professor of Dogmatic Theology at the Catholic Theological Faculty of the University of Tübingen until his retirement in 1997. He was the Founding President of the European Society for Catholic Theology and has been its Honorary President since 1995. He is the author of numerous publications and has edited the *Enchiridion Symbolorum definitionum et declarationum de rebus fidei et morum* (Denzinger-Hünermann), Freiburg: Herder, ^{44}2014, and *Herders Theologischer Kommentar zum Zweiten Vatikanischen Konzil*, 5 vols. (co-edited with B. J. Hilberath), Freiburg: Herder, 2004.

Thomas Knieps-Port le Roi holds the INTAMS Chair for the Study of Marriage and Spirituality at the Faculty of Theology and Religious Studies of the Catholic University of Leuven, Belgium. He is the editor of the *INTAMS Review: Journal for the Study of Marriage and Spirituality* and has published on the theology, ethics and spirituality of marriage and family. He has co-edited *Companion to Marital Spirituality*, Leuven: Peeters, 2008; *The Household of God and Local Households: Revisiting the Domestic Church*, Leuven: Peeters, 2013; *Being One at Home: Interchurch Families as Domestic Churches*, Zürich: LIT, 2015.

Serena Noceti is Professor of Systematic Theology at the *Istituto Superiore di Scienze Religiose "I. Galantini"* in Florence and also teaches at the *Facoltà teologica dell'Italia centrale* and the *Istituto Superiore di Scienze Religiose* in Arezzo. She is the vice-president of the *Associazione Teologica Italiana.* Among her numerous publications dealing with ecclesiology and the theology of gender is *Trattato sulla Chiesa* (co-authored with S. Dianich), Brescia: Queriniana, ^{2}2005.

Jochen Sautermeister holds the endowed Chair of Moral Theology with a special focus on Moral Psychology at the *Ludwig-Maximilians-Universität* in Munich and became Professor of Moral Theology at the Catholic Theological Faculty of the University of Bonn in 2016. He works as a marriage, family and life counsellor in the Archdiocese of Munich. Among his publications are: *Identität und Authentizität: Studien zur normativen Logik personaler Orientierung*, Freiburg i.Ue.-Freiburg i.Br.: Fribourg Academic Press-Herder, 2013; *Organspende – Herausforderung für den Lebensschutz* (co-edited with K. Hilpert), Freiburg: Herder, 2014; *Selbstbestimmung – auch im Sterben? Streit um assistierten Suizid* (co-edited with K. Hilpert), Freiburg: Herder, 2015.

Eberhard Schockenhoff is a priest of the Diocese of Rottenburg-Stuttgart, Germany. He has been Professor of Moral Theology at the University of Freiburg since 1994, and a member of the German Ethics Council (*Nationaler Ethikrat*) since 2001. Among his many publications are: *Grundlegung der Ethik:*

Cinisello Balsamo: San Paolo, 2012; *Indissolubile? Contributo al dibattito sui divorziati risposati*, Assisi: Cittadella, 2014.

Peter Hünermann was professor of Dogmatic Theology at the Catholic Theological Faculty of the University of Tübingen until his retirement in 1997. He was the Founding President of the European Society for Catholic Theology and has been its Honorary President since 1995. He is the author of numerous publications and has edited the *Enchiridion Symbolorum definitionum et declarationum de rebus fidei et morum* (Denzinger-Hünermann), Freiburg: Herder, [44]2014, and *Herders Theologischer Kommentar zum Zweiten Vatikanischen Konzil*, 5 vols. (co-edited with B. J. Hilberath), Freiburg: Herder, 2004.

Thomas Knieps-Port le Roi holds the INTAMS Chair for the Study of Marriage and Spirituality at the Faculty of Theology and Religious Studies of the Catholic University of Leuven, Belgium. He is the editor of the *INTAMS Review: Journal for the Study of Marriage and Spirituality* and has published on the theology, ethics and spirituality of marriage and family. He has co-edited *Companion to Marital Spirituality*, Leuven: Peeters, 2008; *The Household of God and Local Households: Revisiting the Domestic Church*, Leuven: Peeters, 2013; *Being One at Home: Interchurch Families as Domestic Churches*, Zürich: LIT, 2015.

Serena Noceti is Professor of Systematic Theology at the *Istituto Superiore di Scienze Religiose "I. Galantini"* in Florence and also teaches at the *Facoltà teologica dell'Italia centrale* and the *Istituto Superiore di Scienze Religiose* in Arezzo. She is the vice-president of the *Associazione Teologica Italiana.* Among her numerous publications dealing with ecclesiology and the theology of gender is *Trattato sulla Chiesa* (co-authored with S. Dianich), Brescia: Queriniana, [2]2005.

Jochen Sautermeister holds the endowed Chair of Moral Theology with a special focus on Moral Psychology at the *Ludwig-Maximilians-Universität* in Munich and became Professor of Moral Theology at the Catholic Theological Faculty of the University of Bonn in 2016. He works as a marriage, family and life counsellor in the Archdiocese of Munich. Among his publications are: *Identität und Authentizität: Studien zur normativen Logik personaler Orientierung*, Freiburg i.Ue.-Freiburg i.Br.: Fribourg Academic Press-Herder, 2013; *Organspende – Herausforderung für den Lebensschutz* (co-edited with K. Hilpert), Freiburg: Herder, 2014; *Selbstbestimmung – auch im Sterben? Streit um assistierten Suizid* (co-edited with K. Hilpert), Freiburg: Herder, 2015.

Eberhard Schockenhoff is a priest of the Diocese of Rottenburg-Stuttgart, Germany. He has been Professor of Moral Theology at the University of Freiburg since 1994, and a member of the German Ethics Council (*Nationaler Ethikrat*) since 2001. Among his many publications are: *Grundlegung der Ethik:*

Ein theologischer Entwurf, Freiburg: Herder, 2007; *Theologie der Freiheit*, Freiburg: Herder, 2007; *Ethik des Lebens: Grundlagen und neue Herausforderungen*, Freiburg: Herder, 2009; *Chancen zur Versöhnung? Die Kirche und die wiederverheirateten Geschiedenen*, Freiburg: Herder, 2011.

Clare Watkins is a lecturer in Ministerial Theology at the University of Roehampton, London, UK, and teaches part time at Allen Hall, the Westminster Seminary in London. She has researched, taught and published in the areas of ecclesiology and sacraments, and, more specifically, on marriage, the baptismal vocation, Christian education, and the 'domestic church'. Publications include: *Living Baptism: Called out of the Ordinary,* London: Darton Longman & Todd, 2006; *Talking About God in Practice: Theological Action Research and Practical Theology* (co-authored with Helen Cameron, James Sweeney et al.), London: SCM, 2010. Clare is married to Guy, and they have four children.